FOUNTAIN VALLEY 1972

Michael A. Joseph, Esq.

Strategic Book Publishing and Rights Co.

Strategic Book Publishing and Rights Co.
12620 FM 1960, Suite A4-507
Houston, TX 77065
www.sbpra.com

For information about special discounts for bulk purchases,
please contact Strategic Book Publishing and Rights Co.
Special Sales, at bookorder@sbpra.net.

ISBN: 978-1-62857-984-0

Book Design: Suzanne Kelly

Writing today has forgotten the problems of the human heart in conflict with itself which alone can make good writing because only that is worth writing about, worth the agony and the sweat.

William Faulkner, Nobel Prize Acceptance Address
in Stockholm, Sweden

In Memory Of

Richard Griffen
Ruth Griffen
Charles Meisenger
Joan Meisenger
Patricia Tarbert
Nicholas Beale
Aliston Lowery
John Gulliver

All murdered September 6, 1972, at the Rockefeller brothers' Fountain Valley Golf Course located on St. Croix, US Virgin Islands, a crime and its scene that became notorious as "Fountain Valley." May the victims' souls be consecrated by this effort to bring some worth to their spineless slaughter in so historic a spot of sun, sand, sea, and serenity.

Contents

Overture

Fountain Valley sent asunder a heritage of first to repel New World conquest; molded the man that made modern America; and built San Francisco's earliest hotel. Ron Chernow's 2004 bestselling biography *Alexander Hamilton* hardened the fall. Hence it is of essence to better know St. Croix. Told is how it sculpted founding father Alexander Hamilton (Alex), and of its freedom from the skin color drama. Deep facts about the murders should by so spared prickly presumptions, save pledge to John Steinbeck's point that "a writer's first duty is to set down his time as best as he can understand it."[1]

Spotlight on tropical societies stirs images of irrelevance, even irreverence. This bias is based only on a "decided and long-standing tradition."[2] Yet, Ron Chernow made full use of it. The biographer declared Alex was "architect of Wall Street," but not before his "near miraculous escape from a tropical hellhole."[3] A "grim catalogue of disasters"[4] allegedly suffered by the founder in the tropics is added to mute his tribute: "My time in St. Croix was the most useful part of my education."[5]

Alex's Caribbean cradle was whitewashed as "a beautiful but godless spot,"[6] and his homage to St. Croix claimed as kudos for the New York-based shipping outpost wherein he worked. Nelson Rockefeller was Chernow's four-term New York governor, and that dimmed Denmark's early commercial ties to St. Croix. Rumors its natives relished ruin of Fountain Valley easier coaxed a contention of island hedonism[7] to position this pinching premise that "while other founding fathers were reared in tidy New England villages or cosseted on baronial Virginia estates, Hamilton grew up in a tropical hellhole."[8]

How then did he amass audacity to confront American slavery? Chernow assumed he sensed its looming chaos within the nation he helped to create and opposed it for political points. Truth is, in St. Croix Alex became parentless at fourteen and placed in custody of a widowed relative whose mistress was a free African. Later on, Alex's wife sponsored a home for African children. And when he was slain those years were saluted, his funeral led by two African boys.

Same bias in which Alex was cast fueled the backlash to Rafie's release, and it paralleled them. Three juries concluded the founder was murdered, but his demise spun into a disguised suicide. Rafie's actual suicide by same token was twisted into a routine drug overdose. It is presumed he lacked sufficient self-lessness to have resolved the qualms about him in favor of the public good, just as Alex's allegiance to Africans was angled as pure politics.

Martin Luther King Jr. noticed that "the arc of the moral universe is long, but it bends towards justice." It being so, perhaps this book will help curve closer to fruition the America for which the founder fought.

Part One presents a primer on the origins of America's skin drama plus opens the color curtain to present strawberry fields of empathy and healing. It also tells of my conscription as courier of the killers' account. Part Two details the slaughter and its slipshod investigation, outlines Rafie's upbringing, and reprints what he penned in prison.

Publications about his release puzzled him. He properly got his second chance and trusted it spoke for itself. Still, the storm it stirred up obliged him to vindicate his supporters:

> What I have read so far is based simply on the three Ps—public opinion, police reports, and the prosecutor's case. Mikey, they really do not know. I will help, but it's on you to write the book.

Rafie's subtle exit entombed his resolve to say no more than suffering waterboarding with other tortures like those of the Khmer Rouge's S-21 prison, and why he forgave his torturers.

Prologue

Overall bereavement daily soaked Mammy's yellow face aching also for her most affectionate Rafie. Steadfast still she was; time soon will whisper his story. Olden humility at last beckoned the bishop, a shotgunned employee, plus the golf course proprietors to pilot the prisoner's fresh start. This healing met copious outcry; his let loose tempted more racial killings. Reared beyond such skin color drama, Rafie empathized even as the pack panic strained his native smile. And then, the heart which had inspired victims to beseech keepers quieted fears and paid penance by his refusing refuge in the plea *I'm only human.*

PART ONE

One: Path to Heart's Content

The Rockefellers set aside Fountain Valley as they did Maine's Acadian Mountains, Wyoming's Grand Teton Valley, and St. John's National Park for public enjoyment. Equally, the Rockefeller Foundation exists for the "well-being of mankind throughout the world." It was therefore staggering their St. Croix expenditure exploded into the only golf course carnage ever. Its shockwaves traveled so fast and far workers at Alexander Hamilton Airport not far from Fountain Valley learned of the calamity in a phone call from Australia. The Sydney talk radio host hoped to be told an error was afoot. Alarm hours earlier of murdered Jewish athletes kidnapped from the Munich Olympics had been overtaken by that even more bizarre bulletin.

Jim Simpson of *ABC Sports* sadly recounted the slaughter of those sportsmen arising from perennial Israeli/Palestinian conflicts, and before the global village could exhale its lament, it was blitzed with the golf course butchery. In rush to figure out its "Why?" the media wove it into a racial massacre. That mistake has dug in. A *New York Daily News* piece on teenager Natalee Holloway of Alabama missing in Aruba since 2005 circulated to millions of readers a reminder about the 1972 golf course murders. Grief Natalee will never be found alive morphed into pulp fiction, Fountain Valley triggered, rising racist killings in the Caribbean.[1]

The US Appeals Court in Philadelphia, which upheld each of the murderers' eight consecutive life sentences, describes the crime:

> On the afternoon of September 6, 1972, a group of young men entered the clubhouse area of the Fountain Valley Golf Course in St. Croix. Sixteen persons,

including guests and staff, were in the clubhouse area at that time. The intruders, armed with a variety of weapons including a machine gun and shotguns, took cash from a clubhouse shop and snack bar, robbed some of the guests, and killed eight persons. Four others were wounded while trying to escape and the remaining four were able to escape unharmed. The survivors reported seeing various numbers of gunmen, agreeing that the men wore masks and fatigue-type shirts and perhaps also fatigue pants. [2]

"Massacre is there in your island!" the Madrid restaurant waiter pained to tell his yearly St. Croix patrons. Frank McNamara's family waved it off: "You have the wrong place. Things like that don't happen back home." Showed a Spanish newspaper, said son James, "In big, big letters was the headline with a picture of people cleaning up blood."

CBS' *60 Minutes* televised it as "a public relations nightmare for St. Croix." *Time* printed a photo of an aghast prosecutor, eyes reflecting scarlet globs.[3] A premier destination coveted by Noël Coward, John Wayne, Maureen O'Hara, the Rockefellers, Kennedy, and their likes had lost its serenity in the blink of an eye. The offense, branded as "one of the most vicious in the annals of Western civilization," was matched to the June 17, 1972 break-in of the Democratic Party headquarters at the Potomac River's Watergate Complex. That felony and Fountain Valley's "seismic impact" were linked because both upscale settings instantly spun into notorious events as well.[4]

Watergate was a black-bag bugging op by agents of President Richard Nixon that imperiled America itself. Fountain Valley crushed its paradise. But they long ago parted ways. Nixon yielded his office and was pardoned on September 8, 1974, by successor President Gerald Ford, who at the time said: "My fellow Americans, a long national nightmare is over." Fountain Valley defies so plain a plot. On December 31, 1984, it spiralled into spook politics. One of the killers, while being transferred to a stateside prison by two armed karate experts, hijacked an

American Airlines DC-10 into Havana. No extradition agreement exists between the US and Cuba, so he is still a fugitive.

Rafie's hard-earned freedom a decade beyond that air piracy was a debacle, a Virgin Islands uproar. CBS and ABC TV deployed crews to capture it. CBS reviewed Rafie's clemency petition and sat down with him. It thereafter concluded the dissent in St. Croix, while not surprising, was unwarranted. ABC refocused on St. Croix's sister island, St. Thomas, where another convict's release incited the skin color drama similar to Fountain Valley's backlash. He'd served a few years, although sentenced to life without parole, for a drug-crazed killing of his "white" girlfriend.

Rafie more than doubled his age in prison and was cleared for release by the US Bureau of Prisons. High-profile citizens such as the VI National Guard's top brass supported him. An ABC crew chief asked me to fly to St. Thomas with my brother because of, he said, interest in his remarkable rehabilitation. Rafie availed himself to John Quinones, whose interrogation lasted late into the night. Back in New York, the crew chief called to apologize. *Primetime's* director had opted to televise my brother's release as part of the rancor in St. Thomas.

Respecting reform rules rescued Rafie by a governor's grace unprecedented in penal history. But the protests toppled potential to share a prisoner's redemption. And his free-world future swiftly slid to suicide. Although blessed with a reservoir of charisma, Rafie's empathy for the hollering overtook his desire to continue the good fight. I lamented to our stepmother about his distant mood and she forlornly replied, "Of eleven children I raised, Rafie was the most affectionate."

Mammy, our natural mother, added, "Rafie is a thinker, just like your father was. Sometimes he drive pass without noticing I'm on the balcony. His head is always full of things."

Their responses stirred recall of Albert Camus' insight that a person's character is in doubt until he dies. Rafie "died" when sentenced to perpetual captivity just after he emerged from the cocoon of his teens. The family, however, remained resolute he'll be free one day. Still we worried he was not tough enough material to survive his high-security penitentiary. Yet, he vindicated himself by trumping unspeakable tests. Prison life does not imitate art; enduring it is an art unto itself. Maintaining dignity in *that place*—as Rafie depicted his penitentiary—required quick thinking, sheer strength, and a thick skin.

Pitifully, within four years of making the prison break of all time he succumbed to his heart in conflict with the doubts of man. His sacred refusal to publicly reveal his role in the massacre was his means of damning the police torture he underwent. At the same time, he saw his skeptics' fear of him as natural. Suicide granted their wish to be free from a perceived threat without him having to give up his. Knowing Rafie's heart and the mistakes good ones make may be good for all hearts.

Had it not been for the skin color drama, he could have shared much.

Racism is often decried, but rarely dissected. Open reflection reveals all people have much to learn from each other. Even the South American Orinoco Indians and Australian Aborigines are as worthy as those "white" men who in 1969 walked on the moon. The Orinoco people are master herbalists. Aborigines crafted the first flying tool (the boomerang) and the three-tiered format (music/visuals/dialogue) for riveting storytelling used today in movies. These people do not add to airborne carbon pollution—300 billion tons as of 2010, says *National Geographic*—proven to be melting the polar ice caps at rates "smashing records that smashed records." To slow this mega-threat we must fast embrace those aboriginals' true reverence for Earth.

Seeing this fragile planet from the moon begot insight we are really one people. "That's one small step for man, one giant leap for mankind," Neal Armstrong intuitively said as he set his foot upon our celestial neighbor. That feat was humanity's most unifying moment ever. His fellow cosmic traveler Mike Collins explains:

> After the flight of Apollo 11 we took a trip all over the world. Wherever we went, people, instead of saying, 'You Americans did it,' they'd say, 'We did it, we

humans, we humankind, we people finally did it!' I've never heard people from different countries use 'we, we, we' as emphatically as I heard from Europeans, Asians, and Africans. I thought that was a wonderful thing. Ephemeral, but wonderful.

Similar gladness resides in realization differences among people are, paradoxically, not even skin deep. The heavens bestowed clarity to comprehend and voiced by Edgar Mitchell of Apollo14:

> The biggest joy was on the way home. In my cockpit window . . . were the earth, the moon, the sun . . . Suddenly I realized that the molecules of my body were . . . manufactured in some ancient generation of stars. And that was an overwhelming sense of oneness, of connectedness. It wasn't them and us. It's . . . one thing! . . . Oh my God . . . an insight, an epiphany.

Such appreciation of mankind's singleness must be assimilated into daily affairs. When so, the harmony felt across the globe as images streamed from the moon's Sea of Tranquility will evolve beyond a mere passing peace.

Or else, the skin color drama will continue to revel in its corruption of the kindred spirit. The hindrance is based on a belief racial prejudice is so deeply rooted it's a foregone human foible. But too many lives have been sacrificed to show such thinking needlessly shrinks the human core and withers the seed which sprouted enlightened astronauts. Lest we betray all of those brave souls, occasion to breach racism's purportedly impenetrable lair must never be wasted. This project offered more than just an opportunity. Unfastening America's skin color drama by revealing its roots will heighten Part Two. As novelist Elizabeth Bowen reassured, "To walk into history is to be free at once, to be at large among people."

The past century was mankind's deadliest. Genocides were seen on a shocking scale in Bosnia, Africa, Cambodia, Poland,

Ukraine, Russia, and Germany, among others. They were ignited by despots who spewed pretences of inferior tribe, race, religion, politics, and whatnot. Oddly, whether Serbs, Africans, Kurds, Croatians, Chinese, Jews, Muslims, Hindus, or Christians became victors or victims, they were hardly racially distinct.

Except for its original people ("the only good Injun is a dead one"), America's system of checks and balances restrained similar fates. Racism is yet shredding its role-model tradition. Its states which kept Africans enslaved on pretext of their "inferiority" were defeated in the Civil War. Lamentably, African skin color once pitied as fit only for subhuman bondage, became an object of scorn for the agony of defeat. So, progenies of the formerly enslaved are wedged between the bitterness of old enemies. That bad blood became as contagious as the flu, infecting points of entry like Ellis Island, where it afforded an advantage for later-arriving Europeans. Though some faced religion prejudice, the newcomers didn't have to worry where they would fit socially. The skin color drama had set aside the bottom class for Native Americans and "blacks." Michelle Alexander's *A New Jim Crow* recently tallied aspects of this bigotry.

Mayhem in its mire, however, is kept on a relatively short leash. Aside from sporadic killing of the defenseless with as many as forty-one (Amadou Diallo) and even fifty (Sean Bell) police bullets, racial reprisals were narrowed to nooses hung in back woods. This is not to say "black" citizens think they are safe from massacres. They have been victims of a few, such as in Phillips County, Arkansas, where two hundred were gunned downed in 1919. That year also marked widespread lynching as far Midwest as was Will Brown's in Omaha, Nebraska. Those yet paled to Tulsa, Oklahoma's pogrom of 1921. Untold numbers were murdered, and its prosperous "Little Africa" was looted before being burnt to the ground. In aftershock of the 2012 perceived racial profile slaying of minor Trayvon Martin, a "black" American bemoaned, "We've come a long way to get nowhere."

Even if so, America's racism has never loomed near the broad brutality of Old World carnages. It more lingers in the theatres of the tragic and even of the absurd.

Legal effort to dismantle customs of bondage, segregation, and intolerance are unfinished. Rules to repair official racism are missing because of a judicial ideology that says such edicts affront the Constitution. It is held they are wrongly race based, although it was racially classified people that were unchained from almost three centuries of slavery without as much as a clean shirt.

Consequently, while they make up 13 percent of America, they account for 40 percent of its prison numbers. Michelle Alexander draws attention to this in her book's subtitle, *Mass Incarceration in the Age of Colorblindness*. She charts that these fledgling "blacks" are used as cannon fodder in the war on drugs, which was instigated to appease "whites" crestfallen by civil rights reform. Though "whites" and "blacks" equally indulge in illicit drugs, the latter undergo five times the rate of police contact. They're about one-fifth of regular users yet represent over three-fifths of drug-related imprisonment. Their arrests are at a record high—half is for marijuana, which most Americans believe should be decriminalized. Former senator Jim Webb of Virginia and his Criminal Justice Commission sought to slow the trample. New York Governor Andrew Cuomo hopes to cut the rate of detention. And Attorney General Eric Holder has proclaimed he is scaling back long prison sentences for *all* nonviolent drug offenders.

Still, attempts to advance the special needs of those citizens seldom succeed. Competitors for the American Dream indifferent to them historically denied it file "reverse racism" lawsuits. They allege affirmative action is designed to benefit the "unworthy," deaf to the fact "white" women as victims of American sexism did make great gains under it. Although now so toned down as to cause claims the civil rights movement has been betrayed, the struggle for fairness continues. For more "black" college seats, the Affirmative Action Coalition as well as thinkers like Lani Guinier of Harvard University argue "worthiness" is to be considered in context of barriers unjustly, but legally, inflicted. Guinier also enlightens that if it is legitimate to belittle such citizens as "minorities," then they ought to vote cumulatively. For example, if they can elect five contenders for any political body which includes a "minority," it's fair "minority" voters give their fellow "minority" candidate all five of their votes. In the same vein of struggle, Robert Smith of San Francisco State University has worked to debunk growing belief that racial disparities are due to "black people blunders."

Fortunately, fabrications that fuel racial fantasies are fading in the face of time. Successive generations continue to fragment skin color pressures, mostly through interracial marriages. But it is at a rather slow pace. Vice President Hubert Humphrey in his 1968 campaign for president warned: "For those who say we are rushing the civil rights issue, I say we're late!" Two scores later, in 2008, a "black" was elected to lead the nation. In spite of his distinctive credentials plus a "white upbringing," the new president's skin color remains palpable.

Given the obstinate barriers over which this fresh American leaf has turned, his election was yet uplifting. Its significance is seen in the grit of my "white" friend who waived an absentee ballot to instead vote in person. On November 3, 2008, Richard Balsamo flew to Miami, Florida, from his Caribbean farm. With an on-time arrival he proceeded for connection to Cody, Wyoming. His plan was to drive the following day to the nearby city of Powell and contribute to the extraordinary narrative. This pledge was tested by a boarding pass snafu, and his new route flew him to St. Louis, Missouri. Next, bypassing Wyoming on a Southwest flight, he arrived late at night in Las Vegas, Nevada. Closing his eyes to that city's lure in favor of a short motel sleep, at daybreak he was airborne to Salt Lake City, Utah. After a prolonged stopover in Salt Lake, his next flight again flew past Wyoming to land in Billings, Montana. There, he removed his shoes at checkpoint—mercifully for the last time—in order to welcome his assigned seat to Cody. Finally in Powell, Richard proceeded to do his part, which he says was "to further Martin Luther King's dream that a person will be judged not by the color of his skin, but by the content of his character."

Europeans, too, trusted the new leader's buoyancy by bestowing on him the Nobel Peace Prize in the first year of his presidency. As America's latest promise, however, this optimism is at risk of desertion insofar it is merely hope-based. On April 3, 2009, a C-SPAN *Washington Journal* caller rejected the new president to guest David Brooks of *The New York Times*: "We have to take that black man out to the pasture!"

Brooks rebuffed the racism, but a congressman who shouted "Liar!" at the new president seemed to agree. In July 2011 the national debt ceiling, which before was increased as a matter of course, was flipped into a fiasco against him. It dismayed even foreign observers. *The Globe and Mail* of Toronto urged him to "fight for his values." *The Daily Telegraph* of London advised he not act "too fiscally timid."

At home, columnist Leonard Pitts in August 2011 exhaled "Amen" when the new president was ridiculed as a "tar baby." Another jeered his health care program as resembling a "bone-through-nose witch doctor," a slur rooted in images of the "African savage."

The new president was reelected in 2012 in one of the most racially divided political contests in decades. And before taking his second oath of office, he came under siege of the fiscal cliff.

The Los Angeles Times denounced it. "This intransigence is baffling, given that one of [his] main campaign pledges was to increase taxes on the highest-income Americans. And he won—handily—just a few weeks ago."

It is obvious many hold a view "blacks" are unfit to lead America. In thirty-two years of previous presidents, the Senate blocked twenty of the citizens those presidents decided would best serve the country. But in just five years the new president was denied sixteen *he* similarly selected. *The New York Times* understated this disparity as having "no historical precedent."

Mundane as it may echo, it is patriotic to learn that "blacks" and America are fused at the hip. The *first* patriot to die fighting for its liberties was an ex-slave in 1770. Paul Revere described him as "part Indian, part Negro, and part white." Let's not forget costs for victory over the British were paid in large part from wealth gained off the backs of "blacks." Despite such oppression, they've always embraced America's core values. In

Michael A. Joseph, Esq.

1773 they petitioned for freedom. In 1775 they were part of the militia which first engaged the British in combat. In 1776 they enlisted for the Revolution. In 1780 they challenged *their* taxation without representation. In 1797 they appealed to Congress for American liberties. Clearly, even before the first presidential election, "blacks" were as politically astute as were "whites."

Two high hurdles to a racially cohesive America are mind-sets the Constitution cherished slavery and the Civil War was unjustified. Hence, its embryonic spirit for a more perfect union is being starved by a centrality of skin color which in turn is feeding off of those attitudes.

In December 2008 C-SPAN *Washington Journal* hosted Jon Meacham with his Pulitzer Prize-winning *American Lion* about President Andrew Jackson. Blindsided by criticism Jackson owned slaves, Meacham blamed the Constitution, which, he said, "enshrined slavery." A few months earlier, actor Tom Cruise pressed for election of the new president "because African Americans were considered as only three-fifths of a human being."

In January 2009 a teacher friend bared the depth of that dissonance when he said to me, "John Grisham just sent me an autographed copy of his book *The Appeal*."

Because Grisham's gift is weaving novels out of courtroom rights afforded by America's charter, I responded, "I just wrote a section on why the Constitution is so often dissed. Next time you and Grisham chat, tell him I share his appreciation of it."

The educator flung back that the document was deserving of the damnation.

His letdown wasn't so out of the blue keeping in mind it was framed by, and for, elite Anglo-Saxon males. Then again, many were activists. Alex insisted, "There ought to be a capacity to provide for future contingencies as they may happen." Conceived also on a "We the People" premise, the ten-dollar bill, which depicts Alex along with those three words, echoes it.

Of course human bondage was matted in America, but the Constitution neither promoted its perpetuity nor reduced the souls of the enslaved. Its three-fifths ratio term, cause of Tom

12

Cruise's well-intentioned comment, was inserted to dodge a deal breaker conjured by defensive small slave states. In the end, by suffering for the time being those stubborn yet indispensable states, the charter enlarged liberties.

On September 19, 1787, it appeared in *The Pennsylvania Packet & Advertiser* with a suitable salutation: *We the People . . . in Order to form a more perfect Union . . . and secure the Blessings of Liberty . . .* Clueing it was a work in progress; it emphasized a single word: *amendments.*

Delegate George Mason noted "it certainly will be defective" and proper to that setting; within its first fifteen years it was amended twelve times. Except, the conflict which made for its difficult delivery delayed for sixty-three years the thirteenth one abolishing slavery. This interval was marked by a tremulous truce referred to as the "the slavery question." It split the Constitutional Convention into Northern states which shortly before freed their slaves and Southern counterparts still yoked to 168 years of dependence on them.

It was moralist colonizers, from a Christian kingdom which imposed on them its system of human bondage, who bred the founding fathers. Ergo, they were honest their new nation would start up stained. Slave state delegate Luther Martin was succinct: "Slavery is inconsistent with the principles of the Revolution and dishonorable to the American character."

Slaveholder George Washington, who'd led the convention, agonized over that dilemma: "There is not a man living who wishes more sincerely than I do to see a plan adopted for the abolition of it."

He eventually freed all on the plantation his father had bequeathed him. The charter was thus framed by men torn down the middle. The planter half was born into a way of life they were unable to abruptly abandon. Both camps, having bled in the Revolution, refused to yield to the other. That standoff was calmed by a compromise dividing inhabitants into two groups listed in the Constitution: *free Persons* (citizens) and *all other Persons* (mostly the enslaved). The terms "white," "black," "European," "African," and "slave" will not be found in it.

Michael A. Joseph, Esq.

In slave-free Pennsylvania the first US census (1790) counted a third set: "other free persons." In May 1787, just days before the delegates met to frame the charter, they formed the Free Africans Society. Some founders worshipped in St. George's Methodist Church with its leader Richard Allen. Because other churches were not so worldly, the society built the first African Methodist Episcopal Church in 1794 and started an AME movement.

Myth the Constitution "enshrined slavery" stems from its linking three *free Persons* to five of *all other Persons.* That ratio arose in calculating how many members each state will have in the House of Representatives. This issue was very important because the president would be chosen by state-designated electors "equal to the whole Number of Senators and Representatives to which the state may be entitled in Congress." Without regard to size of their populations, each state got two members in the Senate. With respect to the House of Representatives, however, delegate Benjamin Franklin persuaded, "The number of representatives should bear some proportion to the number of the represented."

His approach was familiar. It was used when English and Scottish parliaments merged in 1707 to create Great Britain. Yet, because states with a higher number of citizens would have more House members and thus more electors of the president, small slave states (of fewer citizens) demanded an edge. In spite their enslaved were held as mere property, they made it clear they would abort quest for the new nation unless slaves were tallied as if they were "citizens." Large slave state delegate James Madison sized up the blade of that sword and lamented, "Great as the evil is, a dismemberment of the Union would be worse."

On the other hand, the South would've gained too much national power if that scheme was given whole number value. This gridlock was loosened by settling on the three-fifths ratio which equated, for the census only, five slaves to three citizens. With it, one thousand slaves were counted as if they were six hundred citizens, a too charitable split. Although slave state Virginia and Pennsylvania had near the same number of citizens, the ratio gave Virginia six more House members. The pro-slavery voice would've sooner been silenced if it was less, like one-tenths. In such case, one thousand slaves would be counted as one hundred citizens and Virginia allowed no more than one additional House member. Sadly, such a plan would've caused grumble that "African Americans were considered as only one-tenth of a person."

The three-fifths ratio is today scapegoated for allegation racism was implanted in the Constitution. But the ratio had nothing to do with racial supremacy. Actually, it aimed to do just the opposite. It was inserted to limit the extra political power those small slave states demanded. In fact, for the reason Africans were known to be no less than "men," the Bill of Rights did not become part of the charter until December 15, 1791. As ardent a slaver as was Charles Pinckney, in arguing against adding it to the Constitution, he reminded, "Such bills generally begin with declaring that all men are by nature born free. Now, we should make that with a very bad grace, when a large part of our property consists in men who are actually born slaves."

Quite a few founders on both sides of the issue were Freemasons faithful to concepts shaped in Africa. And a week prior to publication of the charter, "blacks" started *their* Masonic Lodge. America's first president is honored with an African obelisk, the Washington Monument. The one-dollar bill displays a "black" king's tomb, the Great Pyramid. An attentive eye floats atop it to assure fidelity to Masonic principles. Adding these facts to the reason the Bill of Rights was delayed, claims of African inferiority is an eyes-wide-shut absurdity.

The founding fathers did not indulge in the racism of such slave traders like the Portuguese and Spanish. *They* had been dominated by African Muslims for 450 years before fully recapturing their lands in 1492. On the other hand, America's skin color drama arose from guilt triggered by its flaw of human bondage. How tragic incapacity to fully eliminate it led to the rationale of "black inferiority." But blame for that must not be shifted to the Constitution, which carried a tide against slavery.

The enslaved opportunely fled northward to freedom, and so it mirrored a 1642 fugitive slave law which allowed for recapture of runaway *Persons held to Service or Labor*. More definitively, however, the Constitution empowered a ban on *Importation of such Persons* twenty years after its adoption. This enactment to end the slave trade was its single term not subject to amendment, thereby preventing extension of that period. Reluctance to grant the delay in the first place became clear on March 22, 1794, when Congress banned American ships from supplying slaves to other countries during the twenty-year period. Five days later, the navy was formed to enforce it. Although delegate James Wilson was dispirited, saying, "The period is more distant than I could wish," he was sure it did "lay the foundation for banishing slavery out of this country."

Revulsion that anti-slavery founders had for the slave trade resonated in a magazine of those days:

> The rolling sea hurries the heaving hearts: the sighing souls escape! . . . The groans of a hundred men, the sighs of a hundred women, the cries of a hundred youths are one! . . . Silence prevails, and the dead bodies are thrown to the watchful sharks, whose ravenous jaws are glutted with the flesh of men!

Slaveholder George Mason, too, despised the "infernal traffic," and his warning would prove prophetic: "Providence punishes national sins by national calamities."

Some slaver delegates had argued half of mankind was always in slavery—legal in Saudi Arabia as recently as 1962. Their claim was motivated by fear of financial calamity they'd suffer if the trade precipitously ended. During the 1776 Revolution tens of thousands of the enslaved escaped to freedom or were emancipated by joining it. Slaveholders dug deep into debt to replenish them. It is in this tenor the twenty-year stay in terminating the trans-Atlantic trade was tolerated.

It was banned within its fixed time, a fact indicative of the Constitution's current against slavery. And its tide had signaled support to William Wilberforce's long struggle to end the trade in Britain, where race was even of less significance. One of

Wilberforce's closest colleagues was Olaudah Equiano, a former slave whose book about the horror swiftly sold fifty thousand copies. In the Constitutional Convention, Mason blamed Britain of continuing the "nefarious traffic" for "lust of gain." Soon after the charter's adoption, in an overwhelming vote the British Parliament ended Britain's slave trafficking. Denmark seemed also swayed. In 1792 it decreed it would, and did in 1803, cease shipping slaves to St. Croix.

Still, the twenty-year period in which 170,000 more Africans were imported, plus the edge gained by the three-fifths ratio, tolerated Southern slavery well beyond patience of the American character. Bizarrely, it was prolonged by the fractional elevation of slaves to *free Persons* status. The notorious ratio, therefore, should be judged only for what it actually was—a delay to the fated finish of slavery.

Remarkably, slaveholders joined in to rouse their day of reckoning. In the Confederation Congress they voted on August 13, 1787, for passage of the Northwest Ordinance of 1787. It outlawed slavery north of the Ohio River. That area became the states of Wisconsin, Illinois, Indiana, Michigan, and Ohio. In 1848 Wisconsin joined the Union, and on February 28, 1854, some fifty anti-slavers rallied in Ripon to form a new political group which evolved into the Republican Party. On June 16, 1858, it sponsored Abraham Lincoln of Illinois to run for the Senate. Strikingly, in debating his rival, Democrat senator Stephen Douglas, Lincoln declared, "There is no reason in the world why the Negro is not entitled to all the natural rights enumerated in the Declaration of Independence—the right to life, liberty, and the pursuit of happiness."

He lost that election, but intoned his new party's platform: "A house divided against itself cannot stand . . . the government cannot endure permanently half slave and half free."

The Republicans got Lincoln elected as president in 1860. He entered into a treaty with Britain on June 7, 1862, to seize *all* slave ships, and days later he led the ban on slavery in US territories. When reelected in 1864 Lincoln also advocated that male slaves emancipated by the Civil War be granted the right to vote. Within a mere decade, slavery was crushed by the Republican Party, sown in lands slaveholders had helped to make slave-free.

Reference to enslaved Africans as *all other Persons* by definition asserted their humanity. It was nothing new. James Madison, known as "Father of the Constitution," in 1773 rejected a request to punish his runaway slave Billy. He reasoned Billy coveted the same liberty *he* sought from the British, and of which was "the right & worthy pursuit of every human being." He later wrote why the enslaved were yet treated "in the mixt character of persons and of property." It arose from complex compromises which in effect "regards the slave as divested of two fifths of the man."[5]

This adversity to the blessings of liberty lasted only as long as it took the Constitution to vindicate itself by the war sown in its invention. Delegate Elbridge Gerry declined to sign it because he disagreed with some national powers such as authority over state militias. He had complained to his wife that he was "almost sure they will if not altered materially lay the foundation of a civil war." True to foretell, the Civil War unfolded the bloodiest day in American history with the victory Lincoln awaited to issue the Emancipation Proclamation. And that battle began on the Constitution's seventy-fifth birthday.

The Civil War not only freed the enslaved. It bred the Fourteenth Amendment, granting them equal rights and thereby crushing any idea America was a "white society." Backlash to those upheavals to this day fuels the skin color drama. Being far removed from their African origins, the new citizens unwittingly fed the hostility by foxholing themselves as "blacks." Although no longer in fashion, other tags were "coloreds" and "Negroes." This dermal tangle is seen in Walter Dean Myers' *The Journal of Biddy Owens*:

> Oh yes. I asked Daddy about the question of being Colored, or Negro, or Afro-American. He said he was so busy running from 'nigger' that he hadn't had a chance to grab anything else.

Prior to the New World's conquest people usually were signified from a birthplace standpoint. While in Africa my guide Dr. Yosef ben Jochannan conveyed how a nomadic family introduced to him their four sons. Proud their children had been born in different places, the mother said to Dr. Ben as she pointed to each, "He's Nubian, he's Ethiopian, he's Sudanese, and he's Egyptian."

Those kids would simply be "blacks" in America, where definitions of color adjectives/nouns are: *white*—equals good qualities and even those not so bad; a petty untruth is a "white lie." It is also synonymous with Americans of European descent, or "whites." Compare *black*—opposite of *white*—which refers to Americans of African ancestry, or "blacks."[6]

It is now politically correct to classify "blacks" as "African Americans," but similar tweaking for Americans of European descent has proven unnecessary. According to *Webster's Dictionary of the American Language*, "white" is positive, so Americans of European descent have always been comfortable as "whites." On the other hand, labeling citizens as "blacks" conveys, by definition, negative connotations. Creating comfort zones with tags like "fair-skinned" or "high-color" furthers the yarn. In such instances, it is implied there are others of unfair or low-color skin. Plainly, the people-group nouns "whites" and "blacks" relate to the adjectives "white" and "black," meaning good and bad, respectively. Because it is colorblind, official group labels indicative of negativity offend the Constitution. In February 2013, when the Census Bureau announced it dropped "Negro" from ancestry groupings, it therefore should've also deleted "white" and "black."

Necessity for it was literally driven home in August 2005 when we enrolled our four-year-old in a nearby school, the teachers of which were mainly European Americans. In the first days of pre-kindergarten classes, her mother, born in St. Lucia, West Indies, asked our baby, "How many white kids are in your class?"

"None, Mammy," the confused child declared.

"But I saw some with you," a baffled mom responded.

"People is people, Mammy. Not colors," our little girl insisted.

She lifted a plain sheet of paper and showed her mother. "Look, this is white. None of my friends look like this!"

Revealingly, within two months she asked, "Mammy, will my skin color change when I get older?"

Nudged to explain her question, she calmly replied, "Because when I grow up I want to be white, too."

Her lessons in standard colors were invaded by a specter which sneaked in its shady system. It splashed the starting student with one of its two toxic tints while whispering she must make way for those showering in the other. The alert pupil quickly realized she'd gotten the short end of a skin color ruler. She's comfortable in her golden tone, but her brush with the skin color drama is haunting. She recently reminisced, "I was so annoyed Mammy kept telling me that my friends were white! I thought that was so weird."

Alas, many remain poisoned. On January 30, 2009, several young ladies appeared on *The Tyra Banks Show* for its "Bleaching for Beauty" episode. One was willing to risk even her life for a surgical procedure to make herself "white." Tried as the hostess did, she was unable to change her guests' minds. They insisted that being "white" was "the real McCoy," uneducated it was a "black" inventor, Elijah McCoy, whose fake-proof devices hatched that slogan. Programmed to hate their natural look, they were boasting of their quest to sham it. How ironic *and* pathetic.

In St. Croix, logical with Alex Hamilton fighting for the Continental Army to afford *free Persons* leisure from British rule, "whites" are called "Continentals." Because "blacks" joined the Yankee (Union) Army against the South's Confederate Army to free *all other Persons*, they are "Yankees." And Crucians (St. Croix natives) who migrate to the states are tagged as "Fresh Water Yankees." Their adopted speech is called "Yanking."

The Civil War was fought to equalize America's people at a cost of 625,000 lives. The skin color drama yet makes folly of that incredible American sacrifice. Among its foulness is excluding island citizens from basic rights otherwise present in the "Anglo-American regime of ordered liberty." At dawn of the twentieth century, when several tropical societies including St. Croix came under US dominion, the Supreme Court stated: "The people of those territories did not share the Anglo-Saxon values attached to the [denied] right[s]."[7] So it created the status of "unincorporated territory." How Dred-Scott-esque! It was as indefensible as its *Dred Scott v. Sandford* (1857) case, which declared that Africans were *beings of an inferior order.* Same racism was spewed in the Philippines Islands seized during the 1898 war with Spain. Using the "Home Treatment," it branded native Filipinos as "niggers" and "squaws."

The category of unincorporated territory was conjured by Chief Justice Edward D. White. He did so with his separate opinion in a Puerto Rico tax case. Unlike the Northwest Ordinance of 1787, which provided for admission of states north of the Ohio River, he wrote that Congress didn't express same design for the islands. But absence of a future-state clause in their acquisition treaties didn't exclude them from ever becoming states. Some mainland territories were recognized as "inchoate states" despite lack of formality for future entry into the Union of the United States. And it didn't occur to Justice White that because the Northwest Ordinance of 1787 restricted slavery it was weak support for claiming Congress intended to create in perpetuity a lesser class of citizens.

However, humility of defeat was not about to accommodate as equals those whose skin color harked back memory of the Civil War. Justice White's agony of defeat shaded the fact St. Croix supplied gunpowder for the Revolution as well as Alex Hamilton, a framer of the liberties claimed to be so foreign to islanders. Justice White also failed to notice the first attorney general of the Confederate States of America was St. Croix-born Judah P. Benjamin. He next led its war department before serving as its secretary of state. Called the brains behind the CSA, he was marked on its two-dollar bill. And as did Alex in the Revolution, Judah advised the CSA during the Civil War: "Let us say to every Negro who wishes to go into the ranks, 'Go and fight—you are free.'"

The aggregate number of tropical citizens outstrips the separate populations of half the states. These islanders serve in American wars, and if body-bagged are buried with full military honors. They're always in frontline conflicts as intense as was the Cuban Missile Crisis of October 1962 that brought brink of nuclear disaster. When navy ship *Joseph P. Kennedy* halted the Cuba-bound freighter *Markuba*, St. Croix's Paul Arnold was radio man in the squad deployed to inspect it for nuclear weapons. Romeo Henderson suffered with Senator John McCain in same compound as war prisoners in Vietnam. Others died in the Middle East. But they are denied federal voting rights.[8] Because of this half-vast citizenship, American Islanders can be jaded as people of tropical hellholes and lumps of coral.

Most mainlanders are dumbfounded by this anomaly, which appears to be an offshoot of Native American enslavement. Affairs between Indians and England started with trade and cultural exchanges, mainly among Narragansett and Wampanoag nations. Some had been to Europe years before the Mayflower, sailing for Jamestown Colony (Virginia) was weather blown to Plymouth Rock (Massachusetts). First word its passengers heard from Squanto was "Welcome!" Unaware he'd been to England, they mistook his greeting as God speaking to them through him. When the Mayflower departed for Europe in April 1621, the Indians secured survival of those newcomers. Half had come "for the glory of God," the others for trade. Besides teaching them about their crops, the natives' *wampum* facilitated commerce as their New World initial currency. Settlers who survived that first year adopted the Indians' harvest celebration and invited them to it.

Within a few years, however, natives who mistrusted influx of more Pilgrims/Puritans were preemptively attacked. Alike religious fanaticism seen today in some nations, in 1636 near seven hundred Pequot children, women, and men were trapped and assaulted with a hodgepodge of weapons including fire. Few escaped. The settlers thanked God for the victory in midst of stench of their victims' burnt corpses. By 1676 the Wampanoag people who first befriended them were crushed, their leader

Matacom beheaded. Known also as King Phillip, he was son of Massasoit, who'd assured the well-being of the colonizers. In time, five hundred Indian nations suffered similar doom. As if in remorse for their demise, half the states borrow their names from these vanquished people.

It was not in vacuum cordial relations between England and the Indians evaporated into a fog of barbarism. An ominous future was foretold in 1619 when Africans were unloaded at Jamestown. Being in their own backyards, natives proved too difficult for mass slavery. Still, to match Spain's escalating power financed by gold pilfered from New World kings, evolving standards of human decency were shelved. Spanish gold so flooded European markets, inflation was rampant. Eric Williams' *Capitalism and Slavery* grasped England "would have gone to the moon if necessary for labor. Africa was nearer." Ergo, slavery was driven not by racism, but by economics.

During the Christian Crusades of 1060–1187, when Jerusalem was seized from the Muslims, Anglo-Saxons were enriched by the arts and sciences of North Africa. Scholastic Press' *The Usborne Medieval World* says its people known as Moors "were famous for their civilized way of life. They studied science, mathematics, and astronomy, composed music, and wrote poetry. They also enjoyed playing games such as chess."

A medieval picture portrays two African men playing chess, one playing a harp, and another being served food by a European. A king is dramatized in the 1604 play *Othello the Moor* by Englishman William Shakespeare, who'd courted an African. She was described as dark skinned and of a musically talented London family.

Unlike Alex's guardian's mistress, *she* was not from a slave ship. The Magna Carta of June 15, 1215, and developing common law were intolerant to chattel slavery in England, even if not in its American colonies.

Some colonists had studied Christianity at schools like Cambridge, and it stirred scruples as to how Native Americans and Africans were being treated. To quiet their conscience, contemptuous views of those in slavery were fabricated. However, he who denigrates another degrades himself, and in that ricochet the colonizers started as early as May 27, 1647 to accuse their own as "heretical witches." By the leap day of February 29, 1692, the Salem witch trials were in full swing, and on June 10 Bridgett Bishop was first to be officially executed. Ironically, William Tyndale, religious forerunner of those persecuting Puritans, was burned at the stake in 1539 for his "heretical" views in writing the first English translation of the Holy Bible.

Came as they did, taste of freedoms for which they'd cross a vast ocean survived. By April 18, 1775, the American Revolution began with the "British are coming!" ride of Paul Revere to warn patriots John Hancock and Samuel Adams they were going to be arrested. Instead, the patriots' militia, which included free Africans, gained a victory next day at Lexington and Concord in what is now Massachusetts. That "Shot Heard 'Round the World" was beckoned on March 5, 1770, when a patrol of Britain's Twenty-Ninth Regiment fired into angry patriots in Boston. The English Stamp Act was passed on March 22, 1765, and on October 19 the Stamp Act Congress was created with the cry: "Taxation without representation is tyranny!" Many patriots had joined Britain against France and its allied Indians for control of North America, and to appease them the Stamp Act was repealed a year later. Left in place, however, was the Quartering Act, passed days after the Stamp Act. It compelled colonists to provide lodging for British soldiers, who often forced the wives of patriots to cook and wash for them. So repulsive it was the Bill of Rights later banned soldiers lodging with civilians.

That March 5, 1770 clash against such ever-tightening tyranny is recalled as the Boston Massacre. The patriot who triggered King George III's use of deadly force on that day was Crispus Attucks. Born a slave in 1723, an advertisement in 1750 in the *Boston Gazette* sought his recapture. The ad identified him as a "Molatto Fellow named Crispus" and detailed his classy attire when last seen. Crispus' ancestor John Attucks was a fighter hanged by the Puritans as an Indian spy. With same brave heart, Crispus mocked the British Redcoats as "lobsters."

Upon striking Private Montgomery with a thrown stick, he was killed with two lead balls to the chest.

Samuel Gray, Samuel Maverick, and James Caldwell, felled with Attucks, were all laid to rest in a common grave. Their slayings stirred out more than ten thousand angry mourners who gave them a hero's send-off with church bells ringing in the countryside for miles around.

The patriots formed the Continental Army in June 1775, and, using British belief it would be at rest during the oncoming winter season, secretly deployed cannons in the hills around Boston. With defeat a certainty, the Redcoats on March 16, 1776 filed out of the city. Thomas Jefferson's Virginia adopted a bill of rights on June 12; the Continental Congress declared freedom from Britain on July 2, approved Jefferson's Declaration of Independence on the fourth, and on September 9 changed the name "United Colonies" to "United States."

That boldness did not chill King George; he had marshaled his forces to once and for all crush the rebellion. He filled New York City's harbor with four hundred ships and dealt the patriots a severe blow in the Battle of Long Island. In torrential rains of August 27 the British and its German allies outgunned them, and two days later the patriots took flight. Leaving lit campfires as decoys, they simply vanished into the night. In another retreat General George Washington on December 8 crossed Delaware River from New Jersey to Pennsylvania. Tenacity triggered him to read to his soldiers the powerful words of Thomas Paine, such as: "These are the times that try men souls." It inspired them to shake off their fatigue. On Christmas Eve Gen. Washington crossed back the ice-filled Delaware to launch a surprise assault and seized one thousand Hessians from Germany in the Battle of Trenton. This gave him standing to sway his troops, whose duty ended on January 1, 1777, to reenlist although their pay would be delayed. And fought more they did, gaining victory on January 3 in the Battle of Princeton.

Capture of five thousand British troops on October 17 in the Second Battle of Saratoga sufficed to induce France it need no longer await Spain's assent to help the Revolution. On February

6, 1778, the French signed up. Little known is the patriots were already receiving secret help from Spanish Louisiana's Governor Bernardo de Galvez. He'd been supplying ammo, medicine, and Spanish flags for safe sailing of patriot supply ships. In June 1779 Spain declared war on Britain with a four-year siege of Gibraltar. So, Galvez seized forts in British Florida, gaining control of the lower Mississippi River and safety of patriots' ships. For this he's honored with a city in his name, Galveston, Texas, and a statute in Washington, DC.

On the urgings of Alex Hamilton, also fighting were slaves who "got their freedom with their muskets." Free Africans had enlisted on January 16, 1776. It was this coalition that led to ultimate victory with defeat of Lord Cornwallis in the Battle of Yorktown on October 19, 1781.

How special it came sixteen years to the very day the Stamp Act Congress was convened. As remarkable, shortly after British colonialism was renounced, the abolition of slavery started. Vermont led the way by outlawing it on July 2, 1777—first anniversary of the patriots' self-rule resolution.

Massachusetts continued with anti-slavers leaders, mainly the Adams family. Samuel of the anti-British Sons of Liberty became its governor. His cousin John served as the nation's second president. Also, John's son, John Quincy, was sixth president. He studied in Paris plus the Netherlands yet rejected global ambitions of fifth president James Monroe. Quincy negotiated the Treaty of 1819 with Spain for Pacific Ocean trade, but in a Fourth of July speech he warned the nation not to seek world power by way of the "Monroe Doctrine." Massachusetts next nurtured Susan B. Anthony, women's rights advocate and abolitionist who collected three hundred thousand signatures to end slavery. Notably, its flag honors the Indians' early charity. And who'd have guessed the state of Patriot Pride would twice elect Governor Deval Patrick, a progeny of African slaves?

Nevertheless, in absence of a collective grasp as to how human bondage injured the American spirit, affairs between descendants on both sides of the iniquity remain stressed. Mississippi did not ratify the Thirteenth Amendment of 1865 ending slavery until 1995. And when Dr. James Watson, who with Francis Crick got a Nobel Prize for decoding DNA, criticized *some* of Africa's leaders as dismally incompetent, he was called a racist. But it was Watson's work with genetics which led to a survey that linked all mankind to an African mother. Media icon Walter Cronkite, in narrating a documentary about it, affirmed with his trademark emphasis, "Europeans are migrant Africans. And that's the way it is."

Today's global population of nearly seven billion descended from a mere eighty thousand ancestors, DNA has proven. Ergo, ideas of racial superiority cannot be biologically justified. Cutting-edge research specifies it is the thumb finger that sets mankind so apart from other species. It stimulated brain growth to facilitate the many activities it afforded. These discoveries deserve two thumbs up.

Dr. Watson, my dear, your comment seemed to me a wake-up call on inter-African genocides. Military observers reported in May 1994 slaughter of 200,000 Rwandans. Compared to 200,000 Bosnians murdered in 1995, in Rwanda more than 800,000 were eventually slain! And in April 1995 refugees fleeing a Zaire camp trampled each other as soldiers gunned them down by the thousands. Those brutalities leave millions of civilian casualties! Women are subjected to sexual terrorism so cruel as to make murder a merciful gesture! A UN press release reveals in the Democratic Republic of the Congo more than a thousand are raped each day! Piling salt into their wounds is the cruel scorn each afterwards suffers. A September 2011 BBC broadcast described their plight as "a grotesque, vicious circle." So it has been in Darfur, and in Sierra Leone, where limbs were hacked off. In Zimbabwe mine managers fed tied-up men to dogs trained to attack their genitals. The monstrosities continue in the new nation of South Sudan.

In sentencing a vigilante killer of poor people, a Brazilian judge's revulsion for his crimes barely suffices for those African rapists and murderers: "Such evil demeans all values of human existence!"

Genocidal colonialism may've set the pattern. Mark Twain ridiculed Belgium's King Leopold II, who in 1885 accepted at the Berlin Conference the Congo State. While promoting himself as benevolent, he allowed millions of Africans on rubber plantations along the Congo River to be killed. Hands often were hacked off and nailed to the rubber trees from which insufficient sap had been collected. So unthinkable that was, its echo in Joseph Conrad's *Heart of Darkness* was thought to be fictional. In 1916 Belgium started a system of tribal rivalry in Rwanda which led to its 1994 genocide. As if the horror is never enough, on November 21, 2012, the UN reported Rwanda and Uganda were aiding M23 rebels in Eastern Congo. The beat goes on in Central African Republic, and Nigeria's self-centered politicians turn a blind eye to mass kidnapping of schoolgirls. These crimes against humanity are so self-destructive it causes some to excuse them as a collateral damage of African colonization. Even if that is the case, Bob Marley's guidance must be heeded: "Emancipate yourself from mental slavery. None but ourselves can free our minds."

An African proverb likewise teaches, "If there is no enemy on the inside, the enemy on the outside can do no harm."

It is troubling the quip from Dr. Watson got a lot of press, but deadly risks taken daily by many charitable Continentals in Africa do not. Assuming the scientist's statement was racist, it's hardly worth the bother when lined up to those machete-hacked and bullet-riddled Africans. Pitifully, before stench of burnt corpses clears, warlords function as minions to foreign financiers of their atrocities. They are destroying Stephen Biko's vision that higher education is the cold steel from which an emergent Africa will be struck. They're also propping up the handful of supremacists who say it proves "black people animalism." Thankfully, that was soundly trounced by an intellectual who declined to accept his Nobel Prize, Jean-Paul Sartre: "Nothing more consequent among us than a racist humanism, for the European has not been able to become a man but by fabricating slaves and monsters."[9]

Breaking away from racism reminds of reptiles whose severed limbs twist and twirl in phantom link to their bodies. Patrick J. Buchanan's *State of Emergency* in a similar way adds credence to Sartre. Pat admitted to the evils of slavery but linked them to his assertion that "Europeans brought immense benefits" to the New World. The political pundit and past White House candidate posed: "Was not Western civilization vastly superior to the indigenous civilizations it encountered and crushed?"[10]

This spin rotates more in histrionics than in Pat's humanity. In 2000 he picked a "black" female as his running mate, thus revealing his bond, even if ethereal, to the greater truth. At the end of the day, there's but one people.

Notice how sprinters of all skin shades dip to break the electric beam at Olympic Games. Human sight is usually incapable of picking the winner due to their equal prowess. As for competition in intellect, a posthumous award in science is deserved for a grandson of slaves, Dr. Percy L. Julian. He over-came 1930s Jim Crow bigotry to register dozens of chemical blueprints including the soybean's alpha-protein, thus aiding its $20 billion trade. His grudging acceptance into the indus-trial chemists' citadel was achieved only after he outclassed Sir Robert Robinson, foremost organic chemist at that time. Julian won their race to synthesize an herbal extract used to treat glaucoma. And weren't it for his keenness, he'd have been hoodwinked. Robinson was declared the winner, but Julian proved his rival's synthesis, unlike his, had a boiling point dissimilar to the natural molecule. Some Harvard researchers' efforts to show Africans were innately inferior was thereby foiled by Julian.[11]

St. Croix librarian Wallace Williams personally knew of Dr. Julian's struggle:

> Percy and his accountant were over at my house all the time. I can hear him even now complaining about discrimination against his patents. My father was his mechanic. As a kid, though, I just admired his account-ant's Porsche. But really, it was my mother's cooking they loved.

Michael A. Joseph, Esq.

Pat Buchanan is uninformed the founding fathers borrowed a political scheme from America's indigenous people. James Madison is credited with arriving three months early in Pennsylvania with the Constitution's blueprint. However, it also incorporated a Native American model. The Six Nations Iroquois Confederation was the New World's first democracy. Unlike the Greeks, who first practiced popular voting, the Iroquois foresaw the harm which sexism and slavery will cause, and its Great Law said: "In our every deliberation, we must consider the impact of our decisions on the next seven generations."

America's slave economy made that paradigm of governance unreachable. Consequently, when the Civil War was ignited, a grandson of second president John Adams observed, "We the children of the third and fourth generations are doomed to pay the penalties of the compromises made by the first."

Let's not forget the founders' political awareness had come solely from kingdoms. Some read portions of Englishman John Locke's liberal writings. A few knew of Frenchman Montesquieu's ideas of balancing powers that made for a republic. And others heard of the judicial role played by the English House of Lords. Still, they remained unsure as to what type of political structure they would enact after the Revolution. During those times, "[George] Washington resisted all calls to become a king."[12]

It was in this setting Alex prompted the Constitution by nudging James Madison to persuade Washington that the 1781 Articles of Confederation created after the Revolution was inadequate. It'd sketched a crumbly congress, no judicial or executive branches, no standing army. As such, it made for domestic volatilities such as the January 26, 1787 revolt of debt-ridden farmers led by Captain Daniel Shays' attempt to seize a Massachusetts arsenal. But Washington had sworn to uphold the Articles. Fortunately, coaxing was part of Alex's skills. His standing at the Constitution Convention is seen in this: While as many as eight delegates signed to commit their states to the document of 1787, Alex's lone signature sufficed for New York. In the next eight months he penned two-thirds of *The Federalist Papers* to sway skeptics such as his influential governor, George

Clinton, into ratifying it. James Madison and John Jay added the other third. Jay focused mainly on foreign affairs and Madison on legislative powers. Alex, though, wrote on states, taxes, war, armies, and the presidency. Thomas Jefferson said *The Federalist Papers* was "the best commentary on government which ever was written."

Alex founded the Federalist Party, which focused on a centralized government. Most members were non-slavers for a standing army and popular voting. Alex pained over the potential abuse of common voters, worried the not-so-literate would serve as pawns for despots. He pondered whether politics should better be left to educated assemblies, or even to a monarch. His June 18 daylong convention speech revealed his conflict; he flirted with the idea Washington should accept the role as a king. Described by Ron Chernow as "the indispensable aide to the indispensable Washington," Alex would've been the proverbial power behind the throne.

Benjamin Franklin proposed a three-person presidential committee because he believed a single chief executive could only lead the country to "despotism." Alex likewise predicted that a single chief executive would sooner or later act as a crowned head. President Andrew Jackson (1829–1837) asserted that he was the "first among equals." Others wielded powers beyond the scope envisioned in 1787, especially in times of crisis. During the Civil War Abraham Lincoln (1861–1865) denied courtroom review of persons jailed, censored speech of noncombatants, and ignored the US Chief Justice's request that he tone down. Franklin D. Roosevelt (1933–1945) in the war against Japan rounded up citizens of enemy heritage and restricted them to guarded camps. Most blatant was Woodrow Wilson (1913–1921), who began on April 11, 1913 to racially segregate all federal agencies. He also welcomed into the White House the movie *The Birth of a Nation* glorifying the vile racism of the Ku Klux Klan. That film revived to unprecedented numbers the murderous KKK!

Executive overreach to the side, Alex opted to risk the power of the people over that of states. To drive home his point for national rule, he said states should be "reduced to corporations, and with very limited powers." On the other hand, slavers like George Washington's contribution to the Revolution was unassailable. Let's not forget its pivotal battle was won in his Virginia. Surely, it was crucial anti-slavers negotiate with the slave states, and that required delicate balancing.

In June 1754, when James Madison was but three years old, Dr. Benjamin Franklin visited the Iroquois democracy and observed its grand council and president-chief structure. When he returned to Philadelphia, he urged the colonies to elect an assembly by popular vote called the "Grand Council," and for that body to appoint a "president-general" to administer its laws. In the 1787 Convention, the "Congress" and the "president" mirrored the Indians' grand council and president-chief scheme. The natives' grand council was elected by popular vote, but the president-chief was chosen by the council.[13] This arrangement became template for electors of the president.[14] Slave states welcomed it; together with the three-fifths ratio it facilitated slaveholders becoming ten of the first fifteen presidents.

Given Alex had so much influence in calling for the convention, why didn't he go all out to abolish slavery? The answer is simple—he knew total purge of human bondage was an unattainable goal. He could not obtain slavers' votes to end it while cajoling them to surrender power to a central government. As Chernow eloquently noted, "Hamilton could not be both consummate abolitionist *and* federalist."

So, he settled for a federal system which he knew would eventually eliminate the scourge, and urged a "We the People" charter. The South insisted on a "We the States" theme well articulated by Patrick Henry of Virginia.[15] His states-first viewpoint, ironically, offered a truer democracy. A faraway seat of control with an executive selected by a fraction of state representatives was much less accountable. Though Henry was elected a convention delegate, he intuited things would not go his way and stayed at home because he "smelt a rat." Federalists, however, were not about to leave slave states to their own devices. This divide was narrowed by the Iroquois model, which gave the South political comfort and hence birth of the nation.

The Iroquois also had balanced male/female interests. Women elected the male-comprised grand council, which then chose from within itself the president-chief, contrasting denial of the vote to US women for the next 133 years.

Native Americans also contributed to George Washington's battlefield training. As an English ally, Iroquois leader Half King tutored Washington when he was a British captain fighting the French for control of North America. Half King "concluded that Washington was good natured but appallingly inexperienced and unwilling to take advice."[16]

Most Indians remained British loyalists during the Revolution, and the patriots' weaponry so devastated them they tagged Washington as "the destroyer of towns." They were hated as much as the British and demeaned as "wild savages." That party line later reached the Caribbean, where festivals featured "wild Indian dance."

Actually, Indians cultivated complex beliefs such as Earth itself is an aware entity. They elevated fellow creatures to Buffalo Nation, Wolf Nation, Eagle Nation, etc. And they learned English easily and spoke it poetically. This was heard in a scolding about slavery decades before the trans-Atlantic slave trade:

> They tore my people apart and sold them as slaves to the Spanish in Bermuda. But I shall speak with a voice of thunder, and I hope it will be heard to the ends of the Earth. He that advocates slavery is a beast. And he who does not turn his face against it is a coward and not deserved to be numbered amongst men.[17]

Quite a few were enslaved in the early colonies. In 1708 Carolina Colony had 5,300 Europeans, 2,900 African slaves, and 1,400 Indian slaves. Albeit Indian blood, sweat, and smarts enhanced the United States, Harlem author James Baldwin noticed that today *they* are the Americans *most despised*.[18] In South Dakota they suffer a joblessness rate of 75 percent on several reservations and only 10 percent of students there graduate from high school. Their abysmal depravation is of no moment to Wall or Main Street.

Rich respect had marked the ties between Indians and Africans. A tribe living along the Missouri River on meeting York, a slave with the Lewis and Clark expedition, thought he was its bravest member. When going into combat they painted themselves with charcoal for courage. On seeing York's color did not wash off with water, he was honored as the best warrior. Word of that African ran like a prairie fire. Later on, European traders were escorted by "black" emissaries as far as the Dakotas for business with Indians. On the other hand, Kim Dramer's *Native Americans and Black Americans* documents that a few native nations were encouraged to, and did, own African slaves. Those were said to be the "civilized tribes." Dramer details other peculiarities like the Buffalo Soldiers. After fighting in the Civil War those Yankees were deployed to destroy Indians for western expansion. They were yet honored by their victims as buffalo-haired with same brave hearts. That irony is wedged in a Bob Marley requiem: "Buffalo Soldiers / Stolen from Africa / Brought to America / Fighting on arrival / Fighting for survival."

Indians faced assimilation *or* annihilation. Ten million buffaloes, their mainstay resource, were tactically slaughtered to near extinction and the natives were offered this option: "Be like the white man or perish like the buffalo." Refusal to bite into that sour apple often meant execution, even if their warpaths were to save themselves from starvation. In one such case, they suffered the largest mass death sentence. Prior thereto, in Denmark Vesey's slave uprising thirty-five were hanged, but forty-seven natives got the noose.

In Pat Buchanan's lyrics, no doubt Indians were encountered and crushed. Often, however, it was by means which would've gotten attention from the International Criminal Court created July 1, 2002 to prosecute genocides and war crimes. Indians were first victims of a biological weapon. As substitute for rare buffalo hides indispensable for winter survival, blankets soiled with contagious diseases were distributed to them. Wickedly exposed to European germs, so many were wiped out as to amount to genocide.[19] It has been written that "all is fair in love and war." For romance that sounds bizarre, and the conviction of Charles Taylor of Liberia for crimes against humanity by the ICC in April 2012 should cause pause in wars. Though the US quickly enacted the Servicemembers' Protection Act to limit the ICC's reach at its soldiers, it did join the global ban on BWs back in 1972. Even Adolph Hitler, who said, "I want to see again in the eyes of youth the gleam of the beast of prey," refused to use BWs. Pat Buchanan's brag is therefore not so noble.

In spite a few native nations became "civilized," their demise was fated. Missionaries welcomed the Indian Civilization Fund of 1819 to make them "good Christian farmers and tradesmen." The Cherokee, Choctaw, Creek, Chickasaw, and Seminole nations, dubbed "the five civilized tribes," cooperated. But President Andrew Jackson dispensed with the program and spearheaded the Indian Removal Act of 1830 notorious for its "Trail of Tears." In winter of 1838–39, during a forced march to "Indian Territory" of sixteen thousand Cherokees and their slaves, four thousand dropped dead. Jackson's callousness was evident in Georgia's 1829 seizure of Indian lands. They sued and won in the Supreme Court, but he dared it to enforce its "stillborn judgment."

Jackson's malice seems rooted in flashbacks to the Revolution and the War of 1812. The first one mangled him when it killed his parents and he taken prisoner for the use of a British officer. A finger-sized sword gash was inflicted on his head when he refused to clean boots. In the other war he was ice cold when he led Union forces against Indians allied with the British. The scarred soldier ignored the rules of war and mercilessly slaughtered them in the Battle of Horseshoe Bend. It was the greatest loss ever of Native American lives in a military conflict. And then, with a coalition of free Africans and the French pirate Lafayette, Jackson dealt defeat to the British on January 9, 1815, at New Orleans. Now evermore bold, in 1818 without authority he ordered an attack on the Seminoles providing refuge for

Michael A. Joseph, Esq.

runaway slaves in Spanish-held Florida. At the British-built Fort Negro, 270 men, women, and children were massacred.

As Native Americans numbers dwindled under federal military might, slavery in the South was steady. Of course, the North was not always slave-free. Those "tidy New England villages of other founding fathers" did not generally outlaw human bondage until 1784.[20] Still, Northern Christians continued to aid the abolition of slavery. Indeed, they prompted the Northwest Ordinance of 1787, thereby speeding up its end. The Quakers as far back as 1688 wielded Christian canons to challenge slavers' conscience. And, albeit some say the "Negro church" did little to end slavery, it cannot be denied many enslaved survived by, and resisted with, their gospels.

To deflect the oddness of Bible-carrying slavers, bizarre defenses were brewed. The Good Book was flipped to shrink the humanity of those in bondage. The enslaved were piously retagged from "beasts of burden" to "the white man's burden." President Lincoln was perplexed by that because "both slaveholders and he believed in the same Bible."

His empathy produced pockets of pundits who insist he was, like slavers he indulged, a racist. This is so although he believed of America's greatest abolitionist, "Frederick Douglass is one of the most, if not the most, meritorious American."[21]

Douglass got Lincoln's highest praise despite in 1852 in Rochester, New York, that activist blistered the nation: "Go where you may, search where you will, roam through all the monarchies and despotisms of the old world, and you will say to me that, for revolting barbarity and shameless hypocrisy, America reigns without rival."

It is also true Lincoln suggested "whites" and "Negroes" might be better off if they were apart and slaves should be freed and returned to Africa. So did many Africans, who felt pride on June 25, 1862, when he extended consular status to Liberia. As Africa's first colony to declare independence in 1847, Liberia was home for many freed slaves. Too bad Lincoln wasn't around when the Berlin Conference of 1885 parceled the remainder of Africa to European countries. It'd have conflicted with his stern opposition to oppression. Despite a dozen prior presidents upheld President Thomas Jefferson's embargo against the Republic of Haiti because it had humiliated France, Lincoln quashed it.

Michael Burlingame of *Abraham Lincoln: A Life* is baffled by critics who insist Lincoln was hypocritical. The doubters are unmindful he respected the separation of powers between Congress and the White House even on the issue of slavery. Perhaps, it's difficult for them to grasp Lincoln grew up in racist surroundings but emerged with a tongue so subtle it veiled his originality. It also seems hard to appreciate the self-educated rail splitter harbored for both slaves and slavers a sympathy he secured within a fortress of shrewdness.

When John Brown was sentenced to be hanged because he stormed an arsenal for weapons to end slavery, Lincoln refused to intervene because he "took the wrong path to the right goal." (As fate would have it, present at Brown's hanging were future confederate general Stonewall Jackson and Lincoln's to-be-assassin John Wilkes Booth.) Nathaniel Gordon's hanging under the Piracy Law for having nine hundred African slaves on his ship also failed to gain Lincoln's intercession.

He buried one of his "black" butlers in the national cemetery reserved for "whites." And though the Supreme Court had ruled an African could never be a citizen, he ordered that the butler's gravestone identify him as one. The day after winning the Civil War he directed the Union Army band to play the Confederacy's anthem "Dixie." His answer to the bewilderment: "Am I not destroying my enemies by making them my friends?"

Lincoln often conceded petty points as a debating tactic. In his 1858 spars with Stephen Douglas he parried spats on "African inferiority" as a red herring. The real issue was whether fruits of their labor should be stolen. If his rival's premise was correct, where was the dignity in robbing a lesser being? He did say he would never marry a "Negress." So what? He was already married. Many "blacks" would have responded in like manner in regards to a "white" woman. Point is, even assuming he didn't care much for "Negroes," slavery was such a "gigantic evil" not even they deserved it. In his fourth debate with Douglas at Charleston, South Carolina, Lincoln agreed states had power to refuse Africans the rights to vote, intermarry, serve on juries, and hold public office. Nevertheless, he was steadfast: "One day I'm going to hit that institution, and I'm going to hit it hard by the will of the Eternal."

Seldom was Lincoln so direct; indeed, he was often too subtle. This trait caused Yankee Lerone Bennett's *Forced into Glory* to appraise Lincoln's status of American Hero as dubious. The Bennett measure with all things considered is too idyllic. The great chronicler overlooks Lincoln was a mortal with foibles, among which was uttering half-baked ideas that muddled his clearer aims. Phillip Magness and Sebastian Page's *Colonization and Emancipation* reveals Lincoln called on Africans to relocate to Central America. He asked ex-slaves to abandon the land that, in Richard Allen's words, "was watered with [their] sweat and blood." In point of fact, as leader of the American Colonization Society, former president James Madison in 1833 urged they be sent back to Africa. Wish to disremember abuse in the country to which they'd been kidnapped must've incited those relocation ideas. As conscientious as Lincoln was, he worried how four million ex-slaves without reparations would survive in a hostile South. And when matched to his tenacity to give them the vote, his relocation talk can be said to be a passing ponder on an out-of-sight, out-of-mind option.

Along same lines, Cherokee Nation is today ejecting Cherokee-Africans, the ancestors of whom were their former slaves. Apparently those mixed-bloods remind of a past wished to be forgotten. A March 13, 2007 letter from the Congressional Black Caucus to the Bureau of Indian Affairs decried it. It is matters as these that cause poets to tell man to make peace with his paradoxes.

The axiom "action speaks louder than words" guided my search for the true Abraham Lincoln to this metaphor: Suppose a 246-pound anvil is placed on a man's chest and a passerby removes it and saves his life. What difference does it make if the rescuer wanted the anvil as a tool, didn't favor the person who placed it, or was a Good Samaritan? The healthy attitude is to be nonjudgmental, if not grateful. This approach is just about compelled when, five days later, in consequence of his act the savior is murdered.

Harriet Beecher Stowe and Frederick Douglass, a Continental and a Yankee, respectively, would agree. Beecher Stowe said Lincoln's martyrdom on a Good Friday proved he was "blessed," for none ever accused him of selfishness. At unveiling of the Freedmen Memorial in 1876 Douglass preached that although activists at times described Lincoln as "dull and tardy," everyone else faulted him for being too "zealous and radical." Prior to then Douglass had written, "In all my interviews of Mr. Lincoln I am impressed by his entire freedom from prejudice towards the colored race."

The humble president foresaw the qualms he would yet leave behind: "If the end brings me out all right, what is said against me won't amount to anything. If the end brings me out wrong, ten angels swearing I was right would make no difference."

America survived because Abraham Lincoln lived. And his Reconstruction plan would've made the civil rights movement less contentious, if not unnecessary. Two weeks after the Civil War the Freedmen Bureau was created to oversee programs such as the "forty acres and a mule" for emancipated slaves. On February 7, 1867 a delegation of freed men led by Frederick Douglass met at the White House with President Andrew Johnson (1865–1869). But Johnson's gratitude—as Lincoln's vice president he, too, was to be killed but was spared by Booth's coconspirator George Atzerodt—set the pattern for institutional bigotry for the next century. The loss ex-slaves felt when Lincoln perished echoes in the lyrics of Marvin Gaye: "Has anybody here seen my old friend Abraham?"

Actually, the Supreme Court validated racism in 1857 when it declared Africans were inferior and unfit to seek justice. It was contrary to its 1842 ruling in favor of fifty-three African slaves. In 1839 they were being carried from one area of Cuba to another in the ship *Amistad*. Joseph Cinque of Sierra Leone took control of it and demanded return to Africa. Instead, it was sailed north to American waters, where it was taken into custody. They returned home after abolitionists retained former president John Quincy Adams to represent them in the court.

And a century later it set a pattern outlawing segregation in all its forms. Still, it has yet to directly uphold affirmative action to repair the holocaust of slavery and legalized bigotry. The equal protection clause, paradoxically, is applied to block such goals. It is one thing to halt longtime harms and another to repair their set-in injuries. The court obviously holds that it is powerless to tackle the latter. Given the clout of Congress to do all things necessary to carry out the objectives of equal rights treatment, it needs to address this dilemma. Lewis Diuguid of *The Kansas City Star* recently pointed out, "The Supreme Court in 1954 outlawed legal segregation. But its legacy persists today with inferior schools, unsafe housing, poor health care, low-paying or no jobs, and few opportunities to go to college."

What in 1857, a decade and a half after its *Amistad* ruling, could have caused the court to utter its vile words against Africans? Perhaps it was insincere talk of their inferiority from founders like Thomas Jefferson. He debased his slaves as quite capable of passion yet not of love, and of good memory but not of logic. He yet fathered five children with his house slave Sally. This is more fact than fiction. Attractive house slaves were highly valued, and there's no record her worth was diminished by her duties to another man and their five children. The widowed, fertile writer would've jotted that down somewhere given the many tasks forced on house slaves. Also, Chernow's *Alexander Hamilton* reiterates, "Jefferson's apparent romance with 'Dashing' Sally Hemings."

The esteemed founder's heart was in conflict with itself. He ordered his slaves be treated "with all the humanity and kindness consistent with their necessary subordination and work." And in 1784 when Virginia deeded lands north of the Ohio River to the Union, he offered a law in Congress to exclude slavery there. Jefferson's soul surely cringed at the screams of slave women helpless as their loved ones were being shifted to other plantations. Slavery's twilight, after all, was cocked in his

Declaration of Independence. Abolitionists like Denmark Vesey referred to his unparalleled work on human rights for justification of their militancy.

Still, Philadelphia's mayor Michael Nutter said Jefferson's reference to Indians as "savages" in the Declaration proved he was a racist. It did accuse King George of using "merciless Indian savages" against frontier settlers in spite of their "known rule of warfare." Several native nations, no doubt, in the hell of battle for their very being did not spare children, women, or elderly. The ruthlessness of the Ponies war group is an example of such savagery. In context, Jefferson was stating another rationale for rebellion; let's not forget he was inciting treason. Dr. Ben Franklin so reminded with his wise words: "If we do not hang together, surely we'll be hung separately." Keen as he was, Jefferson surely respected the native political model which inspired Franklin. And when he invited leaders of the Sioux Nation for reports on the Lewis and Clark expedition, he voiced hope to live along with Indians as if they were "in the same household."

The 1857 court was also influenced by rhetoric it was "God's will" to enslave Africans. Biblical scripture—"Servants, be obedient to them that are your masters"—surely played a part. Certain preachers promoted "blacks" were sons of Ham, who'd been cursed for seeing his father Noah naked. Others claimed they descended from Cain, who'd killed his brother Abel. Adding to such pretexts, Jefferson's draft declaration blamed King George for allowing bondage of "a distant people" in his colonies. His Christian kingdom, slavers asserted, was liable for their religious dilemma. To dispel concern the king could curb slavery to avoid the Revolution; those claims were deleted.

Far more graphic Christian piousness flared up when the South was denied right to resolve the slavery question on its own. In the convention only Southerners possessed slaves. Yet, it was a Northern delegate who declared, "The morality or wisdom of slavery are considerations belonging to the states themselves."

Hence, post-Civil War violence was contrived by angry ex-Confederate officers who mobilized a clandestine army, the Ku

Klux Klan. Its first Grand Wizard, Gen. Nathan Bedford Forrest, set an agenda of racial terrorism for scores to come. Imploring the name of Jesus Christ, they met on December 24, 1865, the first Christmas Eve after their defeat. A hooded outfit similar to one worn by a past Christian sect was donned as uniform. Those "God-fearing" men next relied on hideous acts to avenge the North's "treachery." Among which were the 1951 murders of civil rights crusader Harry Moore and his wife by bombing their bedroom on Christmas night. In 1961 they nearly killed the Reverend Fred Shuttlesworth, also on Christmas night. Most appalling of KKK vengeance was the 1963 "Negro Church" dynamiting that murdered four girls as young as eleven who were studying the Holy Bible.

These atrocities wrapped in the cloth of Christianity must have been driven by a piercing psychic pain. While Southerners in comradeship with Northerners were shedding blood against British tyranny, slavery was okay. To then have been ruined by the North because of it was seen by the South as pure betrayal. Infuriating that passion, the North insisted the South integrate ex-slaves without first extending a pacifying hand. Making matters even worse, while many "whites" were stripped of their vote for raising arms against the Union, ex-slaves were swiftly granted it. Well-being of these newly made citizens for that reason was possible only in presence of federal troops.

President Ulysses S. Grant (1869–1877) did all he could to secure the rising sun of equality. "Tiger Ulysses" spearheaded a law tagged the Ku Klux Klan Act to rope in the terrorist backlash. His Civil Rights Act of 1871 made it criminal to use public authority to racially victimize anyone. It also punished two or more persons for agreeing to deprive someone of a basic right like voting. The weight Grant wielded upon the South was cartooned on November 7, 1874 in *Harper's Weekly* as an elephant, which became the Republican Party's symbol.

But weeks after Grant's successor Rutherford B. Hayes (1877–1881) was sworn, Union troops were withdrawn from the South and Reconstruction came to a dead stop. That produced the gripe that Hayes abandoned the nation's healing. However, he also saved it from postwar chaos. Cravings for covert combat stirred in Southerners persuaded they'd been unjustly attacked. Adding to KKK violence were lawless groups such as the Quantrill Raiders, Reno Outlaws, and the Jesse James Gang, all intent on destroying the North. Within silent support, Jesse James moved around as "commodities broker Thomas Howard." He and his brother Frank sounded the rebel battle cry in a war unfinished. Their crime spree was political. Robert, their father, was destroyed as a small slave farmer. Publisher John Newman Edwards, denied voting rights and self-exiled in Mexico, hyped those bandits to agitate Confederate pride. He spun them as innocent men harassed by "radical Republicans." This scenario was fertile ground for sly assassins heaping horror on top of havoc.

President Hayes' retreat arose from election fraud in three Southern states in favor of Democrat Samuel J. Tilden in the 1876 run against Hayes. Hatred for ex-slaves' right to vote likely caused the swindle. Democrats claimed 52 percent of popular ballots, but Tilden was refused a majority of the electoral votes. A commission created by Congress chose along party line (8-7) to award every disputed one to Hayes, thereby making him president.

Needless to say, the already reeling South was bellicose. That powder keg in war-weary America was buried by settling for removal of Union soldiers from the South. Ex-slaves were relieved a Southerner did not again become president so soon after the Civil War. They didn't need another President Johnson, who'd been impeached for favoring the ex-Confederacy but retained his presidency by a single vote. However, since Reconstruction programs could proceed only in presence of Union troops, in the end it didn't matter Hayes followed Grant as president. This became obvious when the last of the troops left New Orleans on April 24, 1877. In the twelve years of federal protection, ex-slaves built hundreds of towns and schools; now they were set ablaze by those tasting the agony of defeat. Also true, with Union soldiers gone, Southerners regained the dignity of a fresh start and stomachs now less empty. "Strangers" (carpetbaggers) from the North were intercepting aid sent to jump-start the South. Those interlopers no longer could hide behind Northern guns.

Unfortunately, while the average Southerner scrounged for survival, others were proceeding with conspiracies started when Lincoln was popularly elected. Following a foiled assassination plot on him in Baltimore on February 5, 1861, he continued to keep his head down, even after the College of Electors on February 13 declared him president-elect. He entered Washington City on February 23 and on March 4 took his oath of office in secrecy. President Hayes, mindful of Lincoln's second-term assassination, opted to be sworn in by President Grant in the basement of the White House amid federal troops.

The ex-Confederacy was down, but definitely not out.

Disgust for ex-slaves' right to vote had become America's new divide. On April 11, 1865, two days following the South's defeat, President Lincoln was giving a speech from the north portico of the White House. Below was John Wilkes Booth, who'd planned to kidnap him. At the moment Lincoln urged the vote for male ex-slaves, Booth growled to a cohort, "That means nigger citizenship. Shoot him now! This will be the last speech he will ever make."

Within seventy-two hours mankind lost a most decent heart in consequence of it.

On January 8, 1867 Congress enacted male ex-slave voting rights over the veto of President Johnson. On Christmas Day 1868 in what was obviously a useful gift to the South, he pardoned ex-Confederates, thus empowering them back into politics. The ex-slave vote yet paid off. Without it, Grant would not have become president. And his reelection was assured by passage of the Fifteenth Amendment on February 3, 1870, making ex-slaves' vote a basic right.

Nine days later, Utah Territory decided if male ex-slaves got suffrage, so should its women, and extended it to them. But though the Fifteenth Amendment was gender neutral, the Supreme Court in *Minor v. Happersett* (1874) ruled it did not grant national voting rights to women. They'd been fighting for it as far back as January 21, 1648, when Maryland denied it to Margaret Brent despite the fact she owned land. In 1848 Elizabeth Cady Stanton (Susan B. Anthony's best friend) gathered other women rights advocates. While they did not labor as hard as their African counterparts, it was inescapable they, too, were treated as slaves. Stanton's *Sentiments Against Injustices to Women* listed eighteen rights Continental women were denied. However, their demand to vote was mocked as a "Reign of Petticoats fantasy." It was therefore natural the Women's Rights Convention of 1851 featured allied ex-slaves Frederick Douglass and Sojourner Truth, who delivered her famous "Ain't I a Woman" speech.

A few states such as Montana did not wait on Congress to give women political equality. It elected the first woman, Jeanette Rankin, to the House of Representatives in November 1916, four years prior to federal voting rights for her sisters. Their struggle was typified in a March 3, 1913 protest walk to Capitol Hill. Along the way they were brutally attacked, some literally pushed down and stomped upon. A few years later on Election Day they rallied at the White House. Victory finally came on August 26, 1920, when the Nineteenth Amendment granted them the vote.

Southern despair had been thus further provoked by the North's swift political elevation of Yankee males above Continental females.

When the Union troops marched out of the ex-Confederacy, it was able to beat the count. Back on their feet, ex-officers morphed into hooded "Christian Knights" whet for settling a score. The Dixie countryside now carried in surreal union with sensual breeze the stench of burnt flesh. For decades to come, taste for payback would be satisfied by acts long forgotten by Plymouth Rock cousins. Klansmen riding at night under shamed hoods, and driven by vexation of the conquered, targeted the beneficiaries of their defeat.

Descendants of those dumped in the dark depths of coastal dungeons, hauled through the door of no return, and then sardine-packed in bilge water of transporters. Naked women manacled beyond a month on same stench-filled spot. Children strangled by terror of whips in a strange land. And thirty-five thousand more slave ships! Bob Marley echoes the sheer horror: "Old pirates, yes they rob I. Sold I to the merchant ships minutes after they took I from the bottomless pit."

New nightmares included attacks incited by crotch fright: "Wink at her, boy, and you'll die ten times over!" This genital anxiety stemmed from generations of carnal assaults against enslaved women. Not only did the rapists go unpunished, but by law resulting children became property of the victims' masters. Poignantly, as Yankees scaled the barriers of bigotry, proportional fear festered in many Continentals who convinced themselves, "What Negroes really want is not our way of life, but to be with our women."

Pinpointing such paranoia is the 1955 kidnap and murder of fourteen-year-old Emmett Louis Till of Chicago. While visiting Mississippi, and unaware of Dixie's perils, Till whistled at a Continental woman. For it, her husband Roy Bryant and his half-brother J. W. Milam terribly tortured him. They choked the child's tongue out, sliced off his penis, and threw into the Tallahatchie River his body weighed down, ironically, by a cotton gin fan. When Till's mother demanded they be prosecuted, she further suffered: "People began to send me mail by the bushel . . . Dirty pictures, pictures of male organs . . ."

This phallic fright persists. On June 28, 2009 a C-SPAN *Washington Journal* caller griped that the new president was doing no better than his predecessor George W. Bush. Despite so, he said, the media was being seduced "by that black president because of his huge penis."

It is their voting rights, however, which stir the most resentment against Yankees. Consider this: despite ineligibility to vote until fifty-three years after Yankees got that right, the political power of Continental women is unmatchable. A record high of twenty sits in the Senate of the current 113th Congress. Since the end of Reconstruction in 1877, only *four* Yankees have been *elected* to that upper chamber. And none yet from the South! A cause of this chasm was longtime obstacles to the ballot box.

46

To help gain actual access to it, the Voting Rights Act of 1965 banned tactics like literacy tests, and the Twenty-Fourth Amendment barred poll taxes. These were achieved by struggles salient in Martin Luther King's August 28, 1963 "I Have a Dream" speech.

While the skin color drama continues to preempt true political parity, a key part of the Voting Rights Act on June 25, 2013 was ruled to be out of date. Most, if not all, of the Supreme Court justices who declared it so were appointees of the Republican Party, the first president from which lost his life urging the vote for same citizens the act protected. (Perhaps that's why in a 2009 case upholding the act the court hinted to Congress it was yet at risk.)

As to public education for "blacks," US troops were deployed to the South on September 24, 1957, four scores to the year President Hayes withdrew them. President Dwight D. Eisenhower took action two weeks after signing the first civil rights bill since 1877. The 101st Army Airborne Division moved in to enforce an order based on the 1954 Supreme Court case *Brown v. Board of Education of Topeka* for entry of nine Yankee students into Little Rock Central High in Arkansas. Governor Orval Faubus had mobilized his state guard to block it. Eisenhower at times disagreed with the court's rulings favoring Yankees but became intolerant to the "go-slow" on civil rights. His use of the Airborne Division was decried as alike an invasion by Adolph Hitler's storm troopers. The former supreme commander of Allied forces in WWII dealt a devastating blow to the skin color drama. That victory is today celebrated as the Little Rock Nine. For the second time federal soldiers were deployed to support struggles which started with mutinies and suicides on slave ships. Despite so, in 1962 Southern obstinacy took two lives and injury to one hundred US marshals as the cost to have James Meredith admitted to the University of Mississippi. That forced integration pained Governor Ross Barnett as an act of "genocide."

While in law school, a Southern friend shocked the Shiloh out of me when I praised those federal actions. He buzzed my ears with this bicker: "The North's excuse for invading the Confederacy to free the slaves is a blatant lie! The Civil War was about the Mississippi River! Those bastards wanted to destroy our influence in the West! The South's wealth threatened the North!"

The fury in his eyes switched to a glare of hope I'd empathize because of my West Indian origins. They then saddened with an afterthought I'd be indifferent to his pain because I'm a "black." He truly apologized on noticing my "How dare you!" stare. Actually, he was not very far off. Concerns for interstate and foreign trade were as central to the North as slavery was to the South. The December 1773 Boston Tea Party protest wasn't really about tea taxes, which the British had reduced. The true culprits were the East India Company and other English shippers jacking up transport costs on all colonial goods. The fear was "trade would disappear and Americans reduced to fur trappers and lumberjacks." Like today's Suez and Panama canals, the Mississippi River was increasingly crucial to commerce. Early on, George Washington met twice with Spain's envoy for full access to that river. And only three years before the Civil War, James Hammond of South Carolina bellowed in the Senate, "Cotton is king!" Its profits were due to slave labor, machine threshing, and transport on the Mississippi, which still pulses in the song "Ole Man River." Perhaps what was fixed in my Southern pal's psyche was the relief Abraham Lincoln expressed when the North gained total control of the Mississippi River during the Civil War: "The Father of Waters again goes unvexed to the sea."

Also of weighty reflection regarding America's four bloodiest years is the economic contrast between Thomas Jefferson and Alex Hamilton. Alex outwitted years of snub for a State of New York Bank by drafting bylaws for a private "Bank of New York," creating in 1784 the nation's first bank. Chernow noted it "foreshadowed Jeffersonian revulsion against Hamilton's economic programs." Jefferson believed in farms with a honeycomb of interstate bartering and was wary of federal power over the economy: "That government, which governs least, governs best," he said. He also insisted "politicians must be held down by the chains of the Constitution."

Alex urged flexibility "for future contingencies." And his 1791 *Report on Manufactures* heralded industry and banking, which reflected his familiarity with St. Croix's global trade.

Continental Army debts defied first President George Washington (1789–1797), and in September 1789 he handed the West Indian a conductor's baton as secretary of the treasury. In 1791 Alex fashioned the first federal tax, the Whiskey Act, and First Bank of the United States. IOUs held by veterans were settled for pennies on the dollar with merchants who then collected even money from the First Bank. A common currency came with the Coinage Act, which created in April 1792 the US Mint. Weeks later on May 17 merchants started the New York Stock Exchange at 70 Wall Street. Bank of New York stocks continue to be its oldest in trade.

In complete contrast, as the third president, Thomas Jefferson (1801–1809) declared, "I sincerely believe banking establishments are more dangerous than standing armies."

He therefore abolished the First Bank. But fourth president James Madison (1809–1817), though wary of big profits bestowed on financiers by Alex's tactic, initiated the Second Bank. Seventh president Andrew Jackson (1829–1837), first of the Deep South, tried to eliminate it. He believed institutional control of the people's money bred a class of powerful, ruthless, nonelected men. He failed and Congress censured him for removing its funds.

Jackson yet forecasted abuse of the financial system. John C. Bogle's *The Battle for the Soul of Capitalism* tells of fiscal bosses siphoning synthetically high salaries and stock interests. Bogle's concerns seemed counterintuitive until I recalled a luncheon hosted for Loyola University student leaders by the Los Angeles Knights of Columbus. The elder knight urged us to "believe in the system" because "the problem of capitalism is not in itself, but with those who abuse its freedoms." Pope John Paul II likewise said, "Capitalism undisciplined by morality will ultimately self-destruct." Pope Francis decries its use of human beings as an expendable commodity. The 2008 subprime mortgages meltdown, pension fund crashes, and billions in bank bailouts confirmed those weaknesses. James Galbraith's *The Predator State* tells how lawmakers indulge friends with monetary ploys which make the rich richer and the working poor poorer. A dozen years ago in the stealth of a midnight bill, Congress gave shadow banks the go-ahead to fabricate casino-like products such as "credit swaps" that allow financiers to collect cash from bonds they do not own.

Nobel Laureate Paul Krugman traces 2008 Great Recession to reducing taxes on the rich and cuddling banks, but cutting social spending. Acceptable as it is to Southern politicians, that anti-jobs "austerity" attitude would have saddened Presidents Jefferson and Jackson.

Even Ayn Rand, who wrote *Capitalism: The Unknown Ideal*, would've worried about Congress' coziness with crony capitalism. It'd cause her to temper her theme of "personal interests" with the basic point of Adam Smith's *The Wealth of Nations*, which said private enterprise—as distinct from profiteering—is good for society. He is boosted by Nobel Laureate John Nash, whose calculation proved self-initiative coupled with a social progress purpose is better still. What instead seems to prevail, as shown in Michael Moore's film *Capitalism: A Love Story*, are very rich unelected "corpocrats" with power over federal fiscal policies and, ergo, the economy.

Meanwhile, the middle class is shrinking. A July 2013 Associated Press survey revealed this: "Four out of five US adults struggle with joblessness, near poverty, or reliance on welfare for at least part of their lives."

If anything can be termed anti-American, it's that reality. President John Adams said, "Property monopolized or in possession of a few is a curse to mankind." Benjamin Franklin echoed, "No man ought to own more property than needed for his living hood; the rest, by right, belongs to the state." Abraham Lincoln in a letter to Colonel William Elkins voiced concern the Civil War would create "enthroned corporations [that will use] prejudices of the people until all wealth is aggregated in the hands of a few and the Republic destroyed." The penultimate line in Congressman Ron Paul's *End the Fed* rings: "Freedom and centralized banking are incompatible." And a native nation, the Cree, see gloom in America's unbridled capitalism: "When all the trees have been cut down, when all the animals have been hunted, when all the waters are polluted, when all the air is unsafe to breathe, only then will you know . . . you cannot eat money."

Jon Meacham's portrayal of Andrew Jackson as a populist icon was logical. Jackson offered common Continentals confidence in grassroots democracy. The issue of slavery aside, if John Adams, Thomas Jefferson, Benjamin Franklin, Alex Hamilton (who often did free legal work for the poor), and Jackson were alive they'd have joined Occupy Wall Street against policies that cause so few to have so much and so many to have so little.

It's yet unlikely North/South clashing fiscal views prompted the Civil War. Leonard Pitts seemed more precise when he wrote, "Preservation of slavery was the prime directive of the southern confederacy." Still, my Southern friend's doubts about it shouldn't be taken for granted. This is not to defend smugness like flying the Confederate flag atop South Carolina's State House, where it incited memories of Jim Crow atrocities inflicted under its colors. While most Continentals aren't fretful as to where that flag flies, they'd think differently if they were, as Pitts puts it, "black in Mississippi in 1964." On July 1, 2000 it was removed after years of protests. Clash between those for whom the rebel colors symbolizes the worse of their past, and those who seek to honor the lives lost for it, looms. It is on motor vehicle license plates in nine states, but a November 2011 attempt to add Texas met strong resistance. It's ironic the disturbing flag is similar to the patriots' initial bars-and-stars banner.

To be fair, slavery existed in some great African kingdoms of which "blacks" are proud. So, social groups such as Sons of the Confederacy should not be ostracized for recalling their heritage, part of which dealt the same sufferings long familiar

Michael A. Joseph, Esq.

to mankind. Thomas Sowell's *Black Rednecks and White Liberals* notes the universal nature of the travails: "The story of how human beings treat other human beings when they have unbridled power over them is seldom a pretty story or even a decent story, regardless of the color of the people involved. When the roles were reversed, Africans did not treat Europeans any better than Europeans treated Africans. Neither can be exempted from moral condemnation applied to the other."

Such history added more reason to have totally abolished slavery at the 1787 Convention. But as far back as 1635, when Virginia and Maryland navies battled over a boundary dispute, each colony asserted itself as sovereign with respect to the other. Hence, the United States of America reflects the genius of merging two opposing factions consisting of twelve "nations" into a single unit. This new amity swiftly invited Rhode Island—first to denounce British rule but absent from the Convention because of post-Revolution debts issues—into the more perfect union.

Claim the founders dropped the ball in 1787 by failing to fully eliminate human bondage misses the unique dawn of America. Its core loathed slavery, yet had to tolerate it in half of itself in order to give birth to that very core. This paradox, more accurately this gambit, caused political insecurity in the South, since Congress at any time could move to outlaw slavery. The surest way for Southern stability was to flow with the tide towards a slave-free America. But to dodge it, slavers decided to form a separate realm—an option forbidden by the Constitution: "[N]o new State shall be formed or erected . . . by the Junction of two or more States . . . without the Consent of . . . Congress."

The Confederacy was thus created in betrayal of this fundamental. Even leader Jefferson Davis had pangs of conscience about his disloyalty. It is therefore poignant Davis' unexpired Senate term was in 1870 filled by Hiram R. Revels, the first "black" senator. Davis very well knew that of the first fifteen presidents, ten were Southerners required to recite directly from the Constitution the following oath to become president: "I do solemnly swear [or affirm] that I will faithfully execute the office of the president of the United States, and will to the best

52

of my ability, preserve, protect, and defend the Constitution of the United States."

(President Washington added "So help me God" at the end of his oath, and it has since been repeated.)

Given Southerners' twice greater opportunity to defend the charter, it is not unexpected a president from the South was first to threaten use of force against any state intent on leaving the Union. Abraham Lincoln simply showed same firmness in fidelity to *his* oath. It is by this fate he is the misjudged main character of the Civil War.

In spite America banned its slave trading on March 2, 1807 within the Constitution's fixed time, doubts exist about its early will to end slavery. A Yankee college mate insisted my respect for the Great Emancipator was misplaced: "Abraham Lincoln didn't give a damn about black people. He said if slavery would have saved the nation, he would have saved slavery."

So what? Lincoln said so on August 22, 1862 during the Civil War in response to an article in *The New York Tribune* scolding him for not enforcing the Confiscation Acts giving him power to seize slavers' property. That utterance was histrionics in defense of his broader policy to keep the nation from totally unraveling. He had long made clear his resolve to see slavery's demise. In 1854 he described it as "monstrous." In his 1858 campaign for the Senate, and 1860 for the White House, his condemnation of it was very clear. Days before he took office, slaveholders in Congress tried to bar his hindrance of their system, but he didn't oppose them. Though he personally detested slavery, he wasn't an abolitionist. He thought the latter's rhetoric hardened slavers' hearts. Difficult as it was, rights they received for sake of creating America had to be tactically stomached. Besides, as an ex-Whig, Lincoln held that legislative power was the truest part of democracy. Originating 1648 in Scotland, Whigs believed the masses were best served by a body of elected lawmakers. He therefore saw the end of slavery as the business not of the president, but of Congress.

For that reason he refused noncitizen Africans' plea to fight for the Union. He did not want to be seen as attacking the CSA to free its enslaved. Instead, he wanted to be known as fighting to uphold the Constitution. Even then, his grasp of the charter assured him that if he preserved it, slavery's end was surely fated. But the CSA's battle capability forced him to be more practical. Frederick Douglass, whose opinion he "cherished most," scolded him, said historian James Horton, "for fighting with a strong right arm behind his back." Douglass knew Lincoln's ideals would amount to naught if he lost the war. Not long after, the combat skills of Massachusetts' Fifty-Fourth Volunteer Regiment of Free Africans proved to Congress "blacks" must be allowed to fight.

In the end, 365,000 Union soldiers were killed, compared to 260,000 Confederates. Often, casualties of the former approached twice that of the latter. This is seen in the Battles of the Wilderness and Spotsylvania of May1864, where Union losses were more than 35,000 in contrast to the CSA's 18,000. Such huge losses were buffered by the almost 200,000 "black" troops.

Though Lincoln was years older than Douglass, wonder marked their link. When Douglass was invited to the White House and saw on the wall of Lincoln's office the same saying he'd hung in his, he asked "Honest Abe" if spies were sent to his workplace. Abe assured his comrade pure fate arranged for both to share it. It was Shakespeare's: "There's a divinity that shape our ends; rough-hew them how we will."

Same destiny guided Lincoln's prudent use of his commander-in-chief clout. He rescinded military shutdown of *The Chicago Times* and directed his generals that even when they felt the press was a threat to the Union, they were to act with "caution, compassion, and forbearance." He rescinded Gen. John Fremont and Gen. David Hunter's separate orders freeing slaves in certain states. Their noble gestures did not factor the need to prevent Unionist slave states like Lincoln's own Kentucky from shifting to the Confederacy. His foresight was surely on point. Missouri sent thirty-nine regiments into the Civil War — seventeen for the South *and* twenty-two for the North. That peculiarity no doubt spun the war into one of brothers against brothers.

While Lincoln possessed keenness of some military greats, war wasn't to his liking and steadily he tried to end it. On April 10, 1862 an offer of aid was made to every slave state willing to end, even if gradually, its slavery. Making clear the South, too, was his responsibility, he announced on December 8, 1863 his intent to rebuild it. To save the nation from ever again tolerating human bondage, on January 31, 1865, with abolitionists like Senator Charles Sumner and Congressman Thaddeus Stevens, he achieved the Thirteenth Amendment. On February 3 he met with Confederates for peace talks promising liberal pardons. But the South refused a cease-fire unless given autonomy. Point it surrendered just five weeks later proves Lincoln's compassion was not based on any uncertainty as to which side would win.

But reluctance to accept the Civil War was sown by Southern conflicting hearts fester a mind-set that the North betrayed the South for the sake of "blacks." Serious symptoms of this malaise resembles schizophrenia: "The key to the disease lies in the dual personality exhibited by its victims, there appearing to be a cleavage or split of mentality."[22]

This is seen in the Ku Klux Klan's setting afire the Christian symbol of salvation as an act of terrorism. How chillingly conflicting is a crucifixion cross fêted with the fire of hell. Such behavior suggests the Klan and its sundry offshoots are victims of a split-mind malady. When confronted in court, they profess not to burn the cross. They instead swear to be "lighting" it. In their cleaved minds, they believe they shed light by inciting fright. Also is their lingering appetite for lynching. It appears to be penalty transference for the sins of slavery exacted not on progenies of its perpetrators, but upon those of its victims.

Similar upside-down politics dominates the nation in contrast to debates seen in other republics. American lawmaking approaches a scorch-earth paradigm. In May 2012 Cliff Schecter compared a current map of "red" (Southern-bent) and "blue" (Northern-bent) states. He concluded the Union remains a house divided: "It is somewhat dispiriting to look at the map from pre-1860 and realize how relevant it is today, when predicting who will have racially tinged immigration laws, collective bargaining rights, [and] kill-at-will Stand Your Ground laws . . ."

In July 2012 Leonard Pitts laid bare the schism which bogs America down and twists it into: "A nation whose depth of division and lack of unifying principle now poison the very air."

It suffocates even the attempt to create a healthier nation. Call for universal health care was met with lies of its failures in Canada, Britain, and France. In reality, the single-provider systems of those countries afford them life spans which exceed that of the United States. In May 2013 ABC TV reported that an average of eleven thousand babies die each year on the day they are born. This rate is higher than in all other industrialized nations combined!

America's cleavage is rooted in its war of brothers against brothers. Before the Civil War, West Point graduates Ulysses S. Grant and Robert E. Lee were true brothers in arms. Naturally, the armies they led were psychologically unprepared to deploy their one and the same training against the other. Just as bizarre was President Lincoln's request to Lee he lead the charge against Southerners of his heritage. Lee resigned his commission in the Union Army to instead defend his familial homeland. Grant became his archenemy of the North. How heart wrenching chief generals of two opposing forces became duty-bound to kill fellow soldiers who had once swore away their lives to both. This disarray slid further downhill when Grant was pressed to execute Lee for treason after the Civil War.

Grant refused, but that courtesy did not quiet Southern outrage a "radical Republican" was urged to slay a "gentleman officer." In Southerners' minds, at worst Lee defended right of the South to deal at its own pace with its "peculiar institution." At best, he fought federal heavy-handedness.

No less hard-hearted than urgings he be killed, Gen. Lee was made stateless until his citizenship was posthumously returned on July 22, 1975. For a century Southerners were shamed by the fact Robert Edward Lee, the Union colonel who defeated John Brown at Harper's Ferry, was stripped of his nationality. And it was unconstitutional. The Supreme Court in *Trop v. Dulles*

(1956) ruled that divesting even a naturalized citizen of his citizenship as penalty for any crime was cruel and unusual under the Eighth Amendment. Lee's citizenship should have been reinstated back in 1956 because the court acknowledged: "Civilized nations of the world are in virtual unanimity that statelessness is not to be imposed."

This tragic Grant-versus-Lee theatre is for Yankees an odd-man-out drama akin to a family feud in which a stranger becomes entangled. The outsider seldom avoids making enemies on both sides. So deep-rooted is this trait, it transcends skin color. Continental abolitionists were at times targets of that passion as far north as Illinois, where newspaper editor Elijah Lovejoy was mob-hanged. Another barely escaped with his life in, of all places, Boston. Some say this civil chaos was due to fear those anti-slavers might've incited race wars. If that was the concern, it seems limiting their meetings would've been the official response. Instead, those hanging mob arousals were caused by primal feelings imbedded in kinship bond yearning. True to it, Union and Confederate soldiers often got together between their lines after a battle to chat and trade food, etc. Such nostalgia later prompted Northern Continentals to vote for Southerner Samuel Tilden for president without worry about "outsider" Yankees.

Continental/Yankee split knotted in North/South estrangement can be healed with interchanges alike those of South Africa's Truth and Reconciliation Commission. This belief arises from my daylong presence in one such hearing presided over by Archbishop Desmond Tutu. To mend the horrific wounds of apartheid, native Ubuntu was beckoned. Its premise is that when one hurts another, he hurts all, including himself. The protocol was, in return for confessions to crimes as forbidding as torture and murder, compassion was extended. Time has proven forgiveness based on the culprit's remorse heals all. True charity so saturated Cape Town's Parliament Chamber in that summer of 1995 it seemed to be mankind's last hope for harmony.

My optimism wasn't passing passion. In Johannesburg days before, I was up close and personal in an instance of a purging.

The moustached man sitting on the barstool next to mine in the hotel lobby was strangely absorbed, mostly staring at his drink. "Good night," I said, but he didn't even look up.

"Good night again sir, could you tell me something about Jo'burg?"

His blue eyes finally met brown ones of a Caribbean accent and it relaxed him. He offered a handshake.

"Gosh, I could swear you were an ANC hit man targeting me!"

His error wasn't baseless. Hours earlier, I felt very vulnerable on an elevator carrying me to see an African National Congress official. It was suspended several times between floors. I was being scrutinized by separate checkpoints. Those gaps seemed longer than infinity and aroused fear of "What if I'm misidentified?" as I looked up at a security camera coldly staring back at me. When I finally met the officer he said the ANC could not afford to trust *anyone* unfamiliar to it. The new South Africa was not as tranquil as it appeared.

Still shaking my hand, the fellow hotel guest stated he was a major in South Africa's army. Perhaps I telegraphed fright I'd alarmed a soldier, for his next words rang out with a true tone of hospitality:

"No worry about me. Mandela is my boss now. Welcome *you* to South Africa!"

In appreciation of his genuine cordiality, I reassured him I was just the opposite of what he had thought of me by mentioning my 1977 song *The Wheel Keeps on Turning (the Bottom Becomes the Top and the Top the Bottom)*. It urged native South Africans that upon the inevitable collapse of apartheid they forgive its perpetrators for sake of peace.

That night we socialized as would long-lost buddies. We ended up at a casino and I nudged the Afrikaner to mingle with native ladies for the first time in his life. He couldn't believe my nerve at suggesting that, but later he admitted he was glad he did. By then, we trusted each other and spoke for hours on general life in old and new South Africa. I asked him why he was so fearful of the ANC, what apartheid-era harm *he* committed before Nelson Mandela became his "boss." With pledge I'll protect his identity he let me tape our discussions and suggested, as a gesture of gratitude for my caring about his country, I publish it.

My new friend came clean. On June 16, 1976 in Soweto Township he fired war bullets into the backs of young children during their protests against being taught in Afrikaans—the Afrikaners' tongue. Sobbing into his palms as they hid his face, he quietly said again and again, "Some died at my hands."

And my eyes also swamped as I repeatedly asked, "How could you kill those children when you have kids of your own?"

I reminded him those students were heeding martyr Stephen Biko's advice they demand better schooling. To dump education intended to mould maids and miners and instead pursue that of doctors and engineers. The repentant major agreed with me, but pleaded, "At the time, I truly believed if those students were not stopped there, they would next invade Durban where my children would be in danger."

Back in St. Croix I destroyed the recording. At that time, I thought by publishing it I'd be exploiting the Afrikaner's contrition. Actually, I felt that to reveal it I would have to betray the confidence he'd placed in me.

Similar stirring post-apartheid stories are found in these films: Regardt van den Berg's *Faith Like Potatoes*, John Boorman's *In My Country*, Tom Hooper's *Red Dust*, Darrell Roodt's *Winnie Mandela*, and Justin Chadwick's *Nelson Mandela*.

As to racial resolution in America, there's belief reparation for slavery is essential. The second-most senior congressman, John Conyers, perennially offers bill HR 40 to study the subject, but to no avail. It's challenged by queries, the answers to which remain beyond reach so long as HR 40 is snubbed. Typical questions are: who precisely was in control of slavery; who will qualify as claimants; what amounts are due; and why taxpayers unproven to have benefited from it bear its burden. That's countered with examples such as: not all Germans killed Jews in the 1940s, yet Germany paid billions in reparations to Israel and paid $50 million to America in 1979 for sabotaging in 1916 an ammo plant on Tom Black Island, NJ; each citizen of Japanese heritage rounded up and held during WWII got $10,000; in 1976 Japan made its final WWII reparation payment to the Philippines; and Congress set aside $1.3 billion for harm to people and property caused by US nuclear bomb tests in the South Pacific.

Significantly, in freeing his slaves George Washington ordered his estate to care for those too old to work and to educate the rest.

Also, the goal of Reconstruction embraced aspects of reparation. Had Lincoln not been the Civil War's last casualty he might have joined his Republicans, who backed at least partial confiscation of slavers' plantations for benefit of ex-slaves. Others had urged transfer of political power from the planters to them. In fact, because of voting rights granted to ex-slaves in 1868 the majority of South Carolina's state assembly was "blacks."

Understanding the skin color drama is critical to useful debates. Mere mention of "reparation" triggers the blame game. The drama's propensity for face-to-face tensions obscure reality slavery and racism were largely legislated. The issue is therefore of institutional, and not of individual, responsibility. It is failure to see this which provokes anxieties.

Amid the outrage stemming from basketball team Los Angeles Clippers owner's Don Sterling racial remarks, "white" columnist Tina Dupuy in May 2014 wrote that "we've grown adept at being disgusted when hearing racist things." And often a career-busting blow is brought upon the head of the loose-tongue offender. Such contempt, however, borders on the pretentious when lined up to the vastly more significant point Dupuy makes and repeated verbatim here: "We're less willing to talk about, or even acknowledge, that institutionalized racism is a real thing. A word is easy to rally and tweet against: the long-term subjugation of a people based on their skin color is, well, not easy to solve with a catchy hashtag."

Discourse about reparation is best place to find solutions. For it appears the uproar that "casual" racism rouses is an avoidance reflex to the underlying truth: an absence of reparation. Hence, contempt for the N-word should go hand in hand with embrace for the R-word—"R" for Respect, the lodestone of reparation.

Some presume wish for handouts motivates the call for it. That's not surprising given the fact the average wealth of "whites" is near fifteen times that of "blacks." However, the benefits of repairing the holocaust of slavery and ensuing century of government-sponsored bigotry covers more than monetary interests. Progenies of both the enslaved and enslavers stand to gain. Mark Twain's *The Tragedy of Pudd'nhead Wilson* makes clear the evil stole humanity from each. In his *The Narrative of the Life of Frederick Douglass* he tells what happened when his owner's wife caught him reading: "Her tender, warm heart turned to stone. Her smiling face became distrustful. By watching her, I saw how slavery hurts slave owners, too. It had changed her from an angel to a demon."

The impact such perversions have on contemporary America can only be imagined. The good of reparation thus may rest in the simple act of facing the issue, like when the South African Army officer bared his remorse. Our instincts to bypass the blame game paved path to open discourse and mutual respect. Wish to repair past wrongs also appeared when I spoke to a Copenhagen University economics professor about Denmark's debt for St. Croix's slavery. He giggled as if caught with his hand in the cookie jar: "I was wondering when you all will ask for it. The main concern, as I see it, would be structuring a payment plan."

Reparation can also start with reeducation; there's no inherent gap between fellow beings, and all have contributed to mankind. A few big businesses have taken, even if small, steps in this direction. Dow Chemical urged that the most significant component of anything "is the human element: nothing more fundamental, nothing more element." Chevron featured a silhouette of an African hunter stalking the horizon as it noted man's instinct to explore. CBS TV offered racial healing words of President Mandela. In subliminal consensus racism manifests aspects of dementia; journalist Mike Wallace followed Mandela with advice depression is not a disease of shame. None are, not even racism. Nevertheless, by definition all diseases are injurious and treatment, if not cure, is always necessary. Whether it is called reconciliation or reparation, America has got to close its historical wound or it will perpetually ooze the pus of racism. As so powerfully said by Archbishop Tutu, "Having looked the beast in the eye, having asked and received forgiveness . . . let us shut the door on the past, not to forget it, but to allow it not to imprison us."

Compelling versions of this true civility are found in a film and in a novel. In *Grace Card* it was grace, not race, which prevailed in that movie about reconciliation. "For it is by grace you have been saved," it reminds. Harriet Beecher Stowe's *Uncle Tom's Cabin* offered a song by John Newton entitled "Amazing Grace." In real life, Newton was an English slave trader who captained ships, including the *Africa*, that carried away as many as twenty thousand slaves. A powerful ocean storm humbled him into promising God he would give up the slave trade if his life be spared. Convinced his prayer was answered, Newton converted to an anti-slavery evangelist forever praising his deliverance out of the wretchedness. He also became the spiritual force behind abolitionist Member of Parliament William Wilberforce. Beecher Stowe's novel was so moving, on her meeting President Lincoln at the White House during the Civil War, he teased, "So, you're the little lady who started this big war."

Many write about America's lingering divide but few spell a way out. Yet, history is on its side. Pitt's July 2012 column astutely reminded that each time the nation was stirred to reach a unifying goal, from the Revolution to the civil rights movement to walking on the moon, it showed a knack to achieve. As Alexis de Tocqueville noticed, "The greatness of America lies not in being more enlightened than any other nation, but rather in her ability to repair her faults."

That praise will be even more fitting when the skin color fissure is fixed. Ambition to mend it is at times transcendent. In August 2007 at St. Francis Hotel in San Francisco I bought some Democrat Barack Obama White House campaign buttons. It caused a Continental guest from Arkansas, an aide to Hillary Clinton when Bill was that state's governor, to start a chat with me. She concluded with utter sincerity, "The ideal team for the White House would be Fred Thompson [a Republican] and Obama. We've got to heal this nation."

While racism remains a tragic part of America, never has it gone unchecked. A random minutia of anecdotes bears proof. Continentals were jailed for aiding the Underground Railroad, by which slaves fled north to freedom. Lucretia Mott of the Philadelphia Female Anti-Slavery Society refused to be muzzled. In the 1850s, when the slavery question was most contentious, Frederick Douglass was guarded by racially mixed abolitionist groups. On May 28, 1863 Massachusetts' Fifty-Fourth Volunteer Regiment of Free Africans, which inspired the Oscar winner *Glory*, marched from Boston into the Civil War. Their Continental commander Col. Robert Gould Shaw during assembly of battalions for the Battle of Antietam had written home these profound thoughts:

How grand it is to meet all the men . . . ready to fight for their country like the old fellas did in the Revolution. But this time we must make it a whole country . . . We fight for men and women whose poetry is not yet written, but which will presently be as enviable and as renowned as any.

Affairs of heart between European indentured servants and slaves were not uncommon. Whenever there were few European but many African women, the latter became lovers of European men. To a lesser extent the opposite occurred. Such colorblindness was seen when Frederick Douglass married a Continental after his first wife died.

Some extreme racial notions have been voluntarily withdrawn. To "awake the so-called Negro," the Nation of Islam publicized racism was the evil of "white blue-eyed devils." James Baldwin thought it did so as a counter-racist tactic, since people find it hard to accept they are despised even though they've done nothing to deserve it. Hence, many "blacks" didn't accept they were the targets of hidden racism. That prop became less needed when the civil rights movement made clear the extent of latent bigotry. The Nation of Islam's current demand that lands be set aside for "the so-called Negro," by the way, was first urged by Senator Rufus King, who was a delegate at the 1787 Constitutional Convention. In 1825 King introduced a resolution in the Senate to sell public lands and use the proceeds to emancipate the enslaved and move them to empty parts of America.

Gov. George Wallace of Alabama bucked his supremacist views and expressed regret to civil rights groups. In 1976 he gave Clarence Norris, last of the nine Scottsboro Boys 1932 racist rape trials—eight of whom were to die but all got new trials and life sentences—a full pardon. Sen. Robert C. Byrd evolved from Ku Klux Klan leader to recipient of 100 percent positive rating with the NAACP.

In 1956 Continentals of Clinton, Tennessee, risked their lives to help twelve Yankee high school students pierce segregated classrooms a year before the Little Rock Nine. And two scores later, teacher Ron Clark's rescue of students at Inner Harlem Elementary School cannot be overstated.

In 1965 Rev. James Reeb, a Continental marching for racial justice, was murdered in Selma, Alabama. In December 1819 when that state joined the Union it had slavery. But during the Civil War its northeastern people tried to opt out of the Confederacy. There were also "white" Southern abolitionists such as Angelina and Sarah Grimké, who trained foes of the "peculiar institution" to spread this message: "Slavery is a violation of the natural order of things, and no human power can much longer perpetuate it."

John Brown with sixteen other Continentals and five Yankees on October 15, 1859 attacked the federal arsenal at Harper's Ferry to start a war against slavery. Ten days later he was sentenced to death and on December 2 he, two Yankees, and three other Continentals were hanged. Brown was vindicated during the Civil War. The West Virginia courthouse where he was sentenced by a slaveholding judge was seized as barracks for Union soldiers, who slept on the bench from which the hanging edict was barked.

Hillsdale College of Michigan when chartered in 1844 explicitly declared its admission policy was race neutral. Mark Twain, despite his literary use of *nigger*, was the first American writer to note the African was not only equal to the European, but could chastise him for moral flaws. William "Buffalo Bill" Cody of the Wild West Shows, when eight years old saw his father slowly die from a knife wound for protesting against slavery. Supreme Court Justice John Marshall Harlan opposed the unincorporated territory doctrine as being based on islanders' skin color, and was the lone dissenter to the "separate but equal" dogma of *Plessey v. Ferguson* (1896), where he wrote: "The Constitution is color blind, and neither knows nor tolerates classes among citizens."

Fifth circuit judge Elbert Parr Tuttle epitomized the commitment of federal judges who refused to ignore civil rights laws. Judge James Horton forfeited his judgeship by setting aside the retrial conviction of Scottsboro Boy Haywood Patterson.

In 1946 a hard blow to bigotry was dealt by the Brooklyn Dodgers when it first braved a "colored player" on a "white field." A score later, Texas Western University did the same for basketball deep in Ku Klux Klan country. Not to be forgotten are the "white radicals" who sacrificed their affluent lives "to fight racism at home and imperialism abroad." Their heart is described in words of a Continental when asked on TV how she felt about the murder of Martin Luther King Jr. Her response was nothing less than eye-opening: "Our prejudice and ignorance is what killed Dr. King. Many people are mourning him, but we Americans should mourn America."

Publisher McDougal Littell noted that as disillusioned a writer as was James Baldwin, he believed racial conflicts could end through reason and understanding. Its *American Literature* quotes him: "We, the black and white, deeply need each other if we are really to become a nation."

Michael A. Joseph, Esq.

This was clarion call of Abraham Lincoln's Gettysburg Address:

> It is for us, the living, rather, to be dedicated . . . to the unfinished work which they who fought . . . have thus far so nobly advanced. [T]hat these dead shall not have died in vain; that this nation, under God, shall have a new birth of freedom; and that government of the people, by the people, for the people shall not perish from the earth.

Lincoln's vision would likely have come to fruition but for his demise and consequent loss of North/South reconciliation. This much was put forward by former president of the Confederacy Jefferson Davis: "Next to the destruction of the Confederacy, the death of Abraham Lincoln was the darkest day the South has ever known."

In attempt to salvage reunion, in 1867 Civil War veterans from the North founded the Grand Army of the Republic, forerunner of today's American Legion. It was the first national social group to openly integrate. True to its objectives, Post 160 of Cazenovia, New York, elevated a Yankee as flag bearer. He was not a token; fighting shoulder to shoulder with Continentals earned Yankees the title of "comrades." Of course, Southern posts refused to abide by GAR's rule to admit *any* American veteran.

Some Southerners migrated to the Midwest, still soaked in Civil War bitterness. As a matter of fact, the Tulsa holocaust of 1921 begun on May 31 set aside as Memorial Day to honor veterans lost in that war. And more than a few had fought in World War I, gaining skills that enabled them to wreak total destruction.

An earlier sign that anguish over the war between brothers feeds the skin color drama was seen in the decision of a Southern general sent overseas. David Silbey's *A War of Empire and Frontier* tells of occupation of the Philippines following the 1898 war with Spain. Gen. Jonathan Mayhew Wright refused to implement the Home Treatment program designed to break the natives' fighting spirit by tagging them as "niggers" and "squaws." For Gen. Wright, Filipinos were never slaves used as pretext to start the Civil War, nor were they "savages" who pounced on frontier "whites." Hence, in spite of his Southern heritage, he rejected the tactic as misplaced in the Philippines.

The bigotry which plagues America, the racial alignment Gen. Wright refused to impose abroad, is unique to it. There-fore, when members of violent racist groups are convicted for skin color crimes they should be evaluated and treated. Instead, they are handed enhanced penalties for those culture-driven "hate crimes." In prison, their psychosis is so pervasive racial conflicts there appear to be part of protocol.

Still, mankind's innate goodwill cannot be stifled by cages. In September 2007 while listening to Trinity Broadcasting Net-work I dozed off but was pulled out of my slumber by *The Paula Show*. Its host was cheering a prisoner who'd given up racism of his Aryan Brotherhood gang. The ex-AB was beseeching prayers for racial harmony. Convicts, too, can be dreamers. To trumpet John Lennon: "They may say I'm a dreamer, but I'm not the only one."

The skin color drama also features internal spats. They are rare, but deadly. One of proportion occurred between Yankee civil rights icon W. E. B. DuBois and Pan Africanist Marcus Garvey, a Jamaican. It abscessed when Garvey sought help from the Ku Klux Klan for his Back to Africa Movement. Since Klansmen also believed in "Africa for Africans," Garvey thought it logical to request they speed the exodus with financial help. DuBois, however, saw it as insensitivity to KKK crimes against "coloreds." Their disagreement flipped into a tragic fight on nuances of skin color. Garvey claimed "light-skinned Negroes" like DuBois, as was often the case in Jamaica, intended to domi-nate those of purer African ancestry, as was he. He said DuBois would infect Africa with it. DuBois shot back with attacks on Garvey so sarcastic as to be unworthy of repetition. It was a sad time for the up-and-coming struggle for equality. Ironi-cally, DuBois did "go home" to Ghana to rest in peace. Garvey,

Michael A. Joseph, Esq.

weakened by that storm plus wounds from the guards of racism, didn't see his dream come true.

That row triggered trepidations about being accused as an apologist for the horrors of racism. My concern was quieted by a story supportive of opinion hard-core racists suffer clinical dementia in need of empathy and healing. On January 28, 2007 Chicago's WGN-TV aired *The Vernon Johns Story* with James Earl Jones as Rev. Vernon Johns. The truth-based film was about a Southern Baptist minister's fury against a KKK cross-burning at his church's doorstep. He bellowed, "The crucifixion of Jesus Christ was a lynching!" intended to terrorize early Christians just as the Klan planned for his gathering. It got him in trouble with seniors of the church. His sermon, they admonished, was too caustic. In tussle now with church elders and Klansmen, the undaunted Rev. Johns preached to both detractors that instead of the crucifiers quaking Christ, he triumphed to become the Redeemer when he uttered down from his Calvary cross: "Forgive them Father for they know not what they do."

Some aren't so naive. They cleverly exploit the skin drama for political gain. I was not startled by Yankee Berth Bowman's tell-all. He was hearings coordinator for Senators Strum Thurmond and Jesse Helms. During *The Tavis Smiley Show* of July 30, 2008 he revealed those politicians elevated him to their behind-the-scenes manager. In fact, he said, they truly loved him. Tavis was more than befuddled because both Southerners were barefaced segregationists. Bowman coolly responded that they really were not racists. Instead: "They knew what to say to get elected."

The skin drama also involves plots which overshadow skin shades. Islanders face fewer snags in this scene of its final act. In 1968 my high school guidance counselor urged I turn down admission to the local college for a stateside one eager to have students of my profile. Giving me an application, the Continental explained, "You will be admitted with financial aid to this college in Helena, Montana. They need to integrate fast to receive federal funds."

I leaned back, stuttering I wouldn't go where I was not wanted. I explained that what I'd seen on TV concerning how

Yankees were scorned surely will get me in trouble. The good lady assured, "No, no. When you get up there they will not consider *you* black. Whites will treat you differently because you are from the islands."

Somehow I felt there was truth to what she said. Actually, her offer crested fantasies from my comic book days. My hero, the Rawhide Kid, saved Helena when an evil totem pole invaded it. I admired how the Kid won although the monster was immune to his six-shooters. I even pictured myself riding a horse to class. Sheer surprise greeted my arrival in Helena. It was a quaint, quiet city perfect for Christmas cards. There were no horses. No cowboys. I was yet so well received at that "lily-white" college, I sometimes long for Montana.

The wonder of President Barack Obama is similarly rooted in more than intellect and charisma. Many Continentals were prepared to give him the benefit of the doubt because he has no straight link to American slavery. Hence, he was less threatening and got a win by default in the skin color drama games. The tenuous and abstract claim in 2012 that he has a slave ancestor didn't harm his general charm. In contrast, true descendants of slavery continue to evoke payback anxiety seen in automatic smiles from Continentals. If there's disconnection in this paradigm, the drama recedes to something less ominous. The not-so-menacing "person of color" rouses, instead, instincts for harmony.

Otherwise, fear rules. Helpless Yankees fleeing the devastation of Hurricane Katrina were herded off a bridge exiting into a Continental community simply because police feared them. Fear is indeed man's first enemy and panic paints with a broad brush. In World War II Americans of German and Italian ethnicity thought to be anarchists were rounded up. And one hundred thousand Japanese Americans were herded into guarded camps. President Franklin D. Roosevelt ordered it even though in his first inaugural speech he declared of the Great Depression he inherited: "I firmly believe the only thing we have to fear is fear itself!" When his calm returned, however, in granting their request to fight for the stars and stripes he clarified: "Americanism is not, and never was, a matter of race or ancestry." A touching instance of this irony was the patriotism of Ben Kuroki. In respect for taking bombing missions over his ancestral land, the flying fortress on which he served was nicknamed "Sad Sake."

Regarding the decided and long-standing tropical bias, President Obama is exempted from it. Although he originated from an island, it is a state of the Union, plus his mother's heritage is linked to Plymouth Colony. He is instead challenged, he admits in *Dreams from My Father*, by a barely familiar father whose Kenyan grave signifies their early separation.

Despite dissimilarity between paternal bonding and skin color, talking heads caught in currents of the racial drama insist Obama's true albatross is "racial identity." They say he is equivocal as to where his racial heart retires at the end of day. They point to his organizing work in South Side Chicago's "black" community as being a journey for self-discovery. Shelby Steele's *A Bound Man: Why We Are Excited about Obama and Why He Can't Win* was as accurate as is the latter part of its subtitle. Oblivious to Obama's native appeal, Steele now tries to salvage his slip with assertions Obama deployed the skin color drama to guilt-trip "whites" into electing him.

Not all "people of color" are tethered to a "racial heritage" any more than they are to their zoological niche in the spectrum of species. Though aware of the ever-present skin drama, they routinely bypass it. William Strickland, who attended college with me, was that way, although "blacks" were expected to "act like brothers and sisters in the struggle." Many years later on *The Tavis Smiley Show* about a jobs book he wrote, he hadn't changed. His "I wear my own armor" outlook is thematic also in the stage play *Passing Strange* by the musician Swing.

Closer to home, Horace Clarke of the New York Yankees, the only batsman to deny three no-hitters in the ninth, fathered a child on the mainland who partly grew up in St. Croix. His Fresh Water Yankee son shared this: "Skin color issues got my attention only when I went back up to the States for college."

Stateside children of Crucian parentage are typically shielded from the drama. Eunice Tranberg, born in Canarsie section of

Brooklyn, remembers her friendly neighborhood. Sharing each other's homes, she bathed and ate with her Italian girlfriends. When nine years old, her parents purchased a South Ozone Park home in Queens. Riding her bicycle in the new community she smiled and waved at another child. "Don't you look at me nigger!" his tiny voice screeched. The perplexed girl quickly pedaled home: "What is a nigger?" Her mother wasted no time in scolding the boy's racially primed parents, who apologized in a heavy German accent.

Other scenes in this final act of the drama include these sketches: Claude Petersen strolled with two Yankee friends to eat in nearby Fort Jackson, South Carolina, just before their deployment to Vietnam. He chose a restaurant, but his friends didn't enter. "You're going to be ignored!" they warned. Snubbed as said, the soldier demanded service. The owner approached.

"What's the problem?"

"I'm on my way to fight for this country and I'm not leaving until I'm served," Petersen declared in his West Indian accent.

"Are you from Jamaica?"

"No. I'm from the Virgin Islands."

"Oh, I see. You guys are different."

The islander dined while his fellow Yankee soldiers stood outside, quite at a loss. Petersen added he really had no idea what he was up against, "But it was not until years later when I attended the FBI fingerprint school at Quantico, Virginia, did I realize how deep skin color goes in America. Of ninety in our Administrative Advance class, there was only one single Yankee fellow."

Trained at Georgia's Fort Banning before being sent to Vietnam, Spanish-faced Luis Martinez and a Yankee-looking Puerto Rican buddy were playing pool when he ordered two beers. The waitress brought him only one with explanation she couldn't serve his "Negro friend." Luis told her he was really, like him, a Puerto Rican. The young lady asked that soldier to speak some Spanish. He happily did. Without further ado, she returned with another beer.

More pathetic was what befell another Crucian on his way to the war. Continental-looking Christian "Olee" Christiansen at

Michael A. Joseph, Esq.

a diner urged his Yankee military buddies to stand their ground
and demand service. The owner decided Olee was "a nigger-
loving troublemaker" and the police were summoned. When
the cops heard his St. Croix accent he was swiftly arrested "for
impersonating a white man." Olee repeated the incident several
times not because he thought I disbelieved. Each time he mentioned it, he truly enjoyed his own laughter the memory evoked.

I was relatively unaware of racism when arctic chill drove
me out of Helena. Los Angeles exposed me to the sheer shal-
lowness of it. At home for summer break in 1970 I ranted to my
father about its folly and accused him of failing to prepare me.
His precision parried my forwardness: "What is there to be bitter about? Racism existed long before you became aware of it,
and therefore it didn't involve you. If you choose now to notice
it, why let it make you bitter?"

Not grasping the depth of my naiveté, on return to LA I tried
to share my father's wisdom with a Yankee from South Side
Chicago, but he cut me short: "You are a brother, but not a soul
brother. You can't tell me anything about racism because you
haven't suffered in ways I have."

President Obama's early campaign was in the same tone
scrutinized. Harold Jackson of *The Philadelphia Inquirer*
explained, "So, when other African Americans wonder if Obama
is black enough, they're really questioning whether he has been
oppressed enough."[23]

Consider the White House candidacies of Rev. Jesse Jackson, and that of Rev. Al Sharpton. Both were swiftly stere-
otyped. Jesse was tagged by opponent Vice President George
Bush as a "hustler." In a Fox News interview by Bill O'Reilly,
Sharpton was marginalized to the "new suits" his fundraising
made available. These low blows were spontaneously thrown
because *they* are progeny of the past enslaved. Based on a social
contact with Bush and my being familiar with O'Reilly's *Killing Lincoln*, their insults were not really personal. They were no
more so than the "white" men who stomped on "white" women
demanding the right to vote. Those reflexes are rooted in a pas-
sionate resistance to digging up a past preferred to be forgotten.

For when it is exhumed, it releases the stench of bane bigotry. Chancing the nation to one burnt by the stigma of slavery (or sexism) is feared as a potential venting of that odor. Obama's lighter historic layer posed less risk.

At the same time, Ishmael Reed's *Barack Obama and the Jim Crow Media* tells of others pandering stale prejudices. Its chapter "From Jubilation at Election Night . . . To Cries of Kill Him!" describes the usual suspects darting in and out of the feeding frenzy. That reading was quite comical, setting aside reality there *are* crazies drooling for a chance at the new president.

Contrary to popular perception, the "past" was not that long ago. Masters like Faulkner knew there truly is no such thing. As John Berger reiterated, "The time that was continues to tick in the time that is."

I have heard the actual voice of an ex-slave tape recorded the year I was born. He therefore shared *this* lifetime with tens of millions of Americans. And the last child of a slave, Emma Faust Tillman, died on January 28, 2007, just seven years ago.

So long as the "past" remains unresolved, the skin color drama will dance till dawn. In its loose cannon days it ignited open assaults on the dignity of Yankees. Their unbending intent to bide time and not get themselves killed is awe inspiring. In Ken Burns' documentary *The War*, one fresh from WWII met the racism he hoped to be spared on account of his combat duty. But it was not. Walking home late at night from his janitor's job, a policeman harassed him and barked, "You take that hat off your head when you talk to me boy!"

The death penalty would've raised its ugly head had the veteran flashbacked to the Battle of the Bulge, where Nazis disguised themselves in GI uniforms, and ripped that racist cop apart. Instead, the forbearing soldier complied. Only people of special fortitude could suppress the natural instinct to fight back. Jackie Robinson typified it. The former university athlete and military officer became the first "colored" major league baseball player. Time after time he stomached public and on-field cruelties. Never once did he react.

Such capacity for self-control no doubt rattles bigots' sense of worth. A documentary, *Up from the Rails*, about the legendary Pullman Train Red Caps offers clues. It tells of a wealthy Continental passenger's habit of not ever making eye contact with his Yankee Red Cap porter, who provided him extended services. The man of "wealth and class" simply would walk away and then, as a tip, toss a dime over his shoulder. Was the baggage handler perceived to be "the bigger man?" Did his control outclass the rich man's wish he was invisible? Invisible as hoped is "the past"? People unsure of the integrity of their acts tend to test the character of others. In context of past slavery it's this tension that shaped the caveat "Know your place, nigger!" The Red Cap did not did know his; he ignored the dime every time. The miserable Continental seemed to not care his wife always turned back and handed the porter a dollar.

Dissing the Red Cap was meant as a signal to him that he continue to act without "uppityness." In this scenario, the Continental is hoisted by his own petard as regards the theory of evolution that only the fittest of the fittest survives. Was the Yankee porter as an offspring of human beings who endured the Middle Passage entitled to act as fitter of the two? His lineage, after all, was transported in smaller-than-coffin slits so unsanitary the stench of their ship was clear from a mile away, to next suffer bondage often of unspeakable cruelty. As Olaudah Equiano said when asked by William Wilberforce how *he* lived to write about the then ongoing trade, "Survival is a thread; it either breaks or it doesn't."

***

Two astute writers' views of the skin color drama deeply diverge. James Baldwin thought it is rooted in the awareness a day will come when we will never again see the sun rise. And because African skin tone calls up that darkness of death, an African American has two enemies: a "white" by history, and a "black" by fate. Baldwin stands out as beyond bright, yet he lost me there. I met him through actor Danny Glover in San

Francisco, where his big eyes darted everywhere as he power-pointed his esoteric about the drama. At times, I was completely lost. He invited me to chat and I kept it simple from fear I utter something silly.

For, while awareness of death is constant, in earlier times skin color had little meaning. It was seen as reflection of climatic conditions. Al-Jahiz's chronicle about an African tribe, the Beni Solaim, is enlightening: "These have Greek slaves whose offsprings in the third generation become as black as the Beni Solaim because of the climate."[24]

It is thus difficult to grasp that skin color, being largely a matter of sunshine, the tint most exposed to it is yet despised. Given the viability of the skin-tanning industry, the contrary appears to be the case. Paler shades seek sunlight because baked skin rings the bell of life. Still, Baldwin's take is hard to shake. Some days it just nags me.

Rutgers University professor John A. Williams surmised the tacit password at Ellis Island, gateway for millions of European immigrants, was "nigger." That was intended to poison new laborers by driving a preemptive wedge between those seeking the American Dream and those scraping a way out of their American nightmare. Chance both groups would unionize for decent wages was thereby repressed by reinforcing the racial divide. Ellis Island bureaucrats surely were aware of labor revolts like the May 1886 Chicago Haymarket labor riot. Six policemen were among the dead, and four American Federation of Labor leaders were hanged. One was a Continental, Allan Parsons, who was married to ex-slave Lucy Parsons. Racial unity was clearly egging on labor unrests. Ellis Island pen pushers became proxies for bosses paying famine wages to immigrants. One in Lawrence, Massachusetts, said they "were worked like horses." Lucy carried on Allan's fight. In January 1912 her World Industrial Workers led strikes for twenty-five thousand immigrants from thirty nations. Five months after, Massachusetts became the first state to pass a minimum wage law.

Prof. Williams' insight is shared by a Southerner. I saw a group of thinkers from the South, including Pulitzer Prize author William Styron, discussing the skin color drama. One declared, "Whoever invented racism was a genius. He guaranteed there will always be cheap labor."

Cut-rate wages is therefore an enemy of the American Dream comforted by the skin drama. This point rings in Tina Dupuy's June 2011 column concerning the $13 billion Walmart grabs in profits. She was aghast at the number of its workers who qualify for and receive federal food cards. Even though it's an American icon, Walmart is unresponsive to the first law passed in Jamestown Colony: "Ye who work shall eat." Dupuy thuds its tyranny of profiteering that forces its employees to seek federal aid for adequate nutrition. Leonard Pitts in July 2013 likewise scrutinized the "McBudget" of poorly paid fast food workers. In May 2008 he'd written about the race baiting of working-poor Continentals that sunk Obama's primary run in West Virginia. Obama, on the other hand, might've been more appealing if he had revealed his empathy for Appalachian coal miners, who were exploited worse than were some African slaves.

Labor-related racism was promoted in *Amos 'n' Andy* shows first aired on August 19, 1929 by NBC-Blue broadcasting. Around 1916 and through the 1930s Great Depression, six million Yankees migrated north, where they served as a low-paid labor pool. Job-worried Continentals took comfort in sneering jabs aimed at "those misfits." Racial digs dulled the edge of the anxiety. The insults were alike those Jim Crow blackface minstrel shows mocked up in 1828 to soften slavery's atrocity by portraying Africans as morons. *Amos 'n' Andy* lasted until the mid-1940s, when World War II jobs relaxed the insecurity.

John Williams saw a consequence of what Ron Chernow coined as Alex Hamilton's City of the Future: "Manufacturers and laborers would flock to a country rich in raw materials and favored with low taxes, running streams, thick forests, and a democratic government. And that influx of workers would eliminate one of the most pressing obstacles to American manufacturing: high wages."[25]

John's candor inspired Ishmael Reed, who reviewed his novel *Clifford's Blues*, to say John is "the greatest American writer of the twentieth century." On December 28, 2006 I told him I saw why Reed said so, especially because of his insight on how Yankees and immigrant laborers were manipulated. The teacher teased: "Do you really believe the people at Ellis Island were that smart?"

"Of course, that's why Reed called you the greatest."

"Oh, I paid him to say that."

"You can't fool me, John. A year ago you said, 'Ishmael has a way of exaggerating.'"

He giggled, pleased his former student is still thinking. Suffice it to say, skin shade in and of itself has little to do with the color drama, a reality dictionaries have yet to incorporate. As Harold Jackson concluded, "Black means oppressed."[26]

In this empirical context, given the number of Continentals as skillful as commuter airline pilots whose oppressive wages force them to seek federal food aid, there are more "blacks" in America than supposed.

***

As for tendency to marginalize territorial citizens, Edward C. King, Chief Justice Emeritus Supreme Court of Mariana Islands, observes:

> There is a decided and long-standing tradition in the United States of viewing insular [tropical] areas affiliated with the United States in two unrealistic ways. Many consider these areas to be romantic untouched havens, and also essentially insignificant, even irrelevant to the United States.[27]

In tow, a columnist wrote of American soldiers stationed in the Territory of Guam as "sitting on a lump of coral in the Pacific where brown tree snakes and insects far outnumber the human population."[28]

Literary icon Victor Hugo articulated why such mind-sets are rather naive: "There is no such thing as a little country. The

Michael A. Joseph, Esq.

greatness of a people is no more determined by their number, than is the greatness of a man determined by his height." [29]

Geographical aspects are not the only factors in taking islanders for granted. The disdain is often folded within seductive folklore of slavers, pirates, privateers, and cannibals. So popular is this romanticism, the movie *Pirates of the Caribbean* set a debut record. Forefathers of the people of Dominica, where it was partially filmed, were depicted as cannibals. That was "inaccurate and unfair," said their chief.[30] His mild response reflected Christopher Columbus' chronicled first contact with these relaxed people of the New World: "The King enjoys an estate in such a dignified manner it is a pleasure to see. The villages and the homes are so pretty. No better people or land could there be. They love their neighbors as they love themselves. Their speech is the sweetest in the world. And they are always laughing."[31]

In a twist of faith, on December 24, 1492, off the north coast of present-day Haiti, Columbus' flagship *Santa Maria* ran aground. The natives helped salvaged all which could be saved, and with its timber he built a stronghold for crew left behind, promising his return. Because he had been sponsored by the Spanish crown, he faced severe punishment for loss of that ship—possibly the death penalty. Queen Isabella, after all, pawned her jewelry to finance his try at a new route to India. Columbus opted to save himself on his second voyage in 1493 by pilfering all the gold he could from the very people he'd so admired. History would've been different had *Santa Maria* survived. How tragic after placing so much wealth at the feet of Spain's throne, the Admiral of the Ocean Seas died on May 20, 1506 in abject poverty. As pathetic, his quirk of faith provoked pure plunder, the survivors of which are today defamed as descendants of man-eaters. It started with exaggeration of the fact ancestral bones were hung in island homes nostalgic for departed love ones. Even Shakespeare in his last masterpiece *The Tempest* had been duped by the propaganda of Caribbean cannibalism.

Thankfully, it has been soundly discredited by Professor Jalil Sued Badillo of the University of Puerto Rico and by *500*

Nations, a home video series narrated by Kevin Costner. The sufferings Caribbean people endured were chronicled by Fray Bartolomé de las Casas, who spent forty years in the West Indies. His father traveled with Columbus and Las Casas lived a leisured life at the natives' expense. He renounced their subjugation in 1514 on becoming a priest. He witnessed countless die within two years of slave mining for gold. Las Casas' condemnation shall echo into infinity: "How much damage? How many calamities, destruction of kingdoms have there been? How many lives have been lost in the Indies over the years? How many unforgivable sins have been committed?" [32]

He implored Spain to cease the slaughter of these people (who called themselves Tainos) and returned to Spain in 1540 to advocate on their behalf. He argued that fabrication of the "Carib Indian" was a ploy to degrade *a man* so as to gain consent for his "Catholic conversion," then a euphemism for slavery. [33]

Caribbean tourism competition yet continues to promote fairy tales. A popular one pertains to Columbus' second journey with a seventeen-ship armada carrying a cavalry and war dogs. It is said he was greeted with a "shower of arrows" upon arrival at St. Croix on November 14, 1493. This is promoted to attract visitors by contrasting a primitive past with a hospitable present.

But one of Columbus' passengers, Dr. Guillermo Coma, wrote: "By its position and happy aspect [St. Croix] invited seamen to anchor on her." A native was kidnapped from a canoe and taken unto the flotilla's flagship, the *Marigalante*. Its navigator's journal documented: "The Admiral gave her to me." The woman of Ay Ay (St. Croix's Taino name) fought back fiercely until beaten with a rope into submission and raped by navigator Michele de Cuñeo. He then boasted how the battered soul performed as well as any schooled prostitute from the brothels of Genoa. Hence, the first sexual assault by a European against a New World native occurred on St. Croix. Consequently, so did the first recorded taking of lives between the peoples of the Old and New Worlds. [34]

Masquerading Caribbean myths as history makes for marketable art. Ron Chernow spun it into profits with his setting of a *godless* Caribbean, and Alex Hamilton's St. Croix as a *tropical hellhole*. Still, of all Alex's biographers none cross-referenced the founder's intricacies as intensely as Chernow. His cynical island view simply reflects a vacuum in West Indian history, and thus his use of the decided and long-standing bias. Or, as a *Washington Post* editor at the 2004 National Book Festival publicly teased, he is a frustrated novelist. Artistic license aside, Chernow did point out Alex informed his children that his time in St. Croix was the most useful part of his education. It imbued in him a tiered awareness through which he identified with Africans. This early interaction with them bred his abhorrence for slavery. He must've learned of the runaway slave community that existed for decades before his arrival on St. Croix. And he reviled the extreme penalties suffered by escaped slaves. Danish law linked severity of penalty to time expended for recapture. One day brought a stiff whipping. Longer than that, a cattle brand on the forehead or even a crude amputation inflicted at the knees. James Michener's *Caribbean* is more fact than fiction as pertains to penalties Danish slaves suffered. Some slavers were wicked beyond belief. At times open back wounds were stuffed with hot peppers and salt. Alex must've cringed whenever he saw the whipping post located within bawling distance of the fort where his young mother-to-be was jailed.

This background seeded his leadership in the abolitionist New York Manumission Society. In 1799 Alex caused the decision of New York to end slavery in that state. According to Chernow, it set an example for New Jersey, thereby "helping to set the stage for the Civil War, [as] in a tremendous visionary leap, Hamilton foresaw a civil war between the north and south, a war that the north would ultimately win."[35]

It was more than a vision. Alex appealed for a standing army and beseeched President John Adams he be given command of it. He was murdered soon after, but within a decade of his wife's passing the Civil War was fought. It was made possible by an army willing to enforce federal power over any state, the audacity of Dred Scott to demand the Supreme

Court yank his yoke, and Abraham Lincoln's doggedness that the court's support for slavery must be rejected at all costs for the Union's sake. There was a fourth, albeit more subtle, catalyst. It was President Andrew Jackson. He distrusted men of power, yet tested the judicial and legislative branches more than the six presidents before him combined. For that reason, the twenty-dollar bill portrays his image along with that of the White House.

Dred Scott's appeal to the Supreme Court spun tumbling reactions that helped trigger the Civil War. In March 2007 the National Association of State Attorney Generals honored the 150th anniversary of his case. It lifted Scott to "an American hero," and tied his struggle to Lincoln's success. Scott had moved with his master to Illinois, a non-slave state where he was considered free. He then moved to slave state Missouri and worked as a law office janitor. Inspired by the office key which he kept around his neck, he sued for his freedom under Missouri's law of "Once free, always free." Missouri's highest court instead declared he was still his master's property. Because Indians had been able to seek justice in the nation's top court, Scott hoped for the same dignity. But the Supreme Court used his case to revisit another fiercely fought issue in summer of 1787: the line between state and federal authority. The Ninth and Tenth Amendments—part of the Bill of Rights—retained to the states and to the people all powers not conferred upon the federal government by the Constitution. The court therefore declared it would deny all rights not specifically granted to the Union: "For, although it is sovereign and supreme in its appropriate sphere of action, yet it does not possess all the powers which usually belong to the sovereignty of a nation."

Northern law against slavery was cast asunder in *Scott v. Sandford* (1857) when the court announced Africans were less than human and hence they did not qualify to seek justice as US citizens. And worse, it held Congress was impotent to grant them citizenship. The court thus revived Patrick Henry's "We the States" perspective. It also voiced against a group of people the most disrespectful words ever uttered from men of justice:

They had for more than a century before been regarded as beings of an inferior order, and altogether unfit to associate with the white race, either in social or political relations; and so far inferior, that they had no rights which the white man was bound to respect; and that the Negro might justly and lawfully be reduced to slavery for his benefit.[36]

Some Africans thought just the opposite. An instance of pity they felt for slave owners appeared in David Walker's *Appeal in Four Articles IV, 1829*. He declared that America "is more our country than it is the whites'—we have enriched it with our blood and tears . . . Woe, woe will be to you if we have to obtain our freedom by fighting."

Not only did the court capitulate to the expediency of racism, it betrayed the Constitution by describing Mr. Scott as "a being of an inferior order." Surely, it was aware the charter affirmed Africans were *Persons*. For its betrayal it suffered the embarrassment of misnaming the slave owner in whose favor it ruled. His title was "Sanford," not "Sandford."

Sadly, Chief Justice Rodger B. Taney's opinion did not depart from judicial traditions of the times. Second chief justice John Marshall had accepted a slave as a twelfth birthday gift. In fact, nineteen of the first thirty-four justices owned slaves.

As fate would have it, however, in twilight of his life Marshall warned that unless the Constitution was amended the nation would hold together, if at all, "only by miracles." It could be said one such wonder was the unprecedented deviations of President Jackson. Prior to his emergence, the major parties were Federalists and Democratic-Republicans. Jackson was elected as a Democratic-Republican but soon formed *his* Democratic Party. The major parties were by then fading and a minor party, the Whig, reemerged in 1834 as an alternative to Jackson's new party. Whigs elected the ninth president. He died in office and was succeeded by his Whig vice president. Jackson's party took back the White House with the eleventh. Whigs returned to elect the twelfth but he too died in office. His vice president, the thirteenth, was the Whigs' last. Democrats elected the fourteenth and fifteenth, and Whigs returned to state politics.

In waiting, though, was a Whig from Illinois named Abraham Lincoln. The farmers from his old Northwest opposed any expansion of slavery. That area was conveyed to the Union by Britain after the Revolution, and made slave-free by the Northwest Ordinance of 1787. Congressman Nathan Dane, prodded by Rev. Manasseh Cutler, both of the town of Ipswich north of Boston, caused its passage. It so favored abolition of slavery with surprising help from slaveholders, it was christened the "Ipswich Miracle." That slave-free area sprung the Republican Party when Stephen Douglas in 1854 moved Congress to pass the Kansas-Nebraska Act, opening Louisiana Territory to slavery. Lincoln became a Republican in 1856 and many Whigs followed him. He then beat Douglas to be elected in 1860 as the sixteenth president.

But the footing for the ex-Whig's presidency was set by Andrew Jackson. Midway between Alex Hamilton's economic federalism and Lincoln's federal militarism, Jackson had laid path for the latter.

Destiny sometimes joins the most unlikely souls. Jackson and Alex were both orphaned at fourteen. Alex's mother, Rachael, and Jackson's wife, Rachael, had both suffered scandals of adultery. Alex's second son, James, was Jackson's acting secretary of state and he assisted Jackson's attempt to abolish his father's national bank. Alex's sixth son, Phillip, married the daughter of Jackson's treasury secretary.

Sean Wilentz's *Andrew Jackson* says his populist appeal was due to disdain for what he viewed as a federal government of neo-aristocrats. The slaver yet promoted federal last-word power, the architect of which he knew was the abolitionist Alex. Maybe James and Phillip nudged Jackson to exercise their father's federalism to such an extent as to cause some to tag him as "King Andrew." Carrying two slugs along with ill-fitting dentures in his battle-weary body, "Old Hickory" Jackson was as contrarian a personality as could be found. His future first-term

Michael A. Joseph, Esq.

vice president, John C. Calhoun, in 1818 had moved to censure him for invading Spanish-held Florida without authority. Yet it did not chill his use of force in 1834 to relocate Seminoles to "Indian Territory." And in a most radical act of federalism he sought from Congress the right to use federal troops to implement tariff laws in his kin state of South Carolina. He received it in 1833 by a bill called the Force Act. Under peril of invasion that state backed downed, but passed a resolution decrying the act with grumblings of its right to separate from the Union.

Jackson's Force Act intended to keep the Union from unraveling on his watch. Hence, Jon Meacham posits he was first to reject the option of secession. By so, Old Hickory gave life to the lead line of Alex's *Federalist Papers IX*: "A FIRM Union will be of the utmost moment to the peace and liberty of the States as a barrier against domestic faction and insurrection."

"Firm" meant a standing army as the Union's spine. Jackson's use of this federal power paradigm against South Carolina indicates Lincoln did not blaze first-time use of Union might to preserve *the States*. He simply echoed Jackson when he raised troops to suppress the Confederate States of America—creation of which was an act of insurrection.

The Dred Scott decision having dammed the Constitution's tide against slavery, Lincoln rallied all who distanced themselves from it. At the 1860 Republican Convention in Illinois he noted the court certified America as half-free and half-slaved. He reiterated: "A house divided cannot stand!" At Cooper Union College in New York, Lincoln urged citizenship for Africans. Biographer Harold Holder says that speech was as historically accurate as it was persuasive, and it carried the frontier lawyer into the East Coast fold. He stirred confidence in the victory of good over evil by proclaiming "Right is Might!" So inspiring was his advocacy, the 1860 race for the White House was joined by an abolitionist candidate who split the anti-slavery vote and Lincoln almost defeated himself. With a turnout of 82 percent he mustered barely 40 percent. No Southerner voted for him, but spread of the popular votes gave him a clear majority of electoral ones, particularly from those five Ipswich Miracle states.

Curiously, Alex's New York City voted against the Republican victory three to one. The Abraham Lincoln Institute Symposium of 2007 concluded it was due to its councilmen, who wanted to declare the city a separate state on track to secede from the Union. That is, until they realized they'd be shot for treason. Alex must have turned in his grave, pained by the ease which democracy makes power available to ruthless politicians. On July 13, 1863 in three days of rioting against conscriptions for the Civil War they incited one thousand deaths.

To preempt Lincoln's use of Jackson-like power, eleven slave states circled the wagons and withdrew from the Union. Still singed by the Force Act, on December 20, 1860 South Carolina led the exodus. Lincoln would have none of it: "I hold that, in contemplation of universal law and of the Constitution, the Union of these states is perpetual."

His declaration was taken as an act of war and a Virginian led an attack on federal Fort Sumter in South Carolina on April 12, 1861, thereby igniting the Civil War. The CSA mustered about 850,000 troops. But the Union amassed more than twice that. The rebels yet proved their fighting heart, such as on July 2 when they won the First Battle of Bull Run at Manassas, Virginia. However, on February 16, 1862 Ulysses S. Grant took 14,000 Confederate war prisoners and earned himself the nickname "Unconditional Surrender Grant." The CSA also lost a major gulf port on May 1 in the Battle of New Orleans. Still it came back to win on August 30 in the Second Battle of Bull Run.

On September 17, 1862 the most moving fight arose in the Battle of Antietam. Rebel forces invaded Maryland, which had declined to secede. With 23,100 casualties on that day, it remains the bloodiest battle date in US history. And it happened on the seventy-fifth birthday of the Constitution. Edna Medford of Howard University says Antietam also gave Lincoln the victory he awaited for release of his Emancipation Proclamation. Five days later he declared all slaves in rebel states must be freed by January 1, 1863.

Antietam's momentum was sustained when CSA troops fled on July 3, 1863 after days of carnage in the Battle of Gettysburg.

The combined loss of thirty-seven thousand American lives caused Lincoln to consecrate their souls on November 19 in his Gettysburg Address. Union victory was foretold by its barrages on the South's "Gibraltar of the West," Vicksburg, Mississippi. Following a forty-seven-day siege, Gen. Grant accepted Gen. John Pemberton's sword at the Battle of Vicksburg fittingly on July 4th. On July 9 a small army of rebels was defeated at Port Hudson, Louisiana, south of Vicksburg. And the North was now in control of the Mississippi River.

Gen. William Sherman clinched the win, and Lincoln's ree-lection, on September 2, 1864 when he seized Atlanta, Georgia. Sherman unleashed his November 16th "March to the Sea" along the Atlantic Coast with sixty-two thousand troops. Con-federate president Jefferson Davis and his cabinet (with Jonah Benjamin) fled Richmond, Virginia, on April 2, 1865. The next day, most poetic was "black" reporter Thomas Chester sitting at the speaker's desk in the Confederate House of Representatives writing a dispatch about Davis' dash. And on the day after that Lincoln entered Davis' home, the "Confederate White House," and sat at his desk.

Almost four years to the day it was ignited, the Civil War ended on April 9 when Gen. Lee surrendered to Gen. Grant. However, Texas' slaves didn't know they were free until June 19 when Union Gen. Gordon Granger marched into Galveston. Yankees celebrate it as "Juneteenth."

Incidentally, Alex's Federalists lost the 1800 elections due to its tax drive for an army akin to the one that dealt defeat to the South. His desire to lead it might've been granted as reward for his vote against Aaron Burr, thereby making Jefferson third president. Had Burr not murdered Alex, the Civil War might have sooner been fought, given Alex's disgust for slavery. And his insistence on such army went further. In distractions of the 1800 elections Spain secretly ceded to France the Louisiana Territory. France thus gained practically all the lands along America's western border, which posed a threat to the new nation. Luckily, Haiti's defeat of France in 1803 secured America's ambition for growth by sale of the territory to America to finance France's European military aims.

***

Alex's mother was "Rachael Fawcett Levine (1736–1768)," says her St. Croix tombstone. Irony it is that her loss of social standing afforded Alex freedom from the curse of race and class. His childhood with Africans exposed him to circular counting concepts familiar to them.[37] On the early death of his mom, a Danish judge placed Alex in custody of his first cousin, who had a free African mistress, Ledja.[38] In line with Afro-Caribbean custom, she likely offered him guidance through an African tradition known as *Sankofa*, roughly meaning "to go back and fetch it."

The trans-Atlantic slave trade was but a chapter in Africa's history. To hide its golden years, the Great Sphinx and other icons' noses were smashed. Visits to Giza, Saqqara, Karnak, Luxor, and Abu Simbel temples along River Nile grieved my heart on seeing the attempt to steal those unique times. Frederick Douglass also noticed that effort to usurp African history. In 1854 he demanded Continental writers cease their "fashion . . . to deny the Egyptians were Negroes and claim that they are the same race as themselves. This has . . . been largely due to a wish to deprive the Negro of the moral support of the Ancient greatness and to appropriate the same to the white man."

Not all "whites" set out to steal Africa's truly amazing past. One was an Alex Hamilton (1757–1804) contemporary, Count Constantine de Volney (1757–1820). His travels in the continent proved for him:

[T]he lie the Egyptians was White. When I visited the Sphinx, its appearance gave me the key to the riddle. On seeing the head, typically Negro in all its features, I remembered the remarkable passage where Herodotus says: "As for me, I judge the Colchians to be a colony of the Egyptians because like them, they are black with wooly hair." In other words, the ancient Egyptians were true Negroes of the same type as all native-born Africans . . . What a subject for meditation, to see the present barbarism and ignorance of the . . . descendants of the alliance between the profound genius of the Egyptians and the brilliant mind of the Greeks! Just think that this race of black men, today our slave and the object of our scorn, is the very race to which we owe our arts, sciences, and even use of speech! Just imagine, finally, that it is in the midst of peoples who call themselves the greatest friends of liberty and humanity that one has approved the most barbarous slavery and questioned whether black men have the same kind of intelligence as Whites![39]

It's not surprising skilled Africans were engaged in building the towns of St. Croix. And some never lost touch with their origins. A Crucian family, whose lineage goes back to slavery days, has held on to its Ghanaian name "Sackey."[40] It remains in contact with its native African clan, which includes Quasion Sackey, a former high-ranking UN official.

While the rule was to keep the St. Croix slave class uneducated, some were quite literate. Most familiar is Evangelist Cornelius (1717–1801), who mastered Native Creole, Danish, Dutch, English, and German. St. Croix, unlike America, permitted interracial marriages and African managers of plantations. Slave codes allowed freedom for any reason including being named in a will as an heir, guardian, or executor. Hence the enslaved had great incentive to learn all they could. Given their communal nature, those familiar with commercial practices likely shared it with the outcast but ambitious apprentice Alex Hamilton. Chernow nevertheless asserts it was solely a New York shipping outpost which schooled Alex in "global commerce in an obscure corner of the world." Tagging St. Croix "an obscure corner" is within the decided and long-standing bias. The island by the 1760s had flown six European flags. A Crucian responded to the biographer's narrow view: "If six suitors competed for a single woman, as did those European nations for this island, you can bet she was not only beautiful but also rich."

Colonial merchants as diverse as future president James Madison and traitor-to-be Benedict Arnold made fortunes out of Danish St. Croix. Their routine was to sneak ships packed with its produce into nearby British islands, where the cargo was secretly unloaded then openly reloaded to avoid British tariffs. Knowledge of such shipping practices was what caused Alex to initiate the forerunner of today's Coast Guard.

In its 1493 encounter with Columbus, fruitfulness described St. Croix. When Dr. Coma chronicled "her happy aspect," his fellow voyager Dr. Diego Chanca followed up: "It appeared very nice and apparently well populated, because of the abundant cultivation."

Six flags later, Alex's hometown operated as a global center. Its sugar, cotton, molasses, rum, indigo, spices, and slaves were integral to both European and American markets. St. Croix claims the fifth-richest soil in the world, largest per-square-mile water table, and highest average sugar-content fruits. The Danish West India and Guinea Company, powerfully called "the company," bought the island from the French in 1733 and transferred it to the Danish crown in 1753. The company remained so controlling even as to non-trade affairs, the king was moved to remind it was *he* who was in charge. Its complex dealings primed America's first monetary manager, who lived in the New World's fourth planned city. Only New Haven, Savannah, and Philadelphia preceded Christiansted (est. 1735) as brightly laid out urban areas. And the techniques of Oxholm the Dane in mapping St. Croix to near-GPS accuracy were copied by the Lewis and Clark expedition. The island wasn't a routine agrarian colony. It was full-throttle trade sovereignty. In marking the then-Danish West Indies capital's streets, the company bucked protocol by placing its "Company Street" between King and Queen Streets. In all other Dane towns, streets are in order of "King," "Queen," and "Prince." Telling of its deep history, the company's residual holdings was sold to, and is now operated by, progeny of the slaves it'd once shipped as cargo.

St. Croix rum was passed out to voters as quid pro quo for George Washington and Patrick Henry's elections to Virginia House of Burgesses. So effective it was, a law was enacted to offer the rum *after* voters left the booth. Cruzan Distillery (est. 1760) is among the world's oldest, more senior than even Hennessy Cognac. On October 30, 2006 Gary Nelthropp, whose family for eight generations are its distillers, told me he'd just come from President Washington's Mount Vernon estate, where barrels of Cruzan rum are aging. At the 2000 San Francisco World Spirits Competition it was selected as best across the globe.

St. Croix also provided gunpowder for the Revolution. Chernow said Alex didn't look back on the island, but he would've had a hand in this. His fellow patriots, after all, were taking on the most powerful empire. European gunpowder was superior to that made by the patriots, and they did not have direct access to it until France came to their aid in 1778. Brig *Nancy* sailed into St. Croix to pick up the powder in June 1776 and the island became the first foreign port to salute Betsy Ross' "Stars and Stripes" with a hail of cannon fire.[41]

As a merchant trainee, in November 1769 Alex wrote to a cousin in New York: "I condemn the groveling and conditions of a clerk or the like to which my fortune &c. condemns me . . . I wish there was a war."[42]

At eight, Alex got his first taste of commerce when his mom returned to St. Croix and opened a foodstuff store. I, too, at same age started in my father's grocery selling very alike items. Reaching into casks of beef and pork preserved in rock salt brine similarly irritated our young arms. Scooping beans, rice, cornmeal, and flour from sacks to be pound-weighed was routine in both eras. Comparable was my boredom as an energetic teenager doing clerical work in Grandfather's dry goods store. It offered Parisian cologne. Australian kangaroo leather shoes soft as a baby's face. Fine Italian cloths measured with yard-stick accuracy. English shirts, trousers, and shoes completed its stock-in-trade. Grandfather had also clerked in a shipping and insurance company.

Actually, our father's second name, Lloyd, was borrowed from insurance industry icon Lloyd's of London. And Daddy outsourced to tailors in Hong Kong his Lloyd & Wendell men's suits half a century before that business option was familiar.

But there's more to Alex than business training. His mother, taken as a wife at only sixteen, suffered scorn at hand of her slave-owning husband, Johann Michael Levine. On hearsay she'd been adulterous, a judge ordered her to three months in a jail holding defiant Africans, and Johann took custody of their only child, Peter. Upon her release she left St. Croix for a decade, returning with new sons James and Alex. As bastards they were denied baptism and formal schooling. Other prospects, however, were opened. Alex regularly visited a Jewish schoolmistress who taught him the Decalogue in Hebrew as well as the classics.[43] And he enjoyed a lifetime of interaction with Africans. This was noticeable at his burial procession.

Alex's demise rested in reverence for an unwed mother of thirty-two he suddenly was forced live without. He hinted in a letter to wife Eliza that Rachael had African blood when he referred to himself as a Creole.[44] That term has several meanings, but the context in which Alex used it is revealing. Pondering whether to purchase a basket of crabs or a pie for his wife's ailing sister, whom he was on his way to visit, he opted for the crabs: "Perhaps as a Creole, I had some sympathy with them," he wrote to his wife. His word choice *with*, instead of *for*, indicates more than a fleeting feeling for the crabs. It suggests he paralleled their vulnerability with that faced by "people of color." Interestingly, Harlem's W. E. B. DuBois, who often spoke of Alex as "our own Hamilton," likened political infighting amongst "coloreds" to crabs in a barrel. Besides, New World people of French-African blood are called "Creoles." This is what Caribbean oral history says was Alex's mother's heritage.

Sitting vice president Aaron Burr had held a "predetermined hostility"[45] towards Alex but he didn't bite the bait to duel Burr based on a "despicable comment"[46] supposedly uttered by him

Michael A. Joseph, Esq.

against Burr. In five years of research Chernow could not find it. However, I was befriended by a New Yorker, John Greene, Merit Verbatim Reporter. The highest-skilled craftsman, like Alex, was a Freemason. Their society's initiation involves simulation of a murder. The recruit is required to "feel" a particular grandmaster's slaying for refusing to reveal a password. Ergo, Freemasons made it their business to find out why Alex was shot in New Jersey at 7 a.m. on July 11, 1804 and died around 2 p.m. the next day in New York.

I once released my secretary to John Greene for a New York criminal case which required daily transcriptions of the court record. Perhaps because of that, in the last days of his terminal illness John confided in me the Freemasons' version as to how Alex met his death:

> A few days before he was shot, Hamilton was in a tavern named Fraunces Tavern in Manhattan at a Fourth of July party. He was singing when Aaron Burr went up to him and whispered loud enough for some guests to hear: 'You're a son of a nigger whore!' That's how Burr got Hamilton into that duel.

The court reporter had not read Chernow's *Alexander Hamilton*, but it similarly revealed: "Their final encounter before the duel occurred on the Fourth of July . . . [Alex] and Burr shared a banquet table at Fraunces Tavern . . . Burr was . . . gloomy . . . and sour . . . Hamilton . . . entered in glee and [was] seduced [to sing]."[47]

The biographer didn't write about any barbs between them. But given the tongue-loosening notoriety of pubs it is doubtful there was not even a grumble between those imbibing enemies.

The West Indian was putting off the offer for a duel with letters to Burr described by Chernow as a "tutorial in logic." Alex was certainly no coward. In a battle he led a charge after his horse was shot from under him and scaled an enemy barricade as he shouted, "Rush on boys! Rush on boys!" Because of his accent, his men believed they were being rallied in the name of,

92

and they in turn yelled, "Rochambeau! Rochambeau!" (Jean-Baptiste Rochambeau was a French general aiding the patriots.)

Alex had demanded Burr disclose the supposed insulting remark, a nonstarter since there was none. Burr thus desperately needed a fuse to provoke Alex into the "duel." He revisited his mark's "checkered West Indian past." Rachael is said to have been quite good looking with mixed blood. It is public she had been accused of adultery and flung in jail. Fact no other woman was locked up for so mundane a nuptial suspicion cuts into reality she was truly "white."

Consider William Styron's 1968 Pulitzer Prize-winning *The Confessions of Nat Turner.* That novel was so prickly a retort *Ten Black Writers Respond to Styron's Confessions of Nat Turner* was put out. Turner led America's largest slave revolt on August 21, 1831. That day was the fortieth anniversary of the August 21, 1791 rebellion which blazed the path to Haiti's emancipation. Notwithstanding, Styron insinuated Turner decided to rebel while in a barn masturbating on fantasies of "white" flesh. When Chernow wrote Rachael's mixed-blood reputation was without merit, he did not factor that "Nat Turner mind-set." It is doubtful a beautiful "lily-white" young lady would be jailed within earshot of Africans grunting in dark of night lusting on her Cupid groin. But so bitter an act might be sent against a two-timing racial masquerader, a one-drop adulterer passing as "white."

The Fourth of July "nigger whore" affront upon the Creole son of a tormented mother must have triggered profound pain, the catalyst sought by his assassin. Alex nobly lost his life as a definitive gesture to her. His son Phillip, the family's "brightest hope," had been killed by duel.[48] It caused *The New York Evening Post* cofounded by Alex to call for outlawing gunfights. So, friends unaware of Burr's cruel insult were surprised Alex did the "duel." Chernow endorsed four psycho biographers who studied it in 1978 and opined it was Alex's "disguised suicide."[49] What was factual in 1804, however, the coroner's jury decided Burr *murdered* Alex. And a New Jersey grand jury indicted Burr for *murder.* A New York grand jury also charged Burr with that *murder*.[50] Because the then-law was unsettled as to which state retained jurisdiction, Burr escaped prosecution. Had a trial occurred, an inference of guilt based on flight from the scene might've caused conviction. Since their gunfight was supposedly consensual, why did Burr immediately bolt to a slave plantation off the Carolina coast?

Duel protocol at the time was to throw away the first shot. That is, to deliberately miss your opponent. Alex threw away his. Burr, who'd practiced his aim for weeks, didn't.

It is eerie Abraham Lincoln was murdered at Ford's Theater for leading the war of brothers against brothers while viewing *Our American Cousin*. But it was an irony within a quirk of fate that Phillip Hamilton was dared to duel at a playhouse showing *The West Indian* because he'd critiqued his killer's speech given on a Fourth of July.

General Alexander Hamilton's funeral parade was led by "two small African boys wearing white turbans."[51] Mrs. General Hamilton, as wife Eliza was called in Washington circles, lived on for near another fifty years. She often referred to the South as the "African States."[52] Apparently, Eliza valued Alex's West Indian cultivation. Africans in the Caribbean and in the South practiced the same mode of child rearing. On a TV show of November 30, 2006 Morgan Freeman reminisced about a grade school prank. He happily revealed how he accepted an on-the-spot acting part to spare himself a school spanking. Had he gotten it, he would've gotten an extra one in his Mississippi home for the same misconduct. In St. Croix it'd have been just like that. Tim Reid at the 2007 State of Black America Symposium acknowledged his communal upbringing in Virginia. It streamed northward and Gov. Deval Patrick in a June 20, 2008 speech ascribed his success to similar collective nurturing in Chicago's South Side. St. Croix likely molded Alex within that African child-rearing custom "It takes a village to raise a child."

Chernow, unaware of this synergy, assumed Eliza's reference to the South as the African States was of intent to ridicule it. However, she wasn't inclined to cynicism. Indeed, in Chernow's own words she "was utterly devoid of conceit and was to prove an ideal companion for Hamilton."[53] Eliza, in lyrics of a Southerner, had a "soul, a spirit capable of compassion."[54] She didn't mock even her husband's enemies. Though testy in his defense, she looked down on no one. This was obvious in her going into a debtor's prison for a portrait. It also didn't bother her Alex tendered legal aid to Tories, as British loyalists were called. Eliza was, simply put, an ambassador to humanity, a quality seen in her at an early age: "At thirteen she accompanied her father to a conclave of chiefs of the Six Nations at Saratoga and received an Indian name meaning One of Us."[55]

Those nations included the Oneida people for whom she and her husband later sponsored Hamilton-Oneida Academy, today's Hamilton College.[56]

By referring to the South as the African States, Eliza was calling to mind its wealth made on backs of Africans, and imprint of their collective ways on it. In spite of slavery, Jim Crow laws, segregation, lynching, and convict leasing, many Southerners maintain a steel thread of decency. The tough but caring police officer portrayed by Tommy Lee Jones in the film *Electric Mist* embodies that other side of the South. Pangs of conscience are seen in its referring to itself during the Civil War as the cotton, and not slave, states.

Africans may well have implanted a congenial gene within the helix of its DNA. I once tried a conspiracy case in Montgomery, Alabama. During trial preparation I lunched before heading back home at the Embassy Suites hotel, where I'd drop a fifty-dollar bill. Returning to Montgomery three months later, I was told my money had been turned over to the hotel accountant, who was off during my weekend stay. When I again checked in at same hotel a month later, I was handed an envelope containing that fifty-dollar bill. At trial, eight Continentals and four Yankees returned a verdict of "not guilty" even though I was profusely warned an acquittal was impossible due to Southern bigotry. It seems the jury saw my total faith in their ability to be fair; most of them awaited my exit from the courthouse and greeted me with a round of applause!

I'm not so naive to believe all's well in the South, or in the North for that matter. Albeit my experience might be said to be an exception to the rule, it is nevertheless true. And what puzzled me was that the Southern attorney representing the alleged coconspirator insisted I strike a potential juror he claimed was a skinhead.

"Look at how he's watching you! He doesn't like you."

"Oh no?" I said. "What I see in his eyes is a warning that I not try to fool him. Please don't you strike him! I like jurors that don't want to be fooled."

As it turned out, that juror became foreperson of the jury which acquitted my client but convicted the Southern attorney's client.

St. Croix travels a path where racism is relatively absent. On November 26, 1938 *The West End News* reported that a resolution by the newly convened First Legislative Assembly asked Congress to designate the Virgin Islands as a refuge for Jews who were being persecuted in Europe. Such humanity is reflected in its anthem: "Where all mankind can join today, in friendly warmth of work and play . . . Hold out a welcome for one and all."

On September 27, 2006 in Washington, DC, the VI presented the Alexander Hamilton Distinguished Public Service Award to Sen. Mike Crapo (R-Id) and Rep. Charles A. Rangel (D-NY), "to remind our national leaders of the historic contributions of the Virgin Islands to the development of American democracy."[57]

St. Croix has been a frontline against man's inhumanity to man. As if to ease the horror of its slavery, the island nurtured the largest number of baobab trees in the New World. Known also as the Guinea almond tree, it is Africa's most sacred and many communities center themselves on them. To reiterate, on November 14, 1493 the first loss of lives resisting conquest of the New World occurred in St. Croix. It next aided one of the first Amerindian slave rebellions: "Who in this island [St. Croix] was taught in school that in 1511 there was a Taino rebellion in Caparra, Puerto Rico where the main allies in the coalition forces against the Spanish came from St. Croix?"[58]

Its Maroon Hole runaway slave enclave sustained man's will to be free, and that added to the miasma visited upon its French colonizers. Consequently, in 1695 France moved the balance of St. Croix slaves to its St. Dominique colony (now Haiti and Santo Domingo). This left the Maroons in control of St. Croix until France sold it to the Danish West India and Guinea Company in 1733. The Maroons were finally defeated in 1746 by the Danes, who then brought in more slaves. Those freed themselves on July 3, 1848. Beach sand was substituted in kegs emptied of gunpowder. Faced with inoperative cannons, wet guns, and African drum messages, the overwhelmed Danish governor declared henceforth all slaves free. St. Croix thereby joined Haiti as *only two* of dozens of West Indies slaving locations to emancipate themselves. (Their shared gene pool temps curiosity whether it prescient Haiti's revolt.)

Birth of the Republic of Haiti in 1804 after years of rebellion was seen as a potential provocation for American slave uprisings. President Thomas Jefferson (1801–1809) took special exception to the new nation and wished to see it "starve." In the five years Jefferson lived in Paris he enjoyed a social life within which he "squired around a blond." Haiti's revolution no doubt humiliated his Parisian friends. Little wonder he so swiftly imposed an embargo against it. Flanking that trade barrier, in 1825 America supported France's demand of 150 million gold francs as reparations. Had Haiti resisted it risked invasion by both.

President James Buchanan (1857–1861) withheld from it diplomatic relations and refused to refer to that second New World republic other than by its colonial name, St. Dominique. He wrote it was "Africanized with all its attendant horrors to the white race." Haiti's US ambassador has pointed out that despite President Lincoln lifted Jefferson's embargo his nation remains jaded.

That is so although Haiti gave to America Jean Baptiste DuSable, whose 1774 settlement evolved into its third largest city, Chicago. Let's not forget the secret transfer of Louisiana Territory in 1800 posed a future threat to America until Haiti defeated France. Haiti served as the sanctuary from which

Simon Bolivar launched his 1816 fight against South American colonialism. The Organization of American States, the brainchild of a Haitian, played a major role in solving the 1962 Cuban Missile Crisis. Despite those external roles, food for many Haitians at times is "dirt cookies" of clay, vegetable oil, and salt. It was expected Haiti's catastrophic earthquake in 2010 would bring it better relations. But as of June 2013 two of every three Haitians remain hungry. Jefferson's jinx is surely at work in "the first Black Republic." Its people are optimistic in spite of Tennessee Williams' insight that the average citizen would be straightjacketed if he behaved like governments do.

Interest in the Danish West Indies, now the VI, was different. After it bought Alaska from Russia in March 1867 America attempted to purchase part of the VI in November. While negotiating in St. Croix a tsunami tossed the warship *USS Monongahela* that brought the diplomats into its town of Frederiksted. A dozen soldiers drowned and are memorialized in the St. Patrick's Church grounds. In June 1868 Congress nixed the purchase idea.

But for the tidal wave, the VI might have become, or appended to, a state. It being the plan arose during President Lincoln's tenure, his loyalists would've promoted his goal. For instance, when President Franklin D. Roosevelt died in office his Marshall Plan leaders in rebuilding Europe and Japan proceeded to fulfil in those countries Roosevelt's intention for a second bill of rights of economic and social fairness.

However, territorial citizens suffer similar status Britain imposed on America's founding fathers. This hypocrisy is noticed across the globe. While exiting a conference between People to People delegates and the Academy of Scientists in Kiev, Ukrainian Republic, the academy requested I meet with it alone. That was due to puzzlement on its meeting for the first time a US citizen without a vote in his national government.

Be that as it may, true to St. Croix's legacy of resistance, in 1878 it blazed itself out of Danish serfdom. In 1915 D. Hamilton Jackson founded the first labor union in the West Indies. In fall 2006 the civil rights magazine *Intelligence Report* presented a

1969–2004 timeline of violent racial attacks by supremacists such as skinheads. Its single photo of a "black" fighting back was of *The Geraldo Rivera Show* where Crucian Roy Innis took on several skinheads.

Victor Hugo's assertion that the greatness of a country has no relation to its size is seen by naming some other Crucians. William Leidesdorff built San Francisco's first hotel, the City Hotel, and helped establish California's public school system.[59] A Santa Barbara newspaper featured Rafie as a most effective inmate educator in the federal penal system. Claude Benjamin's songs are heard in voices of Frank Sinatra, Nina Simone, and Elvis Presley, and in Walt Disney Cinema. Christina Allick Hopper of the Sackey family is first "black" female to pilot an F-16 aircraft in combat. The son of six-language-speaker Frank Sr., Gen. Frank Petersen Jr., is first "black" marine aviator. Tim Duncan, San Antonio Spurs' 2005 MVP, was tagged by ESPN as "the best power forward ever" during the Spurs' sweep of the 2007 NBA title. Raja Bell, "the soul" of the Phoenix Suns' 2006 Western Conference finals, and Duncan attained a statistical wonder; both were chosen by coaches for the 2007 All NBA Defensive First Team. It was Duncan's tenth First Team, and 2014 earned his fifth NBA championship ring.

New York Giants catcher Valmy Thomas says hall-of-famer Willie Mays "was the best in the business with a rocket arm that could pick off a runner from the crouch position." Clayton Walker of Grambling State football was among the toughest. Seen on February 5, 2012 by the biggest NFL TV audience ever, New York Giants' Linval Joseph earned a Super Bowl ring. The team's director of media services, Peter Baptiste, got his when the Giants won the Super Bowl in 2007.

Peter Jackson won the Australian and British crowns as first "black" World Heavyweight Champion sixteen years before Jack Johnson was declared so in 1908. Britain was not soft. In 1897 its Bob Fitzsimmons defeated Heavyweight Champion of America Jim Corbett at Carson City, Nevada. Three nephews are boxing champions: Lloyd Joseph II, IBC Middleweight in 2003; Clarence Joseph, All Military Middleweight in 2002 and on

Team USA 2004 Olympics in Athens, Greece; and Livingstone Joseph, 2014 New York City Golden Glove (147 lbs).

My son Jason was High School Wrestling Champion (120 lbs) for State of California.

Rider Kevin Krigger is first of African ancestry to win a $1 million race and to win the Santa Anita Derby. Others include Kerwin John, first of African blood to ride in the Breeders Cup; Victor Lebron won one thousand races in five years; and Julio Felix earned his mounts over $28 million so far. Another statistical wonder: Krigger and Lebron rode in the 2013 Kentucky Derby.

Sprinters LaVerne Jones-Ferrette and Alison Peter, triple-jumper Muhammad Halim, and 400-meter runner Tabarie Henry were competitors in the 2012 London Olympics.

Scholars and activists are: Hubert Harrison of Jeffrey Perry's *Hubert Harrison: The Voice of Harlem Radicalism, 1883–1918*; Yosef ben Jochannan pioneered Egypt's antiquity tourism; Arturo Schomburg of Harlem's Schomburg Center, home of Langston Hughes Auditorium; and Lewis Latimer developed a long-life filament that allowed every household to afford electric lightbulbs. Casper Holstein was a philanthropist who gained wealth from a stock market-based game he invented. Ashley Totten cofounded Brotherhood of Sleeping Car Porters, and in 1937 Pullman Company and his union entered into the first collective bargaining agreement between "blacks" and a major corporation. Frank Crosswaith organized the influential Negro Labor Committee. Johann Clendenin served as a dean of at IE University, Madrid, Spain. Bertha Joseph is first Afro-Caribbean mayor of Brent, England. Harry Fleming led the first "black" world-traveling big band. Frederick Morton via his TV channel Tempo beams West Indian music across the globe.

St. Croix continues to sprout go-getters. Twelve-year old Julisa Mursel made it to the top 7 percent of Scripps National Spelling Bee (2007). Thirteen-year-old Elijah Vegas appeared in Lifetime TV series *Army Wives*. Twenty-one-year-old Eddie Lovett currently holds the NCAA indoor 60-meter hurdles record. Seventeen-year-old Rakeem Christmas was cover story

of *ESPN Rise* (Nov. 2010) as "America's number-two high
school basketball center." He is today a starter with Syracuse
University, which advanced to the 2013 National Championship Final Four, and was a "Sweet Sixteen" going into the 2014
championship.

A relative of Rakeem spoke of the specialness he exudes:
"He has this innate spirit about him." From its Tainos to those
current high achievers, that's what St. Croix instills in its people.

During Chernow's "the man who made modern America"
book (*Alexander Hamilton*) tour he yet appeared before New
York Historical Society and renounced the island: "Hamilton
came out of nowhere." Sean Wilentz mimics it in *Rediscovering
Alexander Hamilton* (a DVD): "Hamilton is a man who, out of
nothing, created an American financial system." Not so at all.
Decades before Alex moved to New York, planters on St. Croix
were financed by Zurich bankers. And its second colonizer, the
Dutch of Amsterdam, had already fashioned the joint stock certificate. Ignorance of such facts is noticed by a Crucian whose
ancestors include Danish king bookkeeper James Bruley plus
Governor DuBois of the Knights of Malta, which in 1651 gave
St. Croix its name. Asked what he thought of the DVD about
Alex, he responded, "Most Americans don't know that when the
colonists were cutting down oak trees to plant tobacco and corn,
we were already drinking fine French wines."

St. Croix itself rebuked the acclaimed Chernow by trigger-
ing in his book a blunder. Of hundreds of sources and char-
acters identified by names in *Alexander Hamilton* only one
is transposed. Chernow misnamed St. Croix librarian Wallace
Williams, with whom he met face to face, as *William Wallace*.[60]
William Wallace led the fight against English rule over Scotland
in the Battle of Falkirk depicted in movie *Braveheart*. Wallace
was hanged on August 23, 1305 for resisting desecration of his
homeland. Chernow's slip offers a field day for fans of Sigmund
Freud.

Still, Fountain Valley fallacies persist. Gen. Petersen implies
it erupted from local Continental dominance.[61] The Fresh Water
Yankee seemed swayed by the colonial cliché: "The natives are

restless." My Continental friend Robert "Bob" Johnson had shared with me an original letter from Washington to Jefferson in Paris signed by Alex. But in 2005 when Bob traveled oversees for a vacation in India, he suffered a hard blow. A British socialite aboard the iconic train Palace on Wheels jerked backwards on learning he was in St. Croix at the time of Fountain Valley. She was even more flabbergasted he still lived in St. Croix:

"Aren't the natives possessed by a murderous hatred for whites?"

That's answered by Travel Channel's Andrew Zimmern. In January 2013 an episode of his *Bizarre Foods America* was filmed on island. When he leaving, he told a reporter, "The best thing about St. Croix is its people."

Our race-neutral tradition influenced these events: In 1968 I was elected freshman class president at Carroll College, followed by a Montana Supreme Court justice inviting me to his home for Thanksgiving. I graduated from Loyola University in 1972 as a top student leader and was awarded the Presidential Citation for Distinguished Service to Loyola University of Los Angeles. In 1974 Golden Gate University in San Francisco offered, and I accepted, a full ride to its law school.

Two: Paradigm of Intent

In the designs of Providence, there are no mere coincidences.

—Pope John Paul II

On learning I was writing this book, a Continental medical doctor cautioned me, "Ever heard of 'hubris,' h-u-b-r-i-s?" I was taken aback. He implied I leave well enough alone and not coddle the conceit that caused demise of mythical Greek heroes. The Vietnam vet had taken to me out of fidelity for his fellow marine, my brother Austin, killed in action. Handed its chapter outline, he changed tone. Days later, a talk radio caller warned, "Michael, you better write the truth!" As for honesty, that's not a problem. But writing honorably is not the same as writing "the truth." Lecturer Anthony di Melo valued this distinction: "The shortest distance between the truth and your heart is a story."

Writing accurately necessarily entails honesty, but it's the agony and sweat expended to find words that tell what is perceived which will define "the truth." James Baldwin sensed this and admitted, "I want to be an honest man and a good writer."

I scurried to Loyola's president Donald P. Merrifield, SJ, PhD, PhD, on the day my adult life became tethered to Rafie's:

"Father, I just heard on the radio my brother Rafael murdered eight tourists at a golf course! He and his friends are being hunted down and I'm scared he'll be killed although I know he's innocent!"

The Jesuit priest always smiled and my ghastly words did not subdue it. Through thick eyeglasses he stared intently beyond my presence as if ushering an inner spirit and, still smil-

103

ing, he softly answered, "I'm sure if Rafael was involved, it was only peripherally."

I gaped dumbfounded at him and inhaled to protest I expected he'd agree my brother was not connected. But the reason I intuitively rushed to *him* came to mind. Merrifield was Loyola's icon, even as we'd tease his separate doctorate degrees in theology and physics were a contradiction of terms. In issues between students and the administration, he could be counted on to not stoop to conquer. Besides, I recalled my concern about Rafie's choice of company now that I was thousands of miles away. Couple days later, I sacrificed graduate school to go home and rescue my brother. The priest's optimism became the rudder for my uncharted journey.

Four years earlier at Carroll College I'd challenge my theology teacher's grade he gave me. He was college chaplain and his class had helped me to become a better student. I ranted until he relented: "Michael, I am going to raise your grade, but . . ."

Whatever he'd added after that "but" was so unhinging and alien it buried itself in isolation of Montana's Christmas snow. Something had occurred, but it'd become a blank spot. Thanks to a phone call from my St. Thomas friend Ralph Smith, who invited me to join him at Loyola from where we drove deep into Mexico for the holidays. In LA, I noticed America wasn't frozen all over during winter and I switched to Loyola.

As a senior there I was reading UCLA student Carlos Castaneda's book about a Mexican Yaqui Indian shaman, Don Juan Matus. They were sitting in the Sonora Desert while Carlos lectured the shaman on his anthropology department's beliefs about Indians' peyote-eating rituals. The Yaqui listened without interruption. Carlos even offered him cash to agree with his teacher's opinion about ingestion of the cactus buttons. When Carlos' rant began to sound like a dying car battery, Don Juan spoke: "Do you think you and I are equals?"

That question caught Carlos completely off guard and it triggered him to think: *How dare this tire-sandal, poncho-wearing Indian to imagine he could be my equal? Heck, I'm a sophisticated university student.*

But eager to get a field-study report Carlos opted to pacify Don Juan by lying that he considered him an equal. However, the shaman was way ahead and preempted the pretence. Before Carlos could answer, Don Juan calmly informed the UCLA pupil, "No. We are not. You are a whore and I am a warrior. Your people sent you to question me for reasons you do not even know, all the while thinking you are all better than me. But if I leave you in this vastness tonight, I assure you will not make it out of here."

That rebuff produced a pressure in Carlos' ears so intense, he wrote, it felt as if a jumbo jet was taking off just inches above his head. He suffered total disorientation. Carlos' narrative freed my blank spot about what occurred when the chaplain agreed to raise my grade and then added, "But you are too honest."

I, too, felt an extreme pressure in my head, the chaplain's office became pitch black, and I heard a worried voice in a fog from which I emerged: "Oh no! Oh no! That's not what I meant. But people will take advantage of you if you are not careful."

Our mind-sets had been crushed! To Carlos, it was categorically nonsensical a poor uneducated Indian could be the equal of a college student. To me, it was beyond bizarre a priest would warn against being too honest. Albert Einstein explains, "Common sense is the collection of prejudices acquired by age eighteen."

The collapse of our "common sense" was so jolting we suffered syncope—interrupted awareness of ourselves and surroundings. Under stress of the inconceivable, we both had blacked out.

The chaplain had wished to save me predictable danger. Don Juan, though, had more personal reasons for shaking up Carlos. The Yaqui was only eleven when his father was killed during an uprooting of his village unto a reservation-bound train. A soldier's bullwhip broke his fingers while he was kneeling next to his father promising revenge. Although over the years he'd freed himself of hate, sorrow, and regret, the shaman still had not shaken off a tad of sadness because, he said, "My parents lived and died as Indians, not knowing that they were, before anything, human beings."

105

Don Juan did not want Carlos to likewise shrink his natural potential. For both he who feels "superior" and he who feels "inferior" lose the inborn joy of simply being human.

Sometime in the early 1990s my theology teacher was on CBS' *60 Minutes*. He'd been defrocked as a priest! The Vatican forgave his fathering children, but it ordered him not to marry their mother. He followed his heart and disobeyed. Against his own advice, he had adopted my fault of being "too honest." In the meanwhile, Carlos Castaneda was assured by Don Juan that a universal force as real as they, which he called the "intent of infinity," had merged their destinies. Carlos became a shaman and wrote eleven best sellers about the teachings of Don Juan Matus. The defrocked priest started his own church. I ignored my father's high school advice I was "too nice" to make a living as a lawyer and became one to save my brother.

The first case I filed was an antitrust class action on behalf of bank tellers in California. State Assembly Speaker Willie Brown Jr. joined me as co-counsel and we removed the barriers to their upward mobility. Returning to St. Croix, I became the legislative director for the Delegate to Congress, where I drafted the Alien Adjustment Act of 1981, which facilitated green cards for thousands of out-of-status VI residents. I was next appointed federal public defender by the US Third Circuit Court of Appeals. One of its judges introduced me to Harvard Prof. Arthur Miller as presenting "the toughest criminal law issues to our circuit."

But when my father asked me what I'd do to make a living I told him I wished to be a musician. To my dismay, he instructed, "You have the talent but nobody is going to pay you for it. Be a doctor, people will pay whatever you charge."

Music is natural to me. I was first musician of the choreographed poem *For Colored Girls Who Have Considered Suicide*. At its debut at Stanford University, creator Ntozake Shange, dancer Paula, and I were loudly cheered. On advice of Stanford's drama director, a few days later Ntozake and Paula (I stayed in law school) moved to New York where *For Colored Girls* won Broadway awards. It is now a movie with Whoopi

Goldberg and Janet Jackson. Nigerian Michael Babatunde Ola-
tunji had asked I not walk away from his Harlem dance company to go to law school. My "impeccable sense of time" would
make me his first drummer, he said. At Minnie's Can Do in
Haight-Ashbury while playing with jazz saxophonist Rahssan
Roland Kirk and moog synthesizer pioneer Sun Ra, the blind
Kirk called out across the stage, "Ra, this boy is playing the
bass line on his drums!" At percussionist Milton Holland's Hollywood home I sang to Chaka Khan my tune *She's Right*. Chaka
gasped, held her stomach, and bent over with sheer surprise.
The diva pleaded for its rights, but her husband/manager (Milt's
son) reminded her of the five-year songwriters' contract with
Warner R&B. Chaka insisted she at least prepare me dinner.
At the Palms Café on Polk Street in San Francisco, a Japanese
lawyer offered a contract of $10,000 per week to leave with him
for Japan to teach and play Caribbean music for three months.
He'd seen me graced on stage with hurled paper money after
singing a Bob Marley tune. But I declined the opportunity. My
brother's freedom was priority. The Japanese doubled the offer
to six months for a quarter of a million dollars! "Where will all
that money come from?" I asked. "Oh, when we fill the venues
you wouldn't have to worry." Still, I just couldn't say yes. He
was stunned. I apologetically told him about Rafie. Thought-
fully, he advised I leave with him and later return to law school.
Still, Rafie's freedom could not be delayed. *Intent* had its plan.

Back in St. Croix, the attorney who volunteered to aid me
had been Rockefellers' Fountain Valley start-up counsel. His
office was in the building where Alex had clerked. And his offer
of help was made in the single town structure named for the
founder: Hamilton House.

In 1968 John A. Williams, as my summer teacher at the
local college, tried hard to make me a career writer. He pointed
out that books like William Styron's *Nat Turner* should not go
unchallenged. Prof. Williams even got permission for me to
stay, on my way to Helena, for a week with him and his wife
in New York City. There, he introduced friends at Doubleday
Publishing. But I had no wish to write until three years after

my brother's 1998 suicide. Yet, thirty-five years after being in his home, John was there to "sharpen my teeth." When I told him that the bishop who assisted Rafie was made a cardinal— the first VI priest to be so elevated since Catholics arrived in 1754—the veteran author replied, "There you go. That's a good omen for your book."

Later on, its publisher informed me it would be edited within the guidelines of a writing manual of which I'd never heard. I became quite worried. Within days, a sudden schedule change allowed me to attend a local judicial conference, where to my surprise a most helpful lecture about writing was presented. And the lecturer had coauthored the editing manual my publisher mentioned a week before. My worries instantly evaporated.

These "coincidences" are convincing of the "intent of infinity" made familiar to Carlos Castaneda by Don Juan Matus, referred to by Pope John Paul II as "Providence," and revealed in Shakespeare's *Macbeth*: "There's a divinity that shapes our ends. Rough-hew them how we will."

PART TWO

Three: Clusters in American Paradise

Mellow jazz of Horace Silver's quintet was vacuumed off the radio that afternoon in Los Angeles. The romantic vibes were as good as it gets until a very anxious voice invaded my room:

"We interrupt this program for a news bulletin! Eight tourists were murdered today at a golf course in St. Croix, American Virgin Islands!"

I scrambled out of bed. *Oh, my God,* I thought, *tourists like to huddle together in bars and restaurants and a hit man took them all out because they were with his target.*

In the nineteen years I grew in St. Croix I never heard of more than one person being shot to death. And that was once in a long while. My mind ran on a Continental tourist couple who three years before watched me in a checkers contest at the Outset, a jazz bar near my house. After they'd left, they sent to me a chess set out of kindness. If they had returned, I figured, they would not be among those killed. They liked mixing with Crucians. My musings were ripped apart when the names of the suspects were called. They were familiar, much too familiar.

In the peaceful island of a founding father, prior to its valley of fountains flowing sacred blood, three clusters had formed. Of five ambiguous outlaws, nine dogged lawmen on hunt for one, and sixteen clueless clubhouse occupants. All were within circle of gunshot echo, yet of mind-sets as far apart as cosmic bodies.

Covertly, the surrounding serene hills had become venue for a private vendetta. The high-value target was on the run after trying to kill two cops. There, on the ridge above the clubhouse, he was within tactical range. A few hours or so before mission accomplished.

But Ishmael LaBeet would escape for a third time. He'd confided weeks before to a fellow Vietnam combat vet that, but for his willingness to run a gauntlet of heavy thorn brush, he'd have been "killed by the pigs." That time was his second slip away.

As the movie *City by the Sea* makes clear, not even a fellow officer's son who shows readiness to kill policemen is given quarter. So, the jungle-trained soldier was sure hell was biting at his heels. He had scuttled to Rafie's camp not far from the clubhouse to hide from the ever-tightening dragnet made up mostly of Vietnam combat vets.

The unbending intent of the posse is seen in the words of retired police lieutenant Marion Jackson ('69) (year of entry into the police force):

> I knew I would possibly be going up against a combat veteran; this man had already expressed a desire to "ice a pig." I was aware that we were up against a forty-five-caliber machine gun in the hands of a person who had only to wait, and who thought he had nothing to lose. My weapon of choice was the thirty-caliber M-1 Carbine with a folding paratrooper gunstock armed with two thirty-round banana clips. I was ready for battle.[1]

LaBeet's frame of mind "he had nothing to lose" arose from his attempt to kill Officer Manuel "Gambo" Camacho ('71) and his partner. Gambo's mother was the sister of two posse leaders: Lieutenant Jorge Torres ('63) and Detective Eleuterio "Tejo" Torres ('68). As elsewhere, an occasional escape is a liability of police work which benefits petty criminals. But he who is a deadly threat never profits from it. As a proven danger to police who refused to lay down arms, LaBeet offered his hunters one option: neutralization with extreme prejudice. The first time he escaped is described by Sergeant Leopold "Polo" Gittens ('58), commander of Frederiksted, where the two officers came under fire. On September 12, 2003 Polo told me, "If I had a car to follow LaBeet—and I knew where he was running to—I'd have pulled alongside and bang! Bang! Bang! That would have been the end of him."

No arrest warrant was sought from a judge on sworn statement LaBeet attempted to take the lives of two officers. A prior warrant for an unrelated alleged robbery had been issued on May 31, 1972 and was still outstanding. It sufficed for mobilization. A covert, private war was now at hand.

In the cluster of outlaws, LaBeet withheld his shooting at two cops. Instead, he pushed for a robbery. Not so much for money as for a dead man's hope his executioners would lose his trail. Warren Ballantine, Meral Smith (Ballantine's brother), Beaumont Gereau, and my twin-like brother Rafael Joseph comprised this group. Ballantine needed cash to afford a boat ride back to the island of Antigua, West Indies, where he had been a week before. Smith and Gereau were drawn into the crime when they brought food to the campsite hours before the slaughter.

Had any known a police group was on LaBeet's heels for trying to kill two, their cluster would've never jelled. Back then, impulse to kill a cop was beyond prospect. In our upbringing police officers were seen as super parents, some dreaded more than others. If during one of our lapses someone shouted "Dratte ['54] is coming!" we didn't worry much about him. "I like to keep the peace," he'd say. On the other hand, Polo was very no-nonsense. We'd often hunted birds on private property about town with our BB guns. If Dratte was spotted, we simply hid. But, if the cry was "Polo coming!" feet were never fast enough. To this day our generation views "the uniform" with same respect.

Prior to Fountain Valley there was no instance of anyone in St. Croix firing gunshots at a policeman. When I learned about LaBeet's assault, Rafie was already dead. Notwithstanding, my brother's upbringing would have caused him to reject outright anyone so insane as to try to kill a police officer. We loved Captain Arthur Brown, ('52) a kind father figure and fence-sharing neighbor of Mammy's humble parents, Modesto Romero and Natividad Nieves de Romero. And, Gambo was a sweet human being. His grocer father purchased wholesale goods from ours. He was so handsome the only challenge he might have given us as our schoolmate was those girls we liked, wanted him instead.

Michael A. Joseph, Esq.

Gambo has not forgotten the bullet whishing below his chin. He gave up police work shortly after. Yet, being of true Crucian class he holds not an iota of ill feeling towards LaBeet, who but for better aim would've by now turned him into clumps of bones.

Besides their high community standing, Rafie was very close to a good number of policemen either as neighbors, relatives, or classmates. Adelbert Bryan ('66) and Douglas Carter ('67) had the highest respect for our father. The mother of David Jackson ('67) and Reinhold Jackson ('71) was godmother to two of our sisters. The father of Frank Jacobs ('68) was one of Daddy's best friends. Franz Christian ('71) and our brother Edwin were in Vietnam. Hubert Brown ('71) and Anthon Christian ('71) were nicest classmates. Larry Oliver ('72) and Ivan Oliver ('71) were also schoolmates. Larry and our brother Austin were marines in Vietnam. Schoolmate Eustace Xavier ('67) loved to test our wrestling skills. Polo was brother-in-law to our sister Mary Soto. Elminio Soto ('65) is her brother. Claude Fredricks ('63) is our niece Michelle's father. Raymond Menders ('58) was first cousin to Mother, Agatha George Joseph, who raised Rafie and me, and Clifford George ('68) was her nephew. Roy Smith ('58) was next-door neighbor. The mother of Ohanio Harris ('68) and Mammy were like sisters. Ralph Johnson ('59) giggled on December 15, 2003 when he conveyed, "For a while Rafie was my 'little beat partner,' walking with me like he was also a policeman."

On January 14, 2004 Ballantine learned for the first time of the hot hunt for LaBeet and was shocked he attempted to murder Gambo. He stared into space with jaw drooping. His cluelessness was so real I thought of John Steinbeck's *In Dubious Battle*. That novel exposed how naive farm laborers' struggles against wretched conditions were manipulated by activists with larger agendas. I also recalled Osama bin Laden boasting that only four of his nineteen hijackers really knew of the 9/11 terror targets.

My macho schoolmate, now realizing he'd been duped, shook the shock and literally spoke to his cell walls: "You know,

I've been asking myself how I ended up with eight consecutive lifetimes when all I was hiding from was only five years of jail time. Really, even if I got five years, in those days I'd get paroled in twenty months. Definitely, I didn't have any information that LaBeet had tried to kill Gambo. I know Gambo. He and I used to drink beer together. We even did a little dice gambling before he was a policeman. He is a good man."

For the record I asked, "If you knew LaBeet had tried to kill Gambo would you have been where he was with Rafie?"

"That's heat, man! Nothing like five years! Trying to kill police is lifetime man! And that's if they don't kill you first! I went to Antigua in early August [1972] for carnival and stayed more than two weeks after that. No problems. I was partying with Bones [Police Officer Ernest Morris ('70)]. We had a good time. He never told me anything about going to jail when I came back. For the first time in a long time I was relaxing and I made good friends over there. That's why I wanted to go back so bad. I was annoyed after I got off the plane and somebody told me police was looking to lock me up and take me to court for sentencing. That's when I tell myself I have to leave this place."

On March 2, 2010 his Fountain Valley co-convict brother, Meral, corroborated Ballantine and himself was in Antigua for its carnival: "I was to leave for St. Croix ahead of him to find out whether he should stay there in Antigua. But we came back together about five or six days before that thing [the murders] went down."

Police Officer Morris passed before I could double check whether he was socializing with Ballantine not long before the slaughter. Based on my knowing him since childhood, it wouldn't have been a big deal for him to be friendly with Ballantine in a carnival setting. Both were in a foreign country and Officer Morris had no duties there. At the local court's 2009 Christmas party I chatted with his daughter, Dr. Patricia Morris, and her brother, Attorney Ernest Morris Jr. They said their father was rather easygoing and saw no reason to disbelieve Ballantine became acquainted with him in Antigua.

Michael A. Joseph, Esq.

Ballantine said he was facing sentence on a guilty plea for breaking someone's arm in a bar brawl. With obvious pride, he repeated several times he had made friends with Officer Morris.

Thereafter, I again spoke with Gambo. I described Ballantine's shock when he found out LaBeet tried to kill him: "As I told you before, I knew those guys. I was one of the few police officers who regularly had friendly conversations with them. I was surprised when LaBeet fired at me. I don't think anyone should believe that Ballantine and Rafie knew that LaBeet had tried to kill me."

Hence, the would-be robbers were unaware a Pied Piper was about to shove them into line fire to draw it away from himself. Pathetically, four of five in the outlaw cluster were as oblivious as were the clubhouse patrons and employees below the ridge. They'd all soon suffer the consequence of a high-value target gripped in fear of meeting Dillinger in hell. This was the setting on that unspeakable day. The golf course victims, clueless cohorts, and the people of St. Croix were about to take a ghastly spin into a long, long nightmare.

The married couples of Richard and Ruth Griffen and Charles and Joan Meisenger were, as a unit, murdered first. They'd played a round of golf, had lunch, and were just departing. Two were on vacation from their jobs with Eastern Airlines. The global carrier's wrath delivered a deathblow to the island's hospitality market. Every travel agency deleted St. Croix out of their brochures and tour plans.

Nick Beale unluckily suffered his last day in paradise because he accepted a spur-of-the-moment repair job. Joan Foster, manager of then-mainstream jeweler C&M Caron, told me she'd excuse him from electrical work at her store to go to the golf course. Hershel Greenaway recalls a noontime phone call from Foster at his Wendy's Bar and Restaurant. He said to me on January 18, 2005, "Nick had come to pick up a bull foot soup and Joan reached him at my place. Fountain Valley needed him to come out and fix their bathroom exhaust fan. The last thing he told me was, 'Hold my soup until I come back.'"

Relocating from Massachusetts only a few months before, John Gulliver, twenty-three, was hired as the golf course landscaping supervisor. John's death was agonizingly slow. His youth and "Paul Bunyan" size eventuated Rafie's suicide and this book.

Patricia Ann Tarbert, Fountain Valley's pro shop manager, was murdered while covering its pro shop as a favor to an employee. She'd just inherited a good sum with which she was to join friend Brenda Henderson and open a boutique store. Brenda's husband, Allan, was to build it for them. Interestingly, Allan Henderson was Rafie's carpentry teacher in junior high. I'll never forget rushing out of my class when told my brother had severely cut his finger. As I ran into Allan's class he was bandaging Rafie's bleeding finger, which had been caught in a lathe. Fate now joined Rafie and a friend of his teacher's wife in murder.

Austin "Junie" de Chabert recalls, "Pat was one of the sweetest friends of our family when I was growing up. She was our neighbor. She always spoke good words about everybody. I cried when she was killed. It was so unreal. How could such a good person be shot down just like that?"

Junie stammered as tearing eyes reflected revisited grief. Our conversation erupted into such sadness, his invitation to later meet to tell more about her was declined.

Those seven were shot first, all so-called "whites." Here, my conclusion the killings were *not* triggered by racial tensions is tested. "I hate you white m'fs!" LaBeet grunted as he sprayed bullets on the couples he'd ordered back inside. Rafie heard the provocative slur. Ballantine heard nothing except machine-gun fire. Rafie was taken by wide-eyed surprise. He was again promised as they descended the ridge there would be no bloodshed.

Ballantine's recall remains: "Fountain Valley was not even the first place we talked about. I told them we should rob someplace far from the camp."

According to Rafie, "Beto [LaBeet] claimed he wanted to make a political statement at Fountain Valley. He was angry about foreigners coming in to take our money and leaving us with crumbs. We never mentioned people as targets. That's why I tried to tell him let's go down at night and mess the place up if he need to make a political statement. We knew people might get hurt if someone panicked, seeing us with all those guns. But somebody said that with so many guns they will all freeze up. Besides, Beto told us the cash registers are emptied every night."

LaBeet's racial slur as prelude to his cruel act was wholly outside our sociology and therefore dubious. Reuben D. Dowling's *Mango Madness* about his growing up in St. Croix reiterates:

> However, since all the teachers, policemen, firefighters, and government workers on the island were Black, Mango did not experience racism. The Virgin Islander never had Jim Crow laws, and he never heard of anyone being discriminated against because of the color of their skin, as he heard had happened in other parts of the world.[2]

LaBeet was raised in an American territory wherein progeny of African slaves controlled local voting rules, all public as well as some parochial schools, hospitals, public health, public safety, welfare, and judicial, legislative, administrative, and executive branches. In fact, his mother Ruth was secretary to a governor cabinet member. In politics, Continentals' power extended only as far as natives yielded it to them.

This is not to discount damage caused by colonialism. Caribbean-born psychiatrist Frantz Fanon's book's epigraph quotes mentor Aimé Césaire's *Discours sur le Colonialisme*: "I am talking of millions of men who have been skillfully injected with fear, inferiority complexes, trepidation, servility, despair, abasement."

However, Dr. Fanon also notes children of European colonizers who equated themselves to the colonized fell into the diagnostic scale of "abnormal." That's because their Eurocentric ways were so rooted in assumed superiority it wouldn't be "normal" to consider the colonized as equals. The converse would seem also true. Crucians, being in control of all every-day affairs, didn't see Continentals as equivalents much less as oppressors. Another distinction is in Fanon's chapter "The Negro and Hagel" concerning perception of self: "One day the White master, without conflict, recognized the Negro slave . . . Historically, the Negro steeped in the inessentiality of servitude was set free by his master. He did not fight for his freedom."[3]

To extent that suggests a self-esteem deficit which creates conflicts with "whites," it ill-fits Crucians because *they* fought for their freedom.

In reasoning LaBeet's slur amounted to pretentious intolerance for Continentals, I do not ignore his appeal to the American Civil Liberties Union alleging racial brutality of him at Fort Dix, New Jersey.[4] It remains, though, in five years following Fort Dix his only known discharge of a firearm was at two St. Croix police officers with whom he had no prior beef. I also concede he was "exceptionally bright [and] discussed Black Power and Pan Africanism." Mindfulness of mainland racial problems was nothing new to Crucians. Our father started the local chapter of Congress of Racial Equality in the mid-1960s. CORE was founded by James Farmer Jr., the fourteen-year-old prodigy portrayed in Denzel Washington's movie *The Great Debaters*. Family friend Roy Innis, then its national leader, authorized Daddy to open a St. Croix chapter to raise awareness about economic self-sufficiency. We walked around town selling newsletters written and printed by our father that focused on such matters. As observed by a scholar on territorial affairs, "Black nationalists leaders are more likely to be supported when speaking of economic issues . . . In these instances, race is more of a surrogate for class."[5]

Raised within earshot of President Eisenhower's Republican politics, I couldn't say our father was a "black nationalist" any more I would say LaBeet was a "Pan Africanist" simply because he saw firsthand America's racialism. In direct contrast to subjugation of Yankees then fighting for the right to be "somebody," our view of that struggle was tempered by gratitude we are our own masters. Crucians are still concerned Yankees are treated as less than full citizens in certain places. Yet we cannot claim to have endured what W. E. B. DuBois called "The Color Line: The Problem of the Twentieth Century."

So, gathered to look at a TV broadcast of a civil rights march, I was pushed to ask, "Daddy, do Continentals really believe they're better than Yankees?" It didn't occur to me the country which we were taught to believe was the greatest in the world was so silly.

My father detected the disbelief in my voice. "Don't fool yourself. Many of them do."

It must've been somewhat painful to have shaken his teen-age son's "racial innocence" with his caveat. Unnoticed by us, the skin color drama was becoming an unwelcome import into St. Croix. Six years prior to the murders, Daddy conveyed to Congress that although it was not part of our heritage, it was approaching. William W. Boyer, the scholar who equated Fountain Valley to Watergate, empathized with the challenge natives faced by that encroachment:

> Testifying before a congressional committee, republican party chairman Lloyd W. Joseph blamed several Unicrat candidates for injecting 'racism' into the 1966 campaign, but he added that whites were responsible initially for implementing racial prejudice in the Virgin Islands where little had existed in the past.[6]

My deduction LaBeet's racial noise was a ruse is made with full awareness of opinions to the contrary. In his chapter "Fountain Valley," Boyer promotes view the murders erupted from perception Continentals were creating a rich-versus-poor condition. He references contemporary articles, letters to editors including *The New York Times*, locally penned books, and summarized:

> The atmosphere of their island was changing. Indeed, St. Croix was no longer their island . . . From the midst of this Crucian malaise reappeared Mario Moorhead .

.. It was Moorhead's thesis that the Virgin Islands had become dominated by Continental whites constituting an alien ruling class. He rejected the contention that the native-controlled government could be relied on to curb the ruling class or that any solution could be found by working within the system.[7]

Moorhead never once urged the use of violence. His style is "conscious music" and "mental emancipation" for social change. As one of the most well-read natives, he is quite aware of Boyer's book. In May 2005 he relayed to me over his talk radio show that he's unable to agree with the gravity of influence he supposedly exerted on Fountain Valley. He was not even on island, but in prison, where he'd been for a while prior to the tragedy.

"I was in solitary confinement at Leavenworth [Penitentiary]. From the time I see how many FBI agents came and pulled me out to ask me all kinds of questions, I knew something really bad had gone down back home."

Even if LaBeet reflected on Mario's politics, given the posse's bullet with his face on it the outlaw must've been driven more by instincts for self-preservation than politics. He knew his hunters were ready to do battle.

Other issues surely were afoot, such as Vietnam. Boyer felt such a connection when he wrote "three of the killers had served in Vietnam."[8] Dead wrong. Only LaBeet did. Gereau refused to kill Vietnamese people and was dishonorably discharged.[9] Speaking with him on November 14, 2011 for the first since his August 1973 sentencing, he confirmed he was thrown out of the army. Ballantine, Smith, and Rafie did not even register with Selective Service upon their eighteenth birthdays.

Lt. Jackson, too, sensed the impact of the war when he came upon the bullet-riddled bodies of the Meisenger and Griffen couples: "My observation of the four dead and the empty forty-five caliber casings [brass] brought me to a quick conclusion: The similar pattern of spent brass consistent with the pattern I had come to recognize from my tour in Vietnam."[10]

The eighth and only non-Continental victim was Alison Lowery, an electrician helper. He died attempting to flee but shot in the lower back.

The muddled nature of the crime is revealed by Ballantine:

> I didn't go there to shoot anybody, only to get some money. When the shooting started I even tried to help a woman, Mrs. Winters, to escape. I wanted her to run away. I knew her husband. He was a taxi driver. I also fired in the air to chase away a heavyset local guy who had a 'conk' [James Brown-styled hair]. You know gun was not my thing. Only a crazy man could think he could kill all those white people and not be hunted down until they find him.

At least one survivor was left with an inkling not all in the outlaw cluster came to kill. Shotgun victim Cletina "Tina" Tuitt in September of 1994 informed me that while bathing with warm water she heard the "clunk" of a shotgun pellet as it popped out of her calf. In spite of that, Tina supported Rafie by writing an unequivocal letter to Gov. Alexander Farrelly requesting his release.

The tragedy, as can be expected, will not be easily forgotten. Denny Fennell, a home security consultant from Littleton, Colorado, offers a clue. He wept as he pondered the twelve students and one teacher killed on April 20, 1999 by Eric Harris and Dylan Klebold at Columbine High School. In an on-camera interview his throat was trembling, wheezing out scattered words: "There is something . . . I guess, something overwhelming about that kind of . . . viciousness, that kind . . . because that kind of predatory action . . . that kind of indiscriminate killing."[11]

A Continental student of Columbine, as if in search of solace to the insanity, emphasized: "And he shot the black kid [Isaiah Shoels] because he was black!"

Though she made this crime-scene statement, there's no media intimation Columbine's massacre was racially motivated.

Her words were understood in context. And even after reading hundreds of pages of the killers' "hate-filled Nazism," the skin color drama was of no moment.

St. Croix wasn't so lucky. Despite FBI and Pentagon investigators concluded no racial mind-set or outside control caused Fountain Valley,[12] there was a rush to broadcast just the opposite. And a tangential, if not dubious, racial slur uttered by a St. Thomas native became a mantra that Crucians are peculiarly inclined to kill Continentals. It didn't matter that after LaBeet ordered, "Kill them all! Don't leave any witnesses!" five locals were shot, one fatally. The fact masks hid their identities indicates his primary objective was to leave as many bodies as possible.

Even so, months after the British socialite's disbelief Continentals are alive in St. Croix, a "black" was warned not fly to it. Brenda Henderson tells how a member of the National Bar Association en route to attend its 2004 Winter Conference was tipped off. During a flight home, she heard a passenger travelling to Puerto Rico caution the Yankee lawyer about Fountain Valley. The island's notoriety had ratcheted up to where any visitor is in danger. Such fairytale not only defamed St. Croix's sociology, it cows enjoyment of her beauty and heritage.

Rockefellers' golf course was designed by legendary architect Robert Trent Jones, Sr. It's cradled in a valley with higher hills to the north and gentle rolling ones to its east and west sides soft to the eyes and warm to the heart. Descending southlands flow towards the horizon. Smooth looking from afar, rich greenery hides hillside craggy sea-floor origins. Settled in this unique basin, the topography scattered warnings of the imminent slaughter.

In a series of interviews, Det. Tejo Torres beginning in July 2003 told me about the hunt for LaBeet. "We could hear voices, but couldn't pinpoint them. What I heard was like quarrelling. There were no paths up there. We had to stay close to each other. Our hand radios were useless in that terrain. And we couldn't risk crossfire."

Half-closed eyes narrowed to prevent puncture from thorn brushes saw precipitous under-footing only at the last moment.

Trickier, though, their target was combat-ready with high fire-power and without scruples to kill by ambush. At the time LaBeet fired at those policemen, he was hiding in an archway.

It was part of landmark Chico's Restaurant owned by Mammy's sister and her husband. Through that arch countless satisfied stomachs filled with tasty Puerto Rican dishes had strolled. Those well-fed spirits perhaps intervened to prevent it spinning into a deadly platform. LaBeet's handgun narrowly missed Gambo and his partner from about 125 feet away.

But on the ridge above the golf course, his miscue did not deter Gambo's uncles' belief they were up against a sniper with Special Forces training. LaBeet's combat skills yet remain a point of dispute. An author on Fountain Valley told me he was merely an infantryman, a "grunt." However, Melwood Civil, a Vietnam vet and National Guard master sergeant, is sure he was with an airborne division: "Yes, LaBeet had more than general training. I was with a supply unit for his division. Sometimes he would send back greetings to some of us he knew. I know he was with airborne because we had the same home base, Long Bihn Replacement Center, which we called 'LBJ' after President [Lyndon B.] Johnson. But we were out in the field in separate places between Nha Trang and Phan Rag."

Luis Martinez saw LaBeet at LBJ, but was not certain he was, like him, a paratrooper. Luis admitted that *he* had done special missions such as extraction of hostages out of Thailand. Two other combat vets advised I may never learn whether the convict was specially trained, or carried out off-record missions. Soldiers were afforded secrecy about certain operations such as assassination of "civilians" suspected of aiding enemies. Others had assignments in Cambodia and Laos, officially neutral countries. Orders like those were placed in "File 13," meaning the wastebasket. The police dragnet wisely took no chances.

To the public, LaBeet was no Fred "Would You Be My Neighbor?" Rogers. Little did they know he may have been just as lethal as was the real Fred Rogers. On September 16, 2005 my specials ops source, a Continental commando who was deployed "to soften up Grenada" before its invasion, told me how deadly specially trained soldiers are: "I bet you think you could've handled that softy, skinny man Mr. Rogers of the children TV show. What a mistake you'll have made. Fred was a Navy Seal with twenty-seven confirmed kills! Most of them in close-quarter combat! These guys are trained to stay awake until *you* fall asleep. I dare you to stay up for two days and still outsmart an enemy in his own backyard."

Our brother Rodney, a navy vet, confirmed, "Fred Rogers was a very deadly sniper."

It had seemed the posse was too afraid of LaBeet. I learned, though, a commando is to a cop, what a cop is to a civilian. On August 24, 2009 the special ops man confirmed it:

> When a policeman on Main Street in St. Thomas was going to slam his nightstick into your brother Rafie for no reason, I simply disarmed him and he seemed to know he was no match for me. Another time at Bailey's Nightclub a policewoman was about to strike a fellow who was sitting down. I took her club, and she reached for her firearm. I was pushing it back down in the holster, but when she forced the draw, I spun the gun out of her hand as I lifted it in the air, empting the six bullets on the floor, and returned her pistol butt-first. All I said to her was, 'Be careful!'"

A further handicap the posse faced was fatigue. Tejo said hunt for LaBeet was relentless. Before gaining proximity to him on the ridge above the golf course they had engaged in an "I sleep, you drive; I drive, you sleep" rotation every two hours. At night they looked for campfires, listened for barking dogs and other noises of alarm. By day, they approached deep-country homes for information.

And psychologically, it must have also been difficult to take down a fellow warrior. Combat vets emerge from the horrors of war with a loyalty amongst themselves that transcends almost all other commitments. This is seen in the movie *Rambo*, in which a Special Forces soldier who went nuts against police brutality benefited from military assistance. Without such allegiance, he wouldn't have survived the lawmen's overkill forces. LaBeet's reputation among police was everything but redeemable. Yet a veteran was in the process of assisting him to reenlist in the army only weeks before Fountain Valley. Exemplary of the caliber of native soldiers David "Billy" Simmiolkjier held back tears as he revealed how painful it was to learn his fellow war-rior was accused of multiple murders: "I was so disappointed when I heard a soldier was involved in that stupid, senseless thing that happened at Fountain Valley. I really wanted to help him. I was helping him shortly before that day. He would have gotten back in the army with my help."

"What was your status with the military, Billy?"

"Commando Sergeant! First, Fifth, and Seventh Special Forces! Airborne! One Hundred and First and Eighty-Second Divisions! I only wish that boy had seen me sooner."

Instinct advised I stop saddening this super fighter. It also told me the posse transferred their unavoidable sense of loyalty to LaBeet by conferring on him maximum military kill-capa-bility. In other words, if they had to bring him down, they saw themselves as taking out, if nothing else, a combatant who did well in Vietnam's jungle for his country.

During the search for him, a murder suspect, Angel Ventura, was deployed by police to help. Ventura was promised leniency for his risk. He found Rafie's camp, and LaBeet. Acting as if he wanted sanctuary, he spent a few nights there. Tragically, before he could report back, LaBeet figured him out as a rat when he stated he had a change of heart and was leaving to give himself up. According to Rafie, "LaBeet simply iced Angel at point blank."

His body was found years later. Bevron Goodwin, a rela-tive of Ventura, informed, "When Angel's body was found, his father, Pastor Ventura, who is my grandfather, refused to bury him in the cemetery because of his sins. Pastor Ventura buried Angel under a tree in his yard in the same box the police brought his body."

Sensing the police were zooming in, LaBeet was trigger-happy. A friend of Rafie with teeth-grinding anger on June 9,

2003 recalled to me his encounter just days before the murders. "That sick m'f! I didn't even know he was up there with Rafie. He put a machine gun right up in my face! LaBeet acted as if he owned the place. Mikey, I ain't joking. If I knew he was going to push that thing at the golf course, I'd have gone back for Dukie [Edwin, our brother] to get him out of there."

Rafie lived quietly in the hills for months prior to the murders. His favorite memory of those days was observing feral dogs as they hunted fleet-footed, high-jumping deer. The dogs ran their quarry in circles until fully exhausted. Crucian naturalist George A. Seaman witnessed, "In St. Croix the deer's chief foe—aside from man—is the so-called 'wild dog.' These, traveling singly or in packs, take heavy toll yearly of the deer population. Fawns, young deer, and pregnant does are particularly vulnerable to these half-starved mongrels."[13]

After my brother recounted those hunts to me, a smile came across his face. I told him I noticed he was smiling. He said when he was depressed in jail, he'd think of the hunts. Prisoners sometimes noticed him beaming and, due to jailhouse perennial paranoia, would probe, "Why *you* smiling?"

He really looked forward to seeing those dog hunts.

"Mikey, if somebody had told me that stray dogs were capable of such intelligent organization, I would have disbelieved. The one thing that got to me about them is that they hunted together, but there was no leader. They'll figure out any escape route and cover it. Sometimes dogs I never saw before appeared out of nowhere just for the hunt, eat, and then go about their own business."

I later realized Rafie's special memory was stimulated by an aspect of his personality. He had an aversion to being led. When needed to help with a chore he didn't wait to be told what to do. *He* decided how best to assist. That attribute makes it most improbable he could be handheld to commit murder. In the countryside, his intent was to be left alone, to mind his own business.

Another myth about Fountain Valley is it was committed by a group of fugitives who formed a Che Guevara-type guerrilla unit.

So seriously taken was this rumor, retired director of nursing Lydia Thomas, while grocery shopping on September 21, 2011, volunteered, "As you know, my husband [former Giants catcher] Valmy was the only federally licensed firearm dealer in St. Croix, and he had a lot of handguns and rifles in our United Sporting Goods store. Police woke us up late in the night after Fountain Valley. They were afraid those guys would break in the store for the guns. They took us with them to remove all the guns and ammunition from the store to secure them until they were captured."

The trial judge ruled Rafie was *not legally* a fugitive, but the police had probable cause to arrest anyone aiding him. This was necessary to justify the seizures of Gereau and Smith on the basis of their taking food to the camp. US District Court judge Warren H. Young wrote:

> The fugitives in question were LaBeet, Ballantine, and Joseph. An arrest warrant was outstanding against at least LaBeet, on a charge unrelated to Fountain Valley, and the police had been greatly desirous of contacting the remaining two about a number of criminal matters. All three had been conspicuously unavailable for some time and were thought to be camping in the hills . . . I know no legal determination of 'fugitivity' has been made, and I do not imply one here.
>
> A bench warrant for [LaBeet] was issued on May 31, 1972, by this court in Criminal No. 44/1972 (robbery). A bench warrant for Raphael [sic] Joseph was not issued until September 8, 1972, in Criminal No. 44/1972 (robbery). The police had been looking for him for some time before then, however. There was no outstanding warrant for Ballantine, but in the latter days of August he had failed to appear for sentencing in Criminal No. 83/1971. A bench warrant in that case was issued on September 8th.[14]

Lawyers have a saying: "Bad facts make for bad law." In the Fountain Valley case, however, they were so awful they also made for bad facts. Despite Judge Young's find-ings about handed-out warrants set forth instantly above, the appeals court, directly after describing the crime as quoted in Part One, asserted, "Prior to the incident at Fountain Valley, arrest warrants had been issued for three of the defendants in this case, Ishmael LaBeet, Warren Ballantine, and Raphael [sic] Joseph, on charges including first degree assault, simple assault and battery, and failure to appear in court after release on bond."

I interviewed near a dozen retired policemen concerning Rafie's flight to the hills. Not a single one was aware of any prior warrant or felony charge, including the alleged robbery in Criminal No. 44/1972. Inspection of that file revealed there's no police report, affidavit, nor complaint in it. It consists of a bare-bones formal charge signed by a prosecutor alleging Rafie and LaBeet robbed a citizen. An arrest warrant is in the file for LaBeet *only*.

Police Commissioner Eric Hansen conveyed, "Before Foun-tain Valley, Rafie was no problem. The only thing that stands out my mind is the day Sunny Isles Shopping Center called us for Rafie and Ballantine."

"What? Were they robbing or attacking people?"

"No, no. They were just looking for other guys they think they could provoke into hand fights. Ballantine, as you know, loved fighting."

"Was Rafie arrested?"

"No. We decided to arrest Ballantine alone. Ballantine was too strong to have us thinking about Rafie too."

Captain Ohanio Harris smiled as he described Rafie's two arrests a few months before Fountain Valley. His bails were set by phone call to a judge, who each time set them at fifty dollars with 10 percent cash surety. It began with unauthorized use of our brother-in-law's car, followed by public drunkenness. Ray Isles, a horse-racing commissioner, said he bailed Rafie out of his second arrest with a five-dollar bill. He described Rafie's final run-in with the police the same night, and which caused him to head out of town:

Frito and your father had made up. Days before that, Rafie—Frito is what I called him—and I worked with your father on the roof of your grandfather's building next to the Royal Dane Hotel. I'll never forget how your father tied ropes around Rafie and my waists just in case we fell off the roof. Anyway, the night Rafie decided to leave town, [retired police captain] Bert Bryan had tried to arrest him for destruction of property. Bert accused him of pissing on an air conditioner behind a store. Frito pushed Bert and ran away. Early the next morning he left to make camp in the hills.

Perhaps my brother's petty provocations with the law were subliminal reactions to a deep void in his life. Emptiness created by a shift akin to that of a child's abrupt designation as an "adult" and forced to separate from those to whom he always was devoted. Edwin, Rafie, and I were born only nineteen months apart. We lived as unit from the time Rafie was a toddler until I went to college in 1968 and Edwin shipped to Vietnam 1969. When I returned home in summer of 1970, friends eager to enjoy Rafie's charm and charisma hung with him. He yet seemed lonely. After I returned to college, Rafie thrust himself onto the steep roof. Our father never allowed much less required us to join him in such perilous projects. Relaxing that rule and placing the anchored rope around Rafie's waist appears to be a gesture of understanding for a son's need to rejoin his family.

This final reunion was short-lived. "Getting into trouble again" crystallized Rafie's decision not to bring further shame to the family. He sought "the country" where our hearts really lived. We'd spent much of our boyhood spare moments in the countryside. The fruit trees, the meadows, the wildlife were our companions. The district court found that Smith and Gereau had carried cases of canned goods to my brother's campsite in the dawn hours before the killings.[15] That shows Fountain Valley wasn't planned until shortly before it occurred, since that much food indicates Rafie was not about to break camp.

He was, in a sense, a cluster unto himself. He was the only truly ambidextrous individual I knew, and with an impeccable handwriting. When the bulletin barged into my bedroom about the killings and "Rafael Joseph" was named I thought another person shared the name. But when that suspect was said to be left-handed, as I am, I knew then it was my brother. St. Croix's population was too few for that coincidence.

Contented in camp as he was, at night Rafie sometimes visited his first child, Afrilasia, born June 14, 1972. Her mother revealed he spoke about discreetly moving in with her and the baby. But an order dated November 3, 1972 denying his request for reduced bail stated, "None of the defendants had real or strong family relationships among their siblings . . . and those who have children neither support nor maintain them nor do they fully perform the father role."

The good judge was uninformed, no less than when he wrote that our brother Edwin was Rafie's "friend."

The heavens seemed to have sent blessings to Rafie's daughter through a cluster of infants baptized within days of Fountain Valley. Lincoln Duval, born six days after Afrilasia, was among them. On Easter Sunday of 2002 *The St. Croix Avis* ran a front-page story about my intent to write this book. Within months, Duval asked for a copy of it because, he said, "I am positive I'm connected to Fountain Valley. I was christened on the day of the massacre."

His memory was too mystic. I recalled movie *The Godfather* where Michael Corleone massacred mob enemies as the church bell rang out his baby's baptism. But Fountain Valley occurred on the Wednesday before Duval's Sunday, September 10th christening. He'd invited me to his home to ask his mom, and she confirmed that day as his baptismal day. My visit jogged her recall of low-hovering helicopters and screaming sirens speeding along roads near her country home. She had worried, *Are those cold-blooded killers nearby?* Though she had fears, she didn't allow it to take over her family:

Governor Evans had come on the radio and TV to tell us the criminals are going to be captured soon. So, I

131

went ahead with the plans for Lincoln's baptism. On the way to pick up his christening cake the Saturday before the ceremony, a police roadblock stopped us and a bunch of men searched our car. Lincoln was sleeping right in my arms. And next day, on the Sunday of his christening, the party was much dampened. Even though we tried not to show it, all of us were worrying because the police was still hunting for the murderers.

Unmoved by his mom's better memory, Duval insisted, "Although I wasn't christened on the exact day of the killings, your brother's daughter's meeting with Vice President Bush tells me that my baptism on the Sunday after Fountain Valley must have blessed her."

On our way to meet his mother, I had told Duval about Afrilasia's meeting in the Governor Ballroom with Vice President George H. W. Bush during his campaign for president. She was crowned "Hal Jackson's Virgin Islands Talented Teen" and in that capacity invited to the reception. The VP of the United States walked Afrilasia to center of the opulent hall for a photo op. He hugged her with glee of showing off a favorite goddaughter. Out of curiosity, on October 21, 2003 I went to a Republican Club meeting to find out the date Afrilasia and Vice President Bush took those pictures. That date was June 20, 1987: Lincoln Duval's fifteenth birthday!

Four: Handsaw and Marbles

We are all born complete. It takes more energy to be
sad than it does to be happy.

—Don Juan Matus

Rafie's boyhood was conjoined with Edwin's and mine. We inflexibly bonded when five, six, and seven, respectively. Our birth dates: myself August 31, 1949; Edwin's September 6, 1950 (Fountain Valley happened on his twenty-second birthday); and Rafie's April 18, 1951. Agatha was Edwin's mother. Isabel was Rafie's and mine. Our father had taken Rafie and me to live with him and Agatha. According to her, we boys "held one head," and she called us "The Trio." One morning when I was in first grade, something was stirring a distraction just outside of my street-level classroom open window. It was Rafie. Naked as he was born. He had shadowed me over the hilly two blocks to school. The Trio likewise always followed each other.

Our father succumbed within thirty-six hours of Fountain Valley. His already fading health couldn't withstand the stress his son was being hunted for the killing of eight. He had provided us strength and character, facilitated the ambitions of others, and pioneered business.

He was first to import BMWs. We learned to drive in brand new "Beemers" while Bayerische Motoren Werke was retooling its image of Nazi warplane builder to trendy car maker. As an automobile connoisseur, Daddy knew they were well engineered. But he was mocked as peddling "matchbox cars." He also became the first BMW renter, having sold only two. Had that business not folded so soon, George and Donna Palmer would have offered sales tips. They'd owned Michigan's oldest Ford dealership, founded by George's father in 1912. Recently while dining at Villa Morales (relocated Chico's) Restaurant, Donna assured, "We'd have been glad to help. St. Croix has been our second home since nineteen seventy-one. We've been dining with your family for more than forty years. I am family here, too, you know."

Our father was as good with his hands as he was with his brains. He took apart and repaired a Beemer's transmission by himself. He also drafted house plans. His designed homes are intact after fifty years and two powerful hurricanes. He made a protégé, Orlando Ramirez, who went on to study engineering. One day Daddy visited his parents' store next door to our home where the teenager was filling and weighing pound bags of white flour. "Do you want to do that for the rest of his life?" "No, sir," was the answer, and that begot Orlando an apprenticeship in house plans with our father. Today he's a building site inspector.

Another is Cecil Benjamin, past president of the local American Federation of Teachers, past labor commissioner, and currently Democratic Party state chair: "It was your father who made me what I am now in the world of labor negotiations. I was able to use bargaining strategies he taught me at conferences as far away as in South Africa. I insist you write this in your book. I owe him that much. He was a great man."

While businessmen were shifting to civil jobs, Christian Lloyd Wendell Joseph was of mind-set native stores were the surest way to survive swelling stateside economic control. He was exclusive dealer for Rheingold Beer, S&W canned foods, and seller of portable carbonated soft drink dispensers. He also was first native to retail household stand-alone freezers, and distribute whole frozen chickens. The preparation of free-roaming poultry from scratch—chasing them up and down, wringing necks, and then plucking feathers—were chores every household gladly gave up. The ready-to-cook ones were sold from our railed-bed truck village to village and vanished like hot bread.

The Trio enjoyed these excursions as we rode shotgun, eyeing chicks of a different sort.

Success afforded him fine racehorses. Those I remember are One-Eyed McArthur, Sir Thomas Moore, and Madam Jenile. They didn't become legends. The one which did was Susan. Lifelong horsemen brag of the fear she bred in stallions, even in those she'd race on their own turf in St. Thomas. The racetrack there is now named after her main jockey, Clinton Phipps. St. Thomas native Silvio Garcia on March 30, 2013 added, "There was a horse named Sunbeam owned by Mr. Daly. He had serviced Susan. I knew your brother Rafie later on when he lived in St. Thomas. He used to exercise horses for the musician Milo Francis. One time Milo's horse by the name of Norman's Castle bolted with Rafie and broke Rafie's leg."

Susan had a colt, Suebeam, from Sunbeam. Daddy sold it and retired from horse racing. To this very day Susan's fans reminisce of her with sheer delight.

Our father wrecked a few new cars in driving challenges. It earned him the nickname "Crash Pilot." Leroy Henley shared, "We students would dash out of class when we heard that roaring engine just to see Crash Pilot's car fly pass our school."

By himself, Daddy built a pickup truck out of a Pontiac sedan he'd crashed. It proved to be a vehicle for making of brave hearts. He'd chopped down its cabin and fashioned "doors" with heavy canvas cloth. By pushing hard against the dashboard we avoided leaning against our "door" or risk spilling out around curves. Of course, we always answered, "Yes, Daddy," when asked, "You boys OK?" Those scary, yet exciting drives afforded us the luxury of controlling fright.

Shortly after Rafie's Fountain Valley sentencing my apartment was Gestapo-like smashed into by lawmen. Instantly looking down the barrel of what I later learned was a .357 magnum pistol, I calmly sized up its nozzle. "Damn, that's a big hole!" I said to the stranger standing over me, truly amazed by its built. He was taken aback. "Who the hell is this guy?" A case of mistaken identity, they grumbled.

Daddy's business savvy manifested a generation later in the person of Ashley Andrews. "When I was a small country boy I was in a store and accidentally bumped into your father's briefcase. I turned around and asked, 'What's that box with the handle?' Your father said, 'It's a businessman's briefcase.' I asked him to explain what he meant by 'business' and to tell me what he had in that briefcase. Your father told me about invoices and his other business papers."

Daddy talked to anyone so long as it was productive and from their encounter, Ashley said he became an entrepreneur. I had the fortune of being involved in local litigation of $60 million in turnkey projects to be built by Rogge Engineering of Germany. Ashley brokered the deal for a $3 million fee. The $60 million was escrowed in New York's Citibank. But the contract was dishonored when a new governor's attorney alleged Rogge was a neo-Nazi. Rogge was represented by a law firm which once partnered with Leonard Hall, past Republican national chairman, and Bill Casey, later CIA director. Ashley caused the firm to retain me as its local counsel. I witnessed him shove away a $1 million banker's check offered as settlement for his fees. Ashley argued that it was unfair he suffered a two-thirds penalty because of an unrelated dispute between the parties. The $60 million had earned $6 million in interests from which the $3 million could be paid, he pointed out. The government's Philadelphia firm did not budge. To my shocking surprise, he walked away from the table and attempted to intervene in the lawsuit. Ironically, I was duty bound to block his tactic and he got not a penny.

I asked Ashley, who'd practiced law in New York for many years, why he threw away a million dollars. "It was important that white people learn that black people, too, know about money. It was a gesture to you, out of respect for your father."

Ashley was away for decades. Yet, on return to St. Croix by chance he located his office in the building directly above Daddy's once-owned La Alhambra Restaurant. That diner seeded the name of a law enforcement center—"Patrick Sweeny Police Headquarters." Hired to play for a while in La Alhambra was a small band from the island of St. Kitts. Its singer was a very handsome and courteous young man, Patrick Sweeny. When the band's visa was up, Patrick asked Daddy to bond him as a bartender so he could stay in St. Croix. Soon he and I were working in the restaurant. Patrick later became a police officer and was killed in line of duty. A new police building was fittingly named in his honor. How eerie Patrick Sweeney Police Headquarters was built to replace King's Hill Police Station from which the submachine gun used at Fountain Valley was stolen

Daddy's youngest daughter seems to have inherited his business genes. Mrs. Christine Joseph-Steinman's brother-in-law, Derrick Steinman, was the editor of the influential financial periodical *American Bankers News*. Maybe one of Daddy's grandchildren will, someday, become a banker.

He was for a long time the lone Republican politician and founded St. Croix Republican Club. He hosted Republican governors and Rafie and I helped serve them. They included Michigan's Gov. George Romney, father of recent White House candidate Mitt Romney. However, the club was snubbed; natives then and now dislike Republicans. President Herbert Hoover (1928–1932) in regards to the 1917 purchase of the VI and the aid it needed from his administration had commented, "We have acquired an effective Caribbean poorhouse."

Nearby Puerto Rico was as much wanting of federal help, but because it was a larger territory fitter for military use, Hoover was less brunt towards it. Nuances aside, his remark was taken as an insult. It mattered little he replaced the islands' naval rule with much gentler civilian officers, or that President Eisenhower appointed John D. Merwin in 1957 as the first native governor.

Besides local dislike, in 1927 mainland Yankees began to stray from their longtime alliance with the Republican Party. As President Calvin Coolidge's commerce secretary, Hoover was assigned to probe violations of civil rights of sharecroppers in the Mississippi Delta. They were herded into forced labor during the Great Flood of April 1927. National Guard soldiers and armed Boy Scouts stood guard as planters made them maintain levees, and provide aid to Continentals. Though he promised to investigate that atrocity which drowned dozens, he never did. Yankees who bothered to vote in 1931 yet gave Hoover 75 percent of their votes against winner Democrat Franklin D. Roosevelt. But when Roosevelt was reelected in 1936 *he* received 75 percent of their votes. That switch was boosted by Roosevelt's 1933 New Deal to lift the lives of the poor.

First Lady Eleanor Roosevelt clinched it by causing the release of Tuskegee Airmen into World War II combat. In a picture seen around the world, she flew with one of those Yankees thereby forcing the military to agree they were fit to be deployed into air combat. Their skills proved to be legendary. A Continental, Don Hinz, even lost his life as a flyer in the Red Tail Project to honor them. They were awarded Congressional Gold Medals in 2006. Two were natives: Henry Rohlsen Sr. and Herbert Heywood Sr. In 1996 Alex Hamilton lost his name at St. Croix's airport to Rohlsen.

Eleanor also served as a board member of the NAACP, founded by Republicans in 1909 on Abraham Lincoln's one hundredth birthday. Her subtle intensity pushed her husband's successor, Democrat Harry S. Truman, to desegregate the armed forces. Truman was the first president to address the NAACP. He had warned his mother-in-law, whose hero was Lincoln's assassin John Wilkes Booth, she'd hate his June 28, 1947 speech calling for an end to racism.

Although President Eisenhower had in 1957 deployed the army against Southern bigotry, Yankees continued to vote Democrat. President Richard Nixon created the EPA for cleaner air and water, and CETA providing first-time job opportunities for tens of thousands of Yankees. But it didn't stem the tide. Those agencies could not offset Nixon's "Southern strategy" recruiting Southern anti-civil rights Democrats into his party.

How ironic. Wayne Perryman's *Unveiling the Whole Truth* tells how Democrats took control of the South when Reconstruction was halted. It was they who used the Supreme Court to render powerless the Civil Rights Act of 1875. President Lyndon B. Johnson (1963–1969) saw his Civil Rights Act of 1964 opposed by a fellow Democrat, Senator Al Gore Sr., who bellowed it was "the same legislation which the Republicans tried to ram down our throats in 1875." Johnson's predecessor, John F. Kennedy (1961–1963), set the pace when he declared that purging racism was a matter of morality and coined the concept "affirmative action." And when Johnson nominated Thurgood Marshall on June 13, 1967 as first "black" to the Supreme Court, it wasn't token gesture. The vast majority of worthy lawyers never get a chance to appear before the court, but here was one who had won nineteen cases before it.

With guidance from civil rights leaders such as Whitney Young Jr., President Johnson's Great Society vision to uplift "folks of all colors" did well to repair his party's racist legacy. On February 29, 1968 Johnson's Kerner Commission warned racism was moving America "toward two societies, one black, one white, separate and unequal." Just days after the April 4 assassination of Martin Luther King Jr., Congress passed Johnson's Civil Rights Act of 1968 banning housing discrimination.

During those shifting times, Daddy remained steadfast for a local two-party system, but his Republicans couldn't muster 5 percent of general election votes necessary to make them an official party. His refusal to abandon the party of Abe Lincoln caused some to refer to him as "Lone Wolf." In the 1966 election cycle he got an offer to switch to Democrat with assurance he'd be seated in the legislature. He refused, and asked me whether he did the right thing. I naively told him he should've said yes. He asked, "Why?" And I said, "Because they outnumber you."

He frowned. "If you were the only horse in a pasture and you came upon a herd of jackasses, would you join up with them simply because you were the only horse?"

How ashamed I felt. It was crushing because Grandfather used to admonish us, "If you boys are going to run up and down in the house, do not be dumb donkeys. Have horse sense!"

On December 30, 2005 I was relieved by an elder from a lingering feeling Daddy had been too politically inflexible. "Your father was a top politician. He was as good as the best. But he was too honest."

His unbending intent to create a two-party system paid off by an act of Congress. With Washington-connected Continentals' help and his testimony in Congress, the Republicans became a legal party by federal law. It then formed a coalition with splinter Democrats dubbed "Victory 66." That led to a Republican being the last appointed, and the first elected, governor.

Sadly, Daddy became a victim of politicians' penchant to forget those who laid path to their lofty positions. Ariel Melchior Jr., then-publisher of *The Virgin Islands Daily News*, complained about it in his commentary of October 2, 1982:

> The late Lloyd Joseph of St. Croix was a staunch Republican at a time many of the same persuasion found it politically suicidal to even be known as a Republican . . . Undaunted by the odds, Joseph maintained his position as a Republican, obviously hoping someday his party would take control of the administration. It happened in 1969 when Richard Nixon won the presidency and appointed a Democrat-turned-Republican, Melvin Evans, to the governorship. And the rebirth of the Republican Party in the Virgin Islands took on a new direction—but without Joseph. Championing the cause of the party netted him no rewards or remunerations and certainly no thanks . . . He became the forgotten man of the local Grand Old Party.

A Continental former member of the local legislature, Holland Redfield, publicly maintains our father is worthy of recognition for creating a two-party system in the VI. He had so informed Vice President Bush the night at Bush's ballroom reception. Daddy's struggle was also appreciated by Sen. Orrin Hatch (R-Utah). As it turned out, refusal to abandon his quest became the political pivot for Rafie's freedom.

Our family was extended alike that of the great Spanish artist Pablo Picasso, who openly enjoyed more than one family. In this regard, Daddy was no different than the financial magnate J. P. Morgan. As did Picasso's, women sometimes scrapped over our father. His children, though, were a single unit. By time I was at Loyola, however, Daddy had changed. When I bragged to him about my two girlfriends, he admonished me, "Today's women are gaining more self-respect. They are with you not because they enjoy that arrangement, but because they love you. Be careful with their feelings."

We didn't know segregation. Three houses away from our birth home, a Continental's living room played classical music nonstop. Two front doors from our grandmother's house lived another Continental. Her son fathered a child with a one of our relatives. A few attended our school when they relocated. If they were shy, we reminded them that "all blood red."

Our upbringing was sheltered. We were never permitted to listen to adult conversations, at least not of a soap opera nature. Whenever family friends visited, we were ordered out of earshot with stern words: "Big people are talking." We did not receive life lessons, a fact noticed by a girlfriend in Los Angeles who said I was "overprotected." We simply were given orders which we obeyed (more or less) under peril of pain. "Who don't hear, will feel!" was the warning. And then, we'd pushed the envelope. Well-placed lashes followed more serious misbehavior. All hometown friends who received this measured discipline are grateful. "No nonsense!" was the standard. Older siblings were always in charge and authorized to inflict corporal tactics. Town elders often had tacit authority to impose discipline on us.

Our father was not petty, and never wasted words. Yet he loved to bargain. One day we looked on as he negotiated an offer to sell his old, heavy security safe. Because of its rust, it could not be opened that day. Yet, for hours on that afternoon the businessman and he argued price and politics in fluent Spanish. Daddy always seemed to know all. In my unconscious, he was beyond human. I actually laughed in disbelief when I saw him in his coffin. I've never heard of anyone who cackled on seeing their truly beloved dad dead. Except, maybe, George Bernard Shaw, who observed, "Life does not cease to be funny when people die any more than it ceases to be serious when people laugh."

Michael A. Joseph, Esq.

For a decade, my psyche refused to accept he'd passed. When I dreamt of him, he'd be unseen only to spring from a secreted place to reprimand us. Both in life and death, his presence meant no "ifs," no "ands," no "buts." Do things his way, or no way. His sharp mind always proved to be accurate. Still, he instilled independence in us. If we needed "spending cash" to go to the movies or to a school dance we asked for permission to do an outside chore. There were already a few chores-for-pay requests from neighbors or family members. Off we'd go to wash a car, water plants, clean a yard, or run errands.

In appropriate moments we'll try to convince Daddy we should have a TV as did our friends. But he'd warn it might change our basic personalities. For his political speeches on TV, he'd direct us to a neighbor to watch him. In our late teens, he finally bought one. It was a Phillips with a splinter-bamboo door that folded back inside its cabinet. It lasted twenty-five years even after being scorched and water damaged in a house fire. It outlasted him by a score, becoming a symbol of his talent for picking quality products.

Rafie didn't care too much for TV. Edwin and I loved switching back and forth the few available channels. Prior to having it, most our spare time was spent riding bicycles into the country, or fishing, or setting bird traps, or figuring out which fruit tree we'd raid before "it was bared." We were never wanting. We needed nothing. We envied no one. We were truly happy. Mother later revealed, "Rafie was the sweetest one of all. He would hide to cry on my lap when he had problems with you and Butchie."

Of course, Butchie (Edwin's nickname) and I didn't know that. Rafie was just as tough. When we'd get a good thrashing, he didn't flinch any more than we did. The most unforgettable whipping came, surprisingly, from a mundane carpenter's tool. That mode of discipline was familiar to those who were apprentices of furniture craftsmen. We had escaped it until the summer break between tenth and eleventh grades. The Trio was assigned to dig beneath a storeroom with pick and shovel two basement bedrooms. Daddy preferred to not change a family legacy by horizontally adding them.

142

It was the stockroom of Grandfather's dry goods store for more than half a century, inherited from his mother, Netta Pryor. He had recently passed, and Daddy decided to convert his two-story Danish-styled home, where we then lived, into a guesthouse of ten units. He single-handedly lifted the second floor off of its first solely with old-fashioned screw jacks. He single-handedly then recast its wooden first floor in cement, reinforced its concrete pillars and second floor mid-beams, then lowered the four-bedroom upper level on its first floor section.

Excavation by hand of the storeroom basement therefore seemed to Daddy a relatively easy task. He hired a retired grave digger to join us, but the work became too much for the old man. The Trio continued the project. Digging, digging, digging, and shoveling, shoveling, shoveling during the hot summer months was miserable, miserable, and miserable. The old man could really dig. But we were glad he was gone. He had a very strong stench about him. Not really stink. It was a one that rather burnt the nostrils. Maybe a stench slaves groomed to remind "Massa" of their inhuman condition. Perhaps it was that smell that caused Thomas Jefferson to disdain some of his slaves. Each time we got a whiff, we giggled. Daddy was always nearby, and giggling while working was a sure path to a slap to the back of the head. But we were masters of the suppressed laughter. We'd forcefully press our hands over our mouths. That pressure in turn produced pooping sounds, the effect of which was to create more laughter concealed with even more pressure. It was a "silent" contorting riot. It is near impossible to describe our sheer joy.

Another scenario for elation was when Daddy told us to go to sleep. One warning was the measure. Next, he'd stand just outside our bedroom with its door ajar creating a long grim reaper-like shadow. Hidden, he thought. Facing threat of lashing forced us to smother more merriment. If the sound escaped, we'd immediately hear, "What was that!?" One of us would have to fess up and say, "Daddy, it's me. I just pooped." Of course, we couldn't say "farted."

The solemnity of Sunday Mass was no buffer to our indulgence for hilarity. While home from Loyola in the summer of

1970 I noticed our St. Patrick's Church had dropped the Latin part of Mass; it was now all celebrated in English. For a good portion of our formative years we attended church every Sunday. Occasionally, the Trio would have to be awakened with drama such as a pitcher of cold water thrown on us by a sweet paternal grandmother named Elizabeth Hardcastle. "Hardcastle" came from father, Henry, a grandson of William Hardcastle, born England in 1804 and migrated to St. Croix in 1830. It was a wonder how such a petite and quiet lady had so hard-hitting a name. Two syllables: an adjective descriptive of strength and a noun suggestive of aristocracy. Yet Granny was all that. She reminded us of upper crust because she was among few afforded private Mass in her living room. Adding to her pedigree, her mother, Arotina McBean, was the niece of Mathilda "Queen Mathilda" McBean, one of four "queens" who in 1878 led the Fireburn out of serfdom. Aunt Mathilda was sentenced to be hanged by the neck until dead for her acts of liberty. Luckily, that penalty was reduced to a life term thanks to the plea of Danish royal women. She was exiled to Denmark on June 19, 1882 to serve her jail sentence and was later paroled.

Granny, no wonder, was stern as she was small. One Sunday she had her fill of our snub at the usual, "Time for church! Please get up boys!" And just as customary, we had been talking and laughing till the wee hours. Granny for some reason bypassed her cold-water treatment. What happened next is both hilarious and fascinating. I could hear through my sleep, which was at its sweetest point, some flat, broad sounds. Whap! "What the hell," I loudly grumbled without opening my eyes. Whap! Whap! Feelings and sounds suddenly merged! "Oh my God!" I uttered as I jumped up. I was being whipped! Daddy moved towards Rafie. Up he jumped. Whap! Whap! Up came Edwin. We'd been "figure-eight," an unprecedented experience. Granny had disturbed her son's slumber in the adjacent house. She knew he'd be greatly annoyed and let loose his umbrage on our backsides. The Trio scrambled into the shower pissed. Quickly we were out, grabbed our readied "Sunday best," and off we went to church, sleepy and irritated. Now in the pews, we had our chance to avenge the humiliation. When the priest started his Latin prayers, out came our trademark belly laughter suppressed by cupped mouths with the farting sounds. For we knew like us, the congregation was largely Latin illiterate. Yet in chorus they'd mumble, "Amen." We laughed more than we had ever done in church until we got the priest's attention. We bowed our giggling heads, got up from our pew, and walked out with knees bended. We sat behind the church and waited until the bell rang that Mass was over. Mind you, we were true believers. "Hail Mary" was our favorite prayer. We'd get down on our knees and pray Daddy wouldn't remember the pasting he'd promised us. Many times it seems to have worked.

Granny showed spunk again when big brother Austin found a huge bullet in the next-door closed cemetery once used as resting place for European gentry and estate overseers. It had become our favorite playground. Austin repeatedly struck the bullet's head with a rock until thunder boomed across our quaint town from that sacred place. Granny knew Austin would never allow his younger brothers to endanger themselves. Therefore, it must've been him who discharged it. He was busted. She tied his hands with those wee arms of hers, drew with chalk on the kitchen floor a circle about one step wide around his feet, and started whipping as she warned him of the dire consequences if he moved out of that circle. He knew she would report him to Daddy, bringing really real hell upon his backside. He contorted, spun, ducked, and wiggled, but he never stepped out.

Even when wrongfully accused, we did not point any finger. Instead, we rode out the storm no matter how painful. An instance of that arose when Rafie and Edwin stole a five-dollar bill out our grandfather's cash box.

Grandfather, Christian Pryor Joseph, was a very proud man. Six days a week he strolled from his home to his dry goods store a third of a mile away in three-piece suit, chained pocket watch, and walking stick. He was a very talkative man who boasted about the quality of his imports and of his health. Sometimes, he stood at his counter and curved his right leg to rest upon the back of his neck alike an Indian guru. According to older brother Rudolph, Grandfather had been a top pugilist. "It is Grandfather who taught me to box. One day he saw me throwing out my hands and asked me, 'You really want to learn? I'll teach you.' That's when he told me he won the Caribbean Heavyweight Champion title in Cuba."

Well-respected "Mr. Christian" was a stalwart of what he called "simple common sense." In spite of advancing age, he never wavered on his right to be right. The unwary who challenged his well-rooted thinking saw a leg lifted across the neck: "Can you do this? As you can see, I might be old but I'm no fool. And I am in perfect health."

Several movers and shakers met often at his store. Among them were: Kai Lawaetz, a farmer for seventy-five years whose family maintains a museum honoring their Danish roots; Canute Brodhurst, free speech activist and owner of *The St. Croix Avis* (est. 1844); D. Hamilton Jackson started the first labor union, and was a judge; Ludwig Harrigan had been an advisor to Marcus Garvey, who returned home to become a legislator of wage laws; and entrepreneur and grocer Alexander Moorhead. Those influential men referred to Grandfather's store as the "war room." A retired police captain who became a legislator remembers it as "Christian Joseph University."

In 1936 Congress granted the Virgin Islands partial self-government, and Grandfather served as a member of St. Croix First Municipal Council. He voted to make the islands a refuge for oppressed European Jews. But he disagreed with the new right of women to vote. Under Danish rule, only men of means could vote; women were simply out of the question. Indeed, women on the mainland had gotten it just fifteen years earlier, and it then met court challenges. So, when that son of a father from Barbados who trained him in the "prim and proper" was told the "weaker sex" would vote, he thought his fellow councilmen had lost their minds. Reminded, "We are now a democracy, Christian," he countered, "A demo what? You mean 'dem who crazy!"

It was within that conservatism he responded to the missing five dollars. He closed the shop, took me down to his house, and a long afternoon began. I was tough, but after what seems

to be hours of whipping I gave in. I'd always wanted a diving "glass" (mask) from nearby Suarez Store. So I told him I
bought a diving glass from Mr. Suarez. He took me to the store
to verify it. The grocer watched me and said, "Boy, what trouble
you're putting me into?" And the lashing for the truth resumed.
Luckily, the patriarch's belts were of rather old leather. He must
have run through three or four, for they kept snapping. And he
was too old to deliver the force I am sure he wished he could.
Finally, he walked me to our new restaurant where Daddy was
doing electrical work and grumbled about his futility with me. I
noticed Rafie and Edwin's awkward faces, but I had been on my
own. We were one for all, all for one. Daddy seemed to know I
was innocent. He told his father he'd take care of it, and drove
him home. Daddy simply put me to work.

Our pedigree includes Mammy's brother Enrique Romero
Nieves. He is the Virgin Islands' most decorated combat veteran.
Even South Korea awarded him military honors. An American
Legion post carries his name. How tragic he died from a tooth
infection. He knew he was among the toughest of "a few good
men." So, death from a toothache was not an option. His wife
begged him to see a dentist. But for our uncle, because North
Korea had been unable to kill him, a tooth couldn't. Rafie was
just as unbending. His lawyer tried hard to convince him to
accept a plea bargain. Since he would have had to point a finger,
he refused and fired that lawyer. Singing for supper was figura-
tively and literally not in our blood.

I often ponder whether capacity to take whippings for each
other imparted a sense pride which made the pain less stinging.
For, we also laughed when the blameless got it. In fact, we made
a joke of it all most of the time, after our hot backsides cooled.
We'd cackle at contortions and grunts that had made their way
to our throats. We did weep sometimes, but never did we lose
our dignity. Lashings were very formal. First, we were questioned, and the quality of our answers determined the number
of strokes. Our bottom was site of impact, but many times we
yielded to an irresistible dare. Reluctant by experience yet with
hope eternal we'd pillow it with our palms. And as always, the

reply was a swift lash across the back. Those truly stung! Still, our palms would again be tempted to intercept the downstroke.

When we lied, we got disciplined less for disobedience than for insulting our parents' intelligence. The stench of lies was least tolerated. Mother often scolded that a liar was more dangerous than a thief: "You can get away from a thief, but you can't get away from a liar."

I later learned her wisdom was rooted in a Benin, Africa, proverb: "You can lock your front door to keep a thief out of your house, but you can't lock a liar out of your bedroom."

Daddy didn't philosophize about it until I crashed the car he kept on St. Thomas. In summer 1970 while working as an Upward Bound counselor at the college, I slammed a tree driving too fast onto campus. "I tried to avoid a pothole!" was the excuse made up. Daddy said he'd fly over and remove it to a repair shop. The following evening he appeared at my dorm door: "Let's go for a walk." He seemed relaxed. I, too, enjoyed the sparkling clear moonlit evening stroll. He'd already removed the wreck I noticed earlier, still in love with the immovable mahogany tree. We casually walked along a rise just above the then-only golf course on the island. Soon we stood at the edge of an overlook where long strings of aqua-violet lights lined the airport runway below. Suddenly he said, "Michael, there is no pothole. You're now a man. You don't have to lie anymore. Maybe only if your life depends on it."

I was speechless with embarrassment. Almost thirty years later I had an epiphany. I could've truthfully responded, "I lied because I was certain you'd kill me."

Corporal punishment was not always the mode. One time we went into Daddy's pants pocket, thinking he wouldn't miss the loot. He calmly took our most treasured possession, our bicycles, and locked them away for what seemed to be an eternity. Another time, Rafie was sent to buy cornmeal nearby. Of course, the Trio marched out the yard. Unknown to us, it was needed instantly to pour in boiling okra water to "turn the fungi." The mission should have taken seven minutes at most. We proceeded to a mango orchard a mile away. We came back nearly two hours later, bellies round with pulp. Daddy had by then arrived home. Thank God he ate something else and apparently was in no mood for dishing out the saddle stirrup strap. But we did not escape. Our plea we did not know the cornmeal was needed right away, and the fact we did bring back some sweet mangoes helped. He directed Mother to find three of her old dresses and have us wear them. At our height, they fitted from neck to ankles. I remember mine being of a dark red poinsettia print with an elastic waist. We were then told to fill a fifty-gallon drum with water from the public faucet a block away. Buckets in hand, we decided to exit the yard to the left. To that side was the Danish graveyard, across from which was the Anglican church. We'd be less noticed, and another faucet was there. To the right, we'd pass several homes on each side of the street. We were overheard, and ordered to go right and receive the scrutiny. At first, we felt humiliated. After fetching the first buckets, we started to look at each other jokingly. For the next dozen trips, we had a jolly good time laughing at each other's garb. Of course, we couldn't be caught laughing. So, as we neared home our faces frowned. We poured out the water, quickly walked away, and resumed broad grins and giggles. It was hard to make us sad for long even in the most trying situations. Like when Mother ordered Rafie to sit in the chicken house as punishment. He began singing so sweet, she says, he warmed her heart and spun her into laughter: "Rafie made me feel so sorry, I called out: 'Oh Lord, Rafie, you can come out now.'"

Our wings of humor were clipped the day we walked to nearby Granny's house for lunch during digging of the basement bedrooms. After the meal, we decided to play marbles to energize our tired muscles, a game we called "Three Hole." Three cup-sized holes were dug in the dirt in a straight line, each at least two feet apart. From a starting end-hole, a marble was rolled in an attempt to get it into the next two holes, turn around, and repeat the same until twelve holes were sunk in sequence. The skill was to strike the opponent's marble which missed its hole as far as possible from it. The first player to successfully make his twelve holes awaited other players to finish. The winner's margin of victory was measured by the number of holes missed by the last man out, something like golf. The winning reward was to strike the loser's knuckles with a marble as hard as possible to the number that reflected each winner's margin of victory. One game was never enough; the loser was entitled to revenge.

We were in our glee playing under the shade of a huge tamarind tree in Granny's yard when suddenly Daddy appeared with a chair and a handsaw. Without a word he placed the chair between the holes and ordered each of us in sequence to bend over the chair. One by one we received his intense strength broadcasted through the saw. Never in our lives did we imagine such force could flow from so flat a tool. It was a shocking new experience. I didn't know humans could survive such awesome force. Confidence he'd never really damage us was the only solace that we would not die. This time there was no doubt as to who was the culprit. This time the Trio got caught in the act. This time there'd be no consolation in bravado, dignity, or comfort crying for each other. Our father finally cooled our heels. We cursed afterwards, outside his earshot of course. But we never felt defeated.

This was learned from "Mr. Yes, Sir Austin." Big brother Austin as the eldest was always in charge. We thought he was the bravest brother ever. He never begged for mercy or sympathy. He agreed to a second combat tour in Quang Tri Province when it was the most dangerous zone for marines. He would place his life on the line for us, but we feared him more than Daddy. Although he never really hurt us, Austin often threatened use of his fists.

Daddy never did, except for a popular West Indian mode of discipline: a slap to the back of the head called a "cuff." It was used for on-the-spot lapses like failing to do our school homework. He'd quiz us and our ignorance would be rewarded with well-placed cuffs.

Rafie ended up back in public school in eighth grade with me. In his sixth, Daddy transferred him to Seventh Day Adventist School and he did two years. I repeated seventh and that's how he caught up with me. (Thanks to the teacher who held me and my friend for another year. He, too, went on to earn a doctorate.) It was hard to articulate why a course like biology got more of my attention than, say, social studies. Courses such as that did not interest me. Mario C. Moorhead's book *She and Me* offers a clue. Our lessons had been split into the objective sciences, and the subjective humanities. Unlike the former, the latter reflects the culture of a particular people. Although St. Croix is historically African, social courses were European oriented. Apparently, that's what the academic dean at Loyola understood when he allowed me to take English for foreign language credits.

Rafie and I were in ninth grade when our father noticed we were falling behind. Daily for about a month, he drilled us in reading, writing, and math with sprinklings of his cuffs. We found school quite boring, but never told him so. It is amazing how clearheaded we became during his lessons.

The cuff of all cuffs was felt a few days after Daddy sat Rafie and me down when he realized we'd turned missing school into an art form. "You're too old to be whipped," he told us. We hadn't gotten one after the handsaw surprise. But neither could he tolerate our truancy so long as we lived with him. He gave us the choice of living with Mammy if dropping out of school was what we wanted. He saw our inkling to leave him for Mammy when we told him we were grateful for his trying to raise us upright. Surprisingly, he responded, "You owe me nothing."

"Your father was a very loving man," family friend Leon Lang told me. "When I was a kid I hung out in his grocery store. Many times I saw him give away foodstuff to people who couldn't pay."

Similar comments came from an apprentice, Herbert David: "Your father taught me a lot. He took me around on his run for US mail from the ships for delivery to the post offices. He was agent for shipping companies. If you wanted something done, just ask Lloyd. He would help people to fill out government papers, and he showed them which office to go to. I never saw him charge them any money. He had a big heart. And as small as he was, he wasn't afraid of any man."

When Daddy told us we owed him nothing, we felt for the first time we could be ourselves in his presence. Rafie seized the moment: "I want to live with my mother." I was more ambiguous, but had not forgotten Mammy's pain when Daddy came for his three sons to live with him and Mother. Rafie was five, and I almost seven. To comfort her, he took four-year-old Christian from the truck cabin and handed him back. Rafie and I stood in the railed-bed truck eagerly awaiting the blasting nighttime breeze against our chubby naive faces. When he asked me, "Do you want to live with me, or of your mother?" I glanced at Mammy's eyes filled with tears but answered, "Yes." All I really cared about on that night was to hurriedly get in the back of the truck to feel the fast wind and its howling in my ears.

Now, I had a chance to make amends. Besides, I could not fathom being separated from my brother, for whom I cried each time he was in distress. One day he fell out of a coconut tree and broke his arm. The huge swelling freaked me out. He groaned, but I began crying audibly. It made him disgusted with me, but he couldn't shut me up. For the next half mile to the hospital, I cradled the ghastly swollen arm in my hands as would a sling, walking sideways. I shamelessly begged every passerby to stop my brother's pain. So, that night we grabbed a few belongings and slowly walked away, saying very little in the long journey of six blocks. We finally arrived, and told Mammy that Daddy said we must live with her because we did not want to remain in school. She began to cry, pleading with me to set an example. She sobbed even more when Rafie made it clear to her that he did not intend to stay in school. She convinced me to return home. I urged Rafie to leave with me.

My younger brother did follow, but bolted after a couple of blocks to stay at Granny's house. Edwin, who had already dropped out, was for that reason living there. A few days later Rafie came to pick up stuff he'd left behind. He couldn't find a few things and accused me of stealing. And we ended up fighting. Perhaps recalling the five-dollar bill episode with Grandfather, I shouted, "I will kill you!" Daddy rushed out of nowhere and landed a cuff across my left ear so hard I saw a blue flash, stars, and heard tweeting birds. It was just like in cartoons. He ordered me through the blue haze and ringing ears: "Don't you dare ever, ever use that word in my house! Ever! Clean up that mess!" I had no idea what he meant, and instinctively looked around to see if we bumped furniture during our fisticuffs. I next noticed I was standing in a puddle of pee. For the first time I'd been hit so hard I urinated. Not even the handsaw thrashing had done that trick.

I've never heard Rafie use the word "kill" in the first person. He was loved by just about all with whom he interacted. One said to me, "Rafie gave out his heart to everybody."

He had no strong position about anything except the right to not be harassed with pettiness. He refused to blindly follow rules set by others. He loathed being lectured by any who lived in a glass house. Daddy smoked cigarettes, so why couldn't he? Rafie rebelled not against good behavior, but against the feeling he was being singled out, perhaps because he was the youngest of the Trio.

Five: Scorpion Is Sprung

Violence is, to human nature, just another way of kill-ing time.

—Don Juan Matus

The sole sound bouncing back from the valley below was the echo of a hammer atop a nearby roof. Then, the carpenter caught crackling pops against its rhythm. While buying a yacht lately, he recalled it:

> When I heard those popping sounds I imagined all kinds of things, but I sense in my heart someone was being shot at the golf course. I stopped working and stayed put. About an hour later, I rode pass on my motor-cycle to get home. The amount of police cars that was there told me lots of people had been shot. All I could do was to keep riding. But I'm glad I didn't leave St. Croix like so many others did.

Of the first police officers to screech tires into Fountain Val-ley was a new lawman and very bright classmate, Steven May-ers. Steve had won the Physics Achievement Award, so it was surprising he bypassed college. He said did not go because, even before migrating from the Eastern Caribbean, all he ever wanted to be was a cop. Unluckily, he was now thrust into a horrendous crime scene to which Rafie was connected.

Officer Mayers had gotten excited by central's broadcast: "Wow, I thought, my first week after graduating from the police academy and I'm responding to a murder scene. Central radioed that a caller had said, 'A crazy gunman jus' killed two people at Fountain Valley.' We requested a repeat. 'A crazy gunman jus' killed two people at Fountain Valley Golf Course. Report immediately to the scene!'"

I stopped him there. "What you must have really heard was 'crazy *gunmen* are killing people at Fountain Valley.'"

Steve's sharp stare sufficed to zip my lip, and listen. "Attorney, you know me from high school. I don't kid around in serious matters. What I heard twice was the singular: 'a crazy *gunman*!'" He continued. "When we got the call, we were in an unmarked vehicle assigned to a captain who was off duty that day. Actually, we were giving a ride to a tourist having trouble finding her way around town. We dropped her off at the Eastern Suburb [Police] Station and raced to Fountain Valley. The drive was darn dangerous. Our siren was malfunctioning; it came on when it wanted to. We engaged it with a floor switch like the older cars' high beam switch. I cursed that siren. We had some near misses. In about twenty minutes we were there. As we jumped out of the car, I saw frightened faces. 'Help us! All the people dead!'"

As the cries pierced Steve's ears, his nostrils picked up the odor of blood. Suddenly the chance to play police as he imagined was overwhelmed by the stark and inconceivable. He rushed across the fifteen feet from the parking lot to the edge of the tiled patio and was slammed with the sight of four bullet-riddled bodies in a circle of clotting blood.

Urgings by survivors to walk further in ratcheted up his horror. Four more victims randomly dominated the clubhouse floor. Reality dug deeper, and Steve shouted, "Jesus Christ! What kind of animal could've done this to these people?"

Allison Lowery, both his fists filled with gravel as if he'd gripped the planet when his spirit took flight, was sprawled facedown at opposite end of the patio. Steve shivered back to the first four bodies: "They had fallen over on each other as if they huddled in the face of their doom."

The still-vibrating love the clinging couples must've swore to each other for the last time caused Officer Steven Mayers to unashamedly yell even louder, "What monster could've done this to these people?"

The extra-high decibel of that bellow caused him to settle down:

> All of a sudden I became cool and started to assess the situation. But a Continental female with a blast under her armpit, spilling her entrails through the other side of her body onto the floor made me nearly vomit. I kept hold of myself. I had a good idea from the victims in what the direction the murderers were heading. I called headquarters to report to the chief that we were going to pursue, but wouldn't engage. To my shocking surprise, my partner and I were ordered to report back to headquarters immediately. I protested, but the chief shouted, 'That's a direct order!' To this day, I don't understand why we were prevented from at least picking up a trail. My partner had experience. That's why I'm still confused.

Steve lost faith that day as to the proper role of a police officer. Not long after, he found himself in a heated argument with an off-duty policeman at their multiple-dwelling apartments. It escalated into deadly threats and the bright officer left nothing to chance. POW! Steve Mayers' single bullet was enough to kill a fellow officer, and a lost life ambition.

On August 23, 2006 police lieutenant Larry Oliver detailed the incident: "The other officer was plain and simple trigger happy. To tell you the truth, I think he had shot three civilians, and had killed a fourth one in separate confrontations. Steve believed he was reaching for his gun, and if Steve had hesitated for a second, he would be dead!"

The seed sown at Fountain Valley by a superior securing Steve from possible harm may have saved his life. He offered more details on December 2, 2006:

> Another policeman who took the officer I had to shoot to the hospital removed his off-duty weapon to

make it look like he was unarmed. They both were friends who grew up together in St. John. Because of that evidence disappearing, I had no choice but to plead guilty to manslaughter. Thank God I served only two of a three-year prison sentence. Would you believe the officer who took him to the hospital later shot his girl-friend, and thinking he killed her, killed himself with the same weapon he had removed from the guy I served time for? That gun's serial number proved it belonged to the officer I was forced to shoot.

Larry explained the chief had ordered Steve to stand down because the killers had heavier firepower. He also told of an incident that occurred while *he* was fetching heftier arms. Under the pressure, he lost his pistol and had to turn back after five minutes of racing to the scene: "My gun must've fallen in the yard when I jumped out."

"The yard" was an open area that was home to the Public Works Department, the Traffic Bureau's vehicle inspection lane, plus the Public Safety Tactical Office, where bigger weapons were stored. Larry had scrambled from his squad car to grab a heavy-gauge shotgun when his revolver came loose, thereby exposing itself to the public. When he swung back into the busy lot, the errant weapon stared at him in such plain view it was difficult to accept it hadn't been removed.

Strangely, this embarrassment was visited upon a police officer who was one of the US Marine's youngest sergeants. He'd volunteered for a second tour in Vietnam, and awarded two Battle Crosses with thirteen commendations. Larry was among the few "FO" (forward observer) trusted to calculate grids for fighter jets and artillery. He was not bragging: "There was another guy who was even better. He was a natural-born FO."

Larry's skills yet exceeded that of his commander, Capt. Charles Robb, the soldier who later married President Lyndon B. Johnson's daughter, and was elected governor of Virginia: "Capt. Robb gave me some calculations which I refused to call in because they were wrong. Although he threatened me with a court martial, I continued to insist that he was calling in a wrong grid. He finally agreed to let me call for the test round I had argued for. I was right! When it came in, Capt. Robb realized his plotting would've killed our own guys."

I asked, "But how could such a marine like you lose your firearm?"

"God made me drop that weapon," answered "the Wolf," as his combat buddies called him.

When Larry finally arrived at Fountain Valley, just about every patrol car was at the scene. To this day, Officer Mayers is certain that mass of police power was mobilized by a dispatcher who broadcasted: "A crazy gunman jus' killed two people at Fountain Valley." This in turn, said the *VI Daily News* on August 28, 2006, was triggered by "LaBeet, who was the ringleader of five gunmen." For sure, men with guns raided Fountain Valley's clubhouse. But what caused Steve to twice hear the singular "a crazy gunman"?

Though the media says the golf course was attacked by five gunmen led by one, the killers were *not* a cohesive unit under a "ringleader." At least not until LaBeet pulled his scorpion out the bag. Four, at most, were of mind-set to simply move in, scare the hell out of the patrons and employees, take cash, and hightail out of there. Three entered side entrances into the snack area and shouted, "Give us your money! No one will get hurt!" They then raided the bar, kitchen, pro shop, and two offices, all of which extended linearly in increasing distances away from the clubhouse entrance.

LaBeet covered that access and the adjacent parking area. Likely because Rafie was reluctant to be there in the first place, he told Rafie to stay with him. The victims were now boxed in, escape possible only by fleeing unto the golf course. The war-wise assassin was now set to execute his spineless diversion: shoot all those innocent "whites" and create a police response of such chaos the posse was bound to shelve their kill bill on him. From a criminology standpoint, Fountain Valley began as two crimes as different as night and day. They merged seconds after the departing couples were herded back by LaBeet into the clubhouse. In surrender, they sat down at the nearest table. "Stand Up!" As they did, he riddled them with his .45 caliber submachine gun. Rafie wobbled, and sat down. LaBeet then shouted, "Kill them all! Don't leave any witnesses!" That ice-cold heart cowed the three who had promised, and word-held, no one would be injured. *Their fright* now steered them into participating in the bloody pandemonium.

The victim calling the police did not suspect the first three robbers would've buckled. The police radio alert—*a crazy gunman just killed two people*—speaks volume about that split-second perception. The clubhouse occupants had resigned themselves to no more than the crudeness of being robbed. Three criminals so far had kept their promise not to hurt anyone. But the other masked man who brought the couples back inside and took their precious lives without slightest provocation had to be crazy! The caller was certain that madman would be restrained by the non-shooting thugs who had pledged to spare them. This was flash frozen in a bubble of faith and submission. Laboring under it, the caller excitedly sounded out the singular *a crazy gunman!*

His partners in crime surely were stealing at gunpoint, but they were not off their rockers. They were not doing any killing. They were just punks looking for easy money. They all had guns, but the one who fired *his* without cause whatsoever shaped the scene. Consequently, not only did the caller uttered *gunman*, but what he'd just done was so preposterous in view of St. Croix's then almost murder-free society, the dispatcher wishfully transposed "two couples" to "two people." Needless to say, there was no second chance to clarify.

Lt. Marion Jackson, who'd been on the ridge above "ready to do battle," made his way down about twenty-five minutes after the gun blast echoes. He offers a theory as to what caused LaBeet to shoot the two couples: "I think LaBeet shouted, 'I hate you white m'fs,' and started shooting because one of the husbands tossed his wallet onto his car seat when he saw the guns. My partner and I did the crime scene forensics. I retrieved an upright, half-open, but unrifled wallet on the driver's front seat."

Michael A. Joseph, Esq.

If LaBeet had seen the victim throw his wallet, why didn't he retrieve it before forcing him back inside? Maybe the intensity of the moment caused a memory lapse. Yet, as cold as ice as he was in taking time to make sure all were dead, he'd recall the easy cash nearby. But to LaBeet, robbery was not even a secondary objective. And so, when the gunfire subsided the war-seasoned murderer took a body count to assess whether a *coup de grace* was necessary. Now clearly the boss, he commanded Rafie to follow him, and directed the others to make their way out. They left.

Next, he focused on John Gulliver, whose pain prevented him from playing dead. His huge middle peppered with bullets, and back slumped against the bar footing, pathetic horror defined his grunts, the only sounds in the otherwise now-unfathomable silence. Thunder of rapid gunfire and screams in every direction moments before had morphed into groans of innocence gripped in an undeserved end. LaBeet looked down at his fellow mortal and growled, "You mother****** ain't dead yet? Rafie, burst him one more and finish him off!"

Rafie yelled, "F*** you! We agreed not to shoot anybody. I told you I didn't want to be here, and now you're asking me to shoot somebody?"

At gunpoint of a "friend" with whom he shared food and shelter, Rafie learned he was but a stranger as expendable as the shredded, sprawled-about victims. LaBeet jammed the .45 caliber submachine gun to his temple. "Shoot! Or the two of you will lay here dead!"

My brother could not believe what he had just heard. He'd seen me cuffed senseless simply for puffing the words "I'll kill you." Now he was being forced to really shoot someone. Without doubt, he knew that LaBeet meant what he said.

A Korean combat vet, too, had been made to feel that chill. On November 5, 2008 retired deputy police chief Elmer James revealed a confrontation he had with LaBeet couple months before Fountain Valley:

> I was patrolling one night by myself and was going up the hill on Prince Street when LaBeet, with two

160

other guys who were familiar to me, turned the corner approaching me. I heard LaBeet say, 'You want us to ice him right here?' and he started to walk alongside me. I said to myself, This is it. I'm dead. All I can do is to take one with me. One of the guys called him back and whispered something. He then turned around and continued walking with them. I really thought I was going to die that night.

At Fountain Valley it became clear to Rafie why Mammy did not want LaBeet to enter her home. According to our brother Sonny, even though he was having an affair with one of our sisters, Mammy warned them, "Never let that man in my house. There is something about him I don't like."

Sonny reminded me our mother always offered food to others she knew. But LaBeet was never invited. Her heart had seen through him. Even before his service in Vietnam, he was a disturbed soul.

A Yankee teacher, Wendell "Hammie" Hamilton, in 1959 began working in St. Thomas at the Department of Parks & Recreation. It was led by John P. Scott, who introduced basketball to the islands. Hammie was hired as his sports director, and shared an office with Scott's secretary, Ruth LaBeet, mother of killer. Hammie went back to college for his master's degree and wrote his thesis on the start up of local basketball programs.

When he returned, he moved to St. Croix and taught physical education to Rafie, Smith, Ballantine, and me. Hammie and I met over several days in July 2003 in the Frederiksted public library. He related how he loved Ruth as a sister. Her boyfriend, she, and he often dined and danced when they were coworkers. He shared what he knew about her son:

That boy, between the age of thirteen and fourteen, was very troubled. I recall Ruth speaking to me and John Scott. She wanted our help to find a suitable military school where she could send him. She couldn't control that boy. She told us how he hit the groundskeeper of the golf course [in St. Thomas] next to the college, upside the head with a rock. The man had warned him several times not to ride his horse on the putting green. The putting area was not really green. Because of dry weather, they could not maintain grass, but instead used a mixture of sand and tar for a smooth surface. The hoof of LaBeet's horse dug holes which had to be laboriously repaired. Simply for being warned not to ride his horse and destroy the golf course, he slammed a rock against the man's head that required a bunch of stitches. Ruth also told us how he'd shoot sharp-tipped arrows into roaming donkeys.

Himself an avid golfer, Hammie knew LaBeet was no stranger to Fountain Valley: "Several years earlier to the killings, the boy was forced to live with his uncle Carl in St. Croix. His father Stanley was divorced from Ruth when Stanley was seriously injured in a car accident. He couldn't handle his son, so he sent him here. Carl worked in the security detail at the golf course. LaBeet sometimes visited his uncle there."

That's how he knew there would be no money in the cash registers at night. Now, he was about to kill a "friend" who gave him sanctuary, and with whose sister he'd slept. Pathetically, Rafie was certain he would also be killed, and there was nothing he could do to save Gulliver.

POW! Another horrendous crackle echoed through the serene valley. Rafie had fired a shotgun blast into the Paul Bunyan of Fountain Valley.

Gabriel Lionel, who had been a landscaper there, also saw LaBeet at the golf course on several occasions. Gabriel was Gulliver's coworker, and had this to tell me:

John was huge. We'd joke that when he walked the ground would shake. He hadn't been with us too long, but they made him supervisor either because he was so big, or because he was white. Gulliver didn't have any landscaping experience. Maybe that's why he felt he had to forget about his wife and go up to the clubhouse. Although we had broken off early that day, he told me he's going to help the electricians. But before that, he had told me that he was going straight home because the water pump he installed in the trailer home they had just bought wasn't working. His wife had called him to tell him hurry home to fix the pump. That guy was so strong he wouldn't give up. They told me that in the emergency room he was crying out for his wife. I don't think she got to see him before he died.

I learned from Rafie the details of his shotgun blast *after* he was released from prison. I reminded him of the prosecutor's plea bargain offer I personally delivered, whereby he'd have served only five years. I asked him why he didn't agree, it being he was forced to finish off Gulliver: "I did not want to rat. Even if I'd told the truth as to what happened between LaBeet, Gulliver, and me, I would have had to call the names of others. Besides, not in this lifetime could I ever dignify the torture the police made me suffer."

On that tragic day, Meral Smith had detoured to his house nearby the golf course, unaware his uncle had already told police he left home with food supplies at dawn with other defendants. By late night an interrogation team had begun their work on him.

Next day's sunrise met Beaumont Gereau sitting on Daddy's old security safe in surrealistic spins. The quiet Fresh Water Yankee made his way back to the relaxed porch of Granny's house and was as detached as when cajoled to "hit up the golf course for Ballantine to throw land [leave] on a boat to Antigua." He did not sleep since visiting the camp with Smith the day before. Gereau was soon seized in an elaborate tale that involved a police officer's fight with another young man that ended up way inside Granny's house, where Gereau was encountered and arrested.

He, too, soon yielded to pain and led the posse of lawmen to Rafie's campsite. Detective Francisco "Paco" Vasquez ('68) was in the squad forcing him to hike with them there. The rough terrain proved near deadly to one of the lawmen from the states. He passed out. They thought he had a heart attack and died.

Paco on December 18, 2005 let loose a laugh as he recounted the haphazard situation:

> I'll never forget that FBI agent. He was a huge Yankee. He held the chain we locked around Gereau's waist as we struggled uphill in the bushes to the camp. Even though I carried that guy's shotgun and water, plus my own shotgun and water, this big guy just fell down and fainted. Rafie—sorry, I mean Michael—after he came to, one of the locals had to take him down the hill. We continued up, but those guys had already hightailed!

Paco stared saucer-eyed at me as he ended his recall.

Smith and Gereau's cohorts were by then identified as LaBeet, Ballantine, and my brother. They stalked their escape well away from the middle path of the rainforest canopy, divided by Mahogany Road. It begins half a mile north of Frederiksted, and ends in the historic village of Estate Grove Place, site of Smith's capture. Naturally, it was the main route for the military and police forces. The search team covered the roads also from Estate Jolly Hill though Estate Oxford, which reconnected with Mahogany Road at Estate Orange Grove. The murderers had naturally gravitated to the truly difficult terrain of Estate Nicholas, northwest of Oxford. Within hours their instincts quickly clued that it being Maroon territory it surely would be searched and they'd be boxed in. Their bush skills matched those of urban kids forged into jungle-trained snipers. Having opted for hideout in the basement bedrooms dug during that unforgettable summer, they sneaked across Mahogany Road into Estates Springfield, Bog of Allendale, Beck's Grove, Little La Grange, and finally into La Grange. An overgrown river bed runs through that latter estate. This heavily canopied depression ends at Estate Concordia, which borders the eastern side of our town. Late night, they entered it passing through the hillside graveyard. Just two blocks away was their sanctuary.

The "safe house" was unoccupied because Mother had moved to Puerto Rico with Daddy during his illness. After LaBeet and Ballantine had settled into the subterranean bedrooms, Rafie sneaked another mile and a half south to Estate Campo Rico. His friend told me he stayed there with her for two days, but returned to the dugout basement because her area was too busy. Family and friends, to whom they of course claimed innocence, provided them food until their September 12 capture.

During their escape, Rafie counted as many as six hunters bumbling through the thickets shielding their eyes from prickly bushes, stepping noisily over low vines. Hanging ones were ready to noose their necks, jerking them backwards as if lassoed from behind. At one point, the killers looked down on their hunters from a huge, thickly branched tree. At another, they laid in underbrush peering at the pursuers who were only a few feet away.

Meanwhile, Chief Ann Marie Schrader and Inspector George A. "Georgie" Farrelly had taken command. And then, drama unfolded. Police procedure, said retired detective Manuel Pereira, was to assign as case agent the detective on full shift closest to the time of a major crime. That was he, and he was "gung-ho to take the case." On February 26, 2003 he spoke freely:

> I was familiar with the pursuit of LaBeet headed by Detective José Torres. Several officers knew he was in that area at the time of the murders. Chief Schrader threw away protocol and ordered me to stand down. She shocked me almost as much as the bodies at the golf course when she told me George Farrelly will be chief investigator for the murders. Farrelly had walked in into the detective bureau just some months before, and told us that he was employed as a detective inspector. We looked at him and said to ourselves, 'What the hell is he doing here?' He was not a police officer before becom-

ing a detective. He never attended the police academy. That was a requirement to become a police officer. And then, officers who followed procedures were upgraded to the bureau after showing their ability to perform good field work with results. So when this man with a briefcase in his hand walked into the bureau and said he was a police officer hired as a detective, we looked at the briefcase. We laughed and said to each other that the briefcase didn't have in police reports because he never did one. We kidded it contained political papers since he had been appointed a detective because his father, Stanley Farrelly, was a big Republican. Republican governor Melvin Evans and his father were close friends.

Stanley Farrelly, one of few local Republicans, was appointed Gov. Evans' St. Croix administrator. Stanley's brother, Alexander, had run as the Democratic candidate against Evans. In an instance of party politics being thicker than blood, Stanley supported Evans instead of his brother. So, when faced with the massacre, Gov. Evans instantly teamed up with Stanley, a former US marshal.

Det. Pereira continued, "That's how George Farrelly, who was not even familiar with writing police reports, was appointed as lead investigator. I confronted Chief Schrader and she ordered me to help him write the reports. Of course, I ignored her."

No debriefings were had with the first responding policemen. Had there been even one, Steven Mayers would've learned retired captains James Parris and Clifford George actually arrived at the scene just before he did. According to Parris (currently rehired as police chief), he and George found two uninjured persons in a locked office behind the pro shop. After assuring more help was on the way, they drove around the eighteen-hole course looking for others who may have been wounded as they fled.

Under the inspector's control, inaccurate police reports were written. And when the specialists stepped in, the media feed was downright misleading. The police posse on the ridge above the crime scene were said to have believed the gunshots were "fire-crackers" and weren't alarmed because "an elementary school was on a field trip in the area."[16]

But September 6 marked start of the school year when student field trips are weeks, if not months, away, certainly not so soon to a golf course. The submachine gun rapid fire and shotgun blasts in that valley must have created unmistakable echoes. The tradesman on the roof across from it knew what he heard was gunfire. The firecracker scenario was a ploy for setting up the interrogation technique: wartime info extraction. Placing fictional schoolchildren near the crime scene was planted to preempt grassroots support for the suspects. Also false were police reports that Rafie was being pursued for a prior armed robbery and our brother Edwin "was being held for first-degree rape and sodomy."[17] There was no arrest warrant of any kind for Rafie until two days *after* Fountain Valley. Edwin was neither held, nor charged, for any rape or sexual assault.

Contacted directly after Pereira's statements, retired detective Roland Tranberg, ex-husband of Inspector Farrelly's sister Joyce, did not bite his tongue: "It is true! George Farrelly never did one bit of field research. He was such a coward, he was afraid of his own shadow. That is why the reports on Fountain Valley exaggerated the dangerousness of your brothers."

On June 3, 2009 Tranberg stood his ground: "Georgie and I did not have any personal gripes. In fact we sometimes traveled off-island together. But as a career policeman, I can't lie and say it was OK to give a man without training that type of police position because of politics. He couldn't even shoot. On the range he never got above a score of even thirty."

As we parted, the air force veteran and blunt lawman made it clear he was doing me no favor: "By the way, for what those boys did to those poor people at the golf course, if it was left up to me Rafie would have rotted in jail."

On July 24, 2012 again I spoke with Tranberg to be sure he was correct when he told me that my brothers were falsely identified as wanted felons due to the inspector's politics in preparing Fountain Valley reports:

Michael A. Joseph, Esq.

As I told you before, Mike, Rafie, and Edwin weren't wanted for any such things. Georgie simply didn't know what he was doing. Our differences were strictly professional. In fact, the only photo in existence with our first four governors together was taken when I married Joyce. It's my wedding photo with Georgie, Governor Evans, Governor Cyril King, Governor Juan Luis, and Governor Farrelly, with Joyce and me. I was chief of security for each of those four governors.

Six: Rise Up, Inspector

One shouldn't speak ill of the dead. Repeating how Inspector (later Commissioner) George A. Farrelly botched Fountain Valley's police reports was therefore uncomfortable. Gov. Alexander Farrelly was his uncle, and the governor in turn was our grandmother Elizabeth Hardcastle's nephew. Besides, we were friends.

On September 28, 2004 neighborhood grocer Ala Hannun lent his ears as my sounding board. Being too young a Crucian to have firsthand memories of the murders, Ala listened long with heightened attention as if an enigma was finally being bared. He had nudged me to keep talking while he cashed out customers. He finally broke his silence. "I remember only one thing. People being killed at ah, that place?"

"Fountain Valley," I assisted. "Carambola" came to his mind, but he was aware that's a new name.

"Yes. When I just left high school and was working, some friends took me out there to play golf. When we were in the clubhouse one of them pointed to the floor and told me, 'A lot of people died here.' But she sounded like it happened a very long time ago."

"No, Ala, nineteen seventy-two," I said, with choked-up sadness.

He turned askew as if to avoid the fact it happened in his lifetime, and softly said, "Oh, the blood still fresh."

With regret that Georgie departed without a chance to respond, I'd been telling Ala what the detective in line to take charge of Fountain Valley had related. Ala slowly again broke his silence as he sat down for the first time during our conversation.

"I liked him. He was a good man. I'll never forget when he died. It's like yesterday. A day or two before that, he came into Zachy's, where I worked. We talked while he was drinking his usual Coors Light. He asked for the plain bagels he always bought. I looked on the shelf. It was empty. I felt bad because he was so respectful to me. I didn't want to disappoint him so I went into the walk-in freezer to get it. I looked, and looked. I couldn't find any. I mean, Attorney, I really, really looked for those bagels. It was a Friday. Then on the Sunday or Monday, he collapsed at a party, or he was going to one."

"Georgie wasn't in the hospital?" I asked, surprised by Ala's hint he died so suddenly.

I'd sat with Georgie about a month before at Luz Armstrong's Princess Kitchen Shack while he heartily ate a mouthwatering plate of stewed Caribbean lobster. I fought back envy. My stewed chicken lunch at only five dollars a plate paled in comparison.

"Sit down, Counsel," the retired commissioner commanded, placing a chair for me. "Don't look so hard. I special ordered this lobster," he teased. There was truly an air of oddity about our encounter. Unlike my usual talkative self, I hardly spoke. I even declined a chunk of lobster he offered. The former inspector was very talkative. Yet, I can't recall what was said.

Ala noticed my downhearted tone in revisiting what had turned out to be Georgie's "last supper." Suddenly, he raised his voice eager to tell me something. "That Wednesday after he collapsed, I went back into the freezer for another customer. Believe me, Michael, as I stepped in I swear I heard a 'psst' sound from my left side. As I looked to my left, there was a pack of plain bagels! I am not fooling!"

Noticing the disbelief on my face, he continued, "I was the one who always packed the freezer. Other employees went into the freezer, but they always asked me for assistance. I am telling you those bagels were not there when I tried my best to please Georgie, because I really wanted to please my friend."

Two days after Ala Hannun told me about the bagels, I saw two friends of Georgie at Jiffy Mart, a grocery where I'd seen him at times. These were Richey Hillier, real estate broker, and a retired corrections officer working as store security, Bobby

Williams. I jokingly mentioned Ala's bagel story. Bobby and Richey looked at me like two kids who just heard something unbelievable and met the right person to tell of another mystery. In a near unison, they excitedly said, "You've seen Georgie chatting with us here. But his mother and sister together came in here yesterday. That was very strange. We can't remember the last time we saw his sister here. And we have never seen his mother in here! And definitely, Michael, those two being in this store together is a first!"

Richey and Bobby obviously believed Georgie had sent his family to say good-bye. Later that evening while I was at a client's gas station, a GAF security agency vehicle drove up to the service window. GAF, as the acronym suggests, was of Georgie's car fleet. I asked the station owner when last he noticed a GAF car.

"GAF doesn't have an account with us. I can't remember the last time I saw a GAF ride come to this station."

The next day, I went to Luz's eatery for details about my lunch with the deceased. She offered, "Georgie and I sat next to each other in church every single Sunday at Holy Cross Catholic Church."

"Do you recall when I came here and he was having his lobster lunch?"

"Sure, that was the last time he had his lunch here. He usually ordered his lunch plus a lobster salad to go on the Thursdays that were government paydays."

We looked at a calendar; that day was May 22, 2004.

"He died the Tuesday after Father's Day. On the Monday night, he dropped down ill after attending Gloria Canegata's birthday party. On the Tuesday that he died, I felt so terrible because I didn't go to the party. On that Sunday [Father's Day] he couldn't lift his hands to write a check for his church offerings. And I wrote it out for him."

Shortly after, I visited his niece Sharon Rivera, whose family for forty-five years owns and operates the only native furniture/appliance store in St. Croix. (Today, few natives are business owners.) I wanted background info. Instead, I was greeted with strange events surrounding the passing of her uncle.

Michael A. Joseph, Esq.

"Would you believe I had insisted Georgie come for dinner the Wednesday before the Tuesday morning that he passed? To my surprise, he came! I invited him many times before, but he never did. I took photographs of him and not a single one came out! They all came out blank! I am not making this up. The prints of others at dinner were OK! He used to tell me how much he loved my house—maybe that's why he kept coming back for nights after he was buried and kept turning on my TV. I would get up, turn it off, only for it to pop back on. I finally figured out how to keep it off. I unplugged it. This happened for many days, and then it stopped."

I next happened upon Gloria Canegata, a prim and proper retired superintendent of education. She's not talkative. But I had to tell her of the incredible tales of her friend's passing. To my surprise, she added more.

"Well, you wouldn't believe this. When he arrived the night of my party, after which he suddenly died, I had said to him, 'Georgie, what you doing here? You belong in St. Patrick Church's graveyard.' He wanted to know what 'f' I was telling him."

She couldn't help enjoying a moment of giggle. I asked what she meant by saying he belonged in St. Patrick Church's graveyard.

"Oh, yes, if you go down there, you will see a tombstone that says 'George Farrelly.' I never noticed it before until a few days before the party night. That same night I even asked him about it, and he said it might be the grave of some great-uncle whom he is named after."

I hurriedly went to see what the educator was talking about. There it was, a tall granite tombstone standing apart and inscribed with the words "In Memory of George Farrelly."

Rise up, Inspector.

Seven: Air Piracy Pounces Patience

That "the arc of the moral universe is long but it bends towards justice" is seen in the results of Meral Smith's letter for reduction of his sentence. It became the green light for Rafie's release. After the Supreme Court declined to review their case, the Fountain Valley Five were left with 120 days to submit motions to lessen their prison time. Any cut time was within sole discretion of the trial judge they'd repeatedly dissed. So, the other four assumed it would be pointless pleading to a man reddened by the obscenities they'd hurled at him. The judge accepted Smith's letter as a valid motion to reduce sentence and, surprisingly, invited the others to file papers joining it even though their time had lapsed. Naturally, they grabbed that second bite at the apple. They all argued eight consecutive life terms denied them incentive for rehabilitation, it being they'd be eligible for parole after an unrealistic eighty years. Rafie also offered certificates showing in five years of jail time he'd reformed.

The Honorable Warren H. Young's February 9, 1978 order rejected their contention because the law allowed them to petition the parole board for an "earlier [parole] eligibility date." Judge Young added that after a substantially greater period of same growth Rafie had showed, he may be a good candidate for early release. So, Rafie toiled even harder to reshape himself.

In spite the court pointed a pathway for all five's freedom, LaBeet lost patience to pursue it. I had no contact since 1973 with him, yet on December 29, 1984 he asked me to visit him at the detention center in St. Thomas. He'd return to the islands for a lawsuit he filed against his federal incarceration for what were local crimes, and lost. LaBeet was not seeking legal assistance, but insisted I fly over to listen to an important message he

173

had for my brother. The next day, the thirtieth, I was standing in front of him. Without ado, he let me know, "They are going to be shipping me out of here to the States any time now. You have to tell your brother and the others don't give up and don't admit to nothing. Sooner or later the truth about how we were tortured will come out, and they'll have to let us go."

That was it. I said nothing, and he walked back to his cell. Couple years earlier, LaBeet used the stateside prison grape-vine—the five couldn't directly contact each other—to warn Rafie not to let me "flip" him. A secretary who'd typed a letter in which I advised my brother to apologize to the families of Fountain Valley's victims had wrongly shared it with LaBeet. His words to me on the thirtieth were therefore predictable. In addition, it was in line with jailhouse thinking. As long as a prisoner does not fess up there is a chance he'll someday be set free as wrongfully convicted. So, I presumed LaBeet merely wanted to impress on me the five would get out of prison by holding on to the fact they were tortured. He wasted my time, I then thought. Rafie had already made it clear to me that reach-ing out to the victims was not an option. It could get him killed for "ratting."

It was nighttime the next day, the thirty-first, when I heard on the radio LaBeet took over an airplane and was forcing its captain to fly him to Cuba. It spun me like a top; he now had crashed all possibility of ever getting Rafie out! And then it hit me. He conned me to visit him as part of a scheme to seek asylum in Cuba as a "political prisoner." His game was to stop me from persuading my brother to come clean. For, if the truth came out his political prisoner ploy could backfire.

Prior to that night, we did not expose Mammy to details about Fountain Valley. Every day tears flowed down her cheeks, and she'd often be taken to the clinic for sedatives. Still, I couldn't help calling her to tell LaBeet took over a plane and was on his way to Cuba, but Rafie had nothing to do with it. I complained LaBeet would be the only one free. I disclosed what Officer Anthony Powell, who had testified the five were tortured, told me: "LaBeet was the first to open his mouth and made the others suffer. He called their names as soon as he got a fist to his face."

Now he was going to let them rot in jail. I told my mother I'd never see my brother a free man but she kept telling me to have faith. In a few weeks my confidence in Rafie's potential to gain freedom returned. Judge Young's clue his early release was probable became my focus once again.

Bureau of Corrections officers Charles Christian and his partner Willie Love were overpowered by a ruthless plan of escape. At the time they were transporting LaBeet, Christian had won the title of Caribbean Full-Contact Karate Champion. Love, a quiet man, was also a karate black belt. But the jungle-tested combat veteran was ahead of both. Christian detailed to me:

> When we went to pick LaBeet up in St. Thomas to connect with the flight out of St. Croix to the States, the prison nurse told us that he was having diarrhea because of a reaction to fresh milk he drank. She told us he would have to go to the bathroom a lot during the flight. That's why we weren't surprise when he said he had to use the bathroom four or five times. Then he came out with a gun. It seems he didn't know which one of the stalls it was in. LaBeet was too smart to come close enough to get our guns. He told a little boy to take our guns out the holsters and bring them to him. He then made us sit on the inside of passengers away from the aisles. We couldn't do much without risking the passengers.

After the convict gained control of the huge DC-10, the hijacked flight into Cuba was otherwise, for lack of a better word, uneventful. But there is nothing ordinary in the crime of air piracy, especially at night. One can only imagine passengers' fear of being shot five miles high in the sky, or the plane crashing into the darkness below with the explosion. And no fire trucks, ambulances, or police cars in sight for those, if any, not murdered on impact. A young lady who was on the flight to visit

Chicago, to this day has not returned to St. Croix. On December 9, 2013 her mother repeated that no amount of coaxing can get her to board an airplane ever again.

Curiosity abounds whether the skyjacker is still in Cuba, and if so, what's going on with him. A journalist friend of whom I have reasons to believe has good contacts, says LaBeet remains in Cuba as a male nurse and married with children. Wanted posters went up on St. Croix when federal marshals learned I was on my way to Cuba. It appears they thought I was going to meet with him. In the year 2001 I visited there for three weeks as a People to People Ambassador. At times, I nudged pleasant security officers, who escorted us to gatherings, to enlighten me. Their smiles were telling. Cuba is wary of anyone asking questions about internal matters. We were truly well hosted as guests. But upon our arrival, each of us had been eagle-eyed by a stern Cuban agent. However, I got some general info about others who'd forced their way into Cuba. If LaBeet was handled like those, probability is he was tried, convicted, and sentenced to ten years for violating Cuban air space. He served seven, during which he was taught a skill for social use. While on parole, he was closely monitored. He was then released into a normal life, but could live only within a prescribed area.

From all I've learned about Fountain Valley, LaBeet's gun just as likely was hidden on the DC-10 airliner *before* it left New York for St. Croix. It is true that after it landed in St. Croix, where it overnighted, that Douglas Commercial-10 was serviced. I've been assured by someone who for twenty-five years worked those procedures that no stranger could've breached it after it was, as final step, sealed. Yet, it's simply assumed the firearm was planted either by his BOC guards, a baggage handler, or an employee from the airport's duty free shop. Evidently, it was secreted by someone sophisticated enough to outfox everybody. Knowing LaBeet would be on board, both crew and airport security was on high alert. When he spoke to me, he did not hint he knew for sure when he was leaving. But a New Yorker with access to the turnaround manifest could've told him. He had sufficient info to call me, plus arrange the tale about drinking milk to throw his guards off even though prisoner travel arrangements are quite short-noticed. Conjecture the weapon was placed in St. Croix seems to rest on the belief LaBeet was well-liked by Crucians. The FBI therefore thoroughly scrutinized his BOC guards and many airport personnel. Truth is the St. Thomas native didn't enjoy such rapport in St. Croix, surely not the same as Rafie. Because rumors about the BOC persist, on January 3, 2013 I met again with Charles Christian:

> I was out from the bureau for a couple weeks installing security cameras in a bank before [Warden] Schrader called me on December thirtieth about a transfer. But I did not want to go because the thirty-first was Boxer's [Christian's brother, Victor] birthday plus New Year's Eve, so it's my best day for partying. I waited until nine p.m. to go to Schrader hoping by then he got somebody else. But I wasn't so lucky. I have to tell you again, if it wasn't for our concern for passenger safety, I don't think it would've been so easy for LaBeet."

A person whom I've known from school days to be forthright revealed to me his and LaBeet's family relations to a Cuban link. As far as that Crucian is concerned, my belief the pistol was placed on board in New York may be on target. The person confided in me, "One of LaBeet's aunts was a secretary to Fidel Castro. She was very pretty and was more than just another one of his many secretaries. She and Fidel go back to when he visited Harlem just after he came to power in Cuba. Don't forget LaBeet had people in New York."

In fact, another person conveyed to me a serious experience he had with LaBeet when they lived and hung out together in the Big Apple.

Eight: Most Unlikely Ally

When civilization reaches that point where we become
our brother's keeper then we shall be perfect as men,
ready for the companionship of God's angels.
                              —Marcus Mosiah Garvey

November 1993. Hotelier Betty Sperber, out of the blue, died. Had she not, it is likely Rafie would have been saved from suicide. Betty would've also reassured frightened Continentals. Without her, their public outcry worked against homecoming of a harmless man. She'd have held Rafie's hand until his feet were firmly replanted. At the same time, she'd have convinced her compatriots the only error in his release were the doubts he changed for the better. Boundless positive energy she possessed was more than plenty to accomplish both.

But Betty departed too soon after we met. It was within a shorter period than it took my brother to persuade me to make her my partner in the struggle to set him free.

In September 1989 Hurricane Hugo, beyond every imagination, bulldozed St. Croix. For six months, Rafie's routine during the prior seventeen years of phoning twice a week was agonizingly not possible. When, at last, we resumed our talks he focused almost exclusively on my contacting Betty Sperber. "She wants to help me," he persisted. This was met with warnings of false hopes. My advice fell on deaf ears. Rafie instead ratcheted up his request to a command I coordinate with her to get him out of jail. This new twist caused me to think he was finally having a nervous breakdown. He had become too fond of thinking his continued captivity was caused by my procrastinations. So, I placated him. A whole year of prodding if I'd yet visit her was met with a worn, "I haven't seen her yet. Please, please don't worry. Other angles are looking good. Don't forget we have to keep these things confidential."

In turn, he'd rant a barrage of reasons why I must connect with his Continental friend. Finally, he had enough of my stalling, and I enough of his wishful thinking. Luckily distance separated us. Our phones literally were overheating. He was unrelenting. Betty and he were pen pals for years and enjoyed each other's confidence. But for me, a retired New Yorker whose nest egg, the Mine Gift Shop, was ruined by Fountain Valley, couldn't be trusted. Surely she'd have ulterior motives, like revenge.

Rafie's supposed supporter no doubt was influential in the slowly recovering tourist trade. She organized "Operation St. Croix" to jumpstart it. That title added to my suspicions. It sounded like something out of Langley. Betty led the Chamber of Commerce and Hotel Association, both of which were practically all Continental. Many members' businesses had been hit hard, if not shattered. Naturally, they were hell-bent the remaining four of the Fountain Valley Five rot in jail. Often, the sense in the air whenever I spoke with any of them was, "One already escaped. What more do you natives want?" Of course, I had to swallow that.

I begged Rafie to realize years of real blood, sweat, and tears were at risk. Associating with a probable saboteur simply was not an option. With self-confidence of a challenged college professor he fired back it was my sincerity which was suspect. His thanklessness so shocked me I slashed for the first time our shared umbilical cord. Although so, during the months of separation I did much to find out who was the person my brother insisted I meet. After all, I'd been away for seven years following my brother's conviction and was unaware of some things at home.

Several of Rafie's supporters also felt Betty was all about herself. She was now running the hotel in which she'd been before the murders merely another retail tenant. She was able to

Michael A. Joseph, Esq.

keep charter cruises to nearby Buck Island when natives were unable to restart theirs. But the grumblings were overshadowed by good words. Her standing with Government House was excellent. I tried cases with Gov. Alexander Farrelly when he practiced, and concluded his and Betty's dealings were mutually beneficial. He was nobody's fool. Besides, only he could free my brother. The closer they were the better. Her help would be exponential, the trump card I'd been hunting for. She would glue those convinced Rafie deserved freedom, while keeping at bay her powerful associates who insisted on the contrary.

Betty had roots in my missed calling. In the mid-1960s Jimi Hendrix relocated from Seattle to New York's Village. He was playing for guitar-case coins singing for supper when she added him to her musician portfolio with its popular anchor act, the Isley Brothers. She helped Jimi fly to England to become a legend, and guided other R & B stars including John Mayall.

My brother's Continental benefactor had also road-managed the musical *Jesus Christ Superstar*. She chuckled while describing how the show at times was heckled by Christian protestors at its off-Broadway venues. This was quite interesting. Soon after Betty relocated to St. Croix, she was befriended by two stalwarts of the Catholic church. So, I had no idea she was Jewish—not that it made any difference—before she passed. I had volunteered to be one of her bearers as soon as I found out she died. But son, Miles, sadly reciprocated, "The most you could do for Mammy now is to place a stone on her grave."

If Betty was an angel, as my brother seemed to say, she had two friends for her wings. These are Ann Christian Abramson and Rita de Chabert Schuster, both kindhearted church icons. I've seen "Teacher Rita" as a saint ever since she taught me in second grade. She exudes a quiet, humble, matchless beauty. She and her siblings constructed one of the largest shopping centers in the Caribbean, and her immediate family still operates the island's oldest purified water business. Yet, in social and civic circles she remains as unassuming a human being as could be found.

Ann Abramson is of like generosity, but firm in her approach. Indeed, in this context they are opposites. Self-made Ann is as savvy as anyone on Wall Street. Of quite advanced age, her health and appearance are astonishingly youthful. She's honored by having in her name one of the most scenic deepwater marine facilities anywhere. Still, she's not too proud to recall her modest beginnings such as traveling on foot eight miles to her first job as a teacher. Nor was she bashful to say, "My father trusted my brother's Catholic confirmation suit from your grandfather's store."

Ann smiled as she recalled those days. On Saturdays, she'd walk a couple miles to Grandfather's shop with payment on account in hand. Proud of it she was. That brother became Judge Alphonso Christian, who fathered physician Cora Christian, MD, and women's rights intellectual Barbara Christian, PhD. After we'd spoken, I hadn't seen nor heard from Ann in more than two years. But on January 9, 2008 just hours after writing about her in this chapter, she appeared in a watchmaker's shop out of thin air. I gasped. I'd been visiting its owner Patrick Ramon on an unrelated matter. Incredibly, the last words Patrick uttered only seconds before Ann entered were, "Michael, it was like a miracle."

The company woman, cool as cucumber, greeted us: "Happy New Year young men! This one will make fifty years since Abramson Enterprises have been bussing schoolchildren. I'm going to sell space in a commemoration booklet and I will donate the proceeds for security cameras in the schools."

In the eeriness of the moment I tried to detail the wonder of her entrance. I told her I'd been writing about her and Betty just a few hours before. She simply replied, "Oh yes, Betty Sperber was my very good friend."

Ann's startling appearance might be brushed off as coincidence. Well, three weeks later on January 28 I was again visiting the watchmaker. An elder entered and pivoted towards me: "Oh! Sorry. I almost walked past your shop. Didn't know exactly where it was. Ann Abramson sent me to you."

Patrick intervened: "I'm the one Ann sent you to, sir."

Because he mentioned Ann in the same place I'd met her, I couldn't help telling the gentleman of my encounter on the ninth with her.

Michael A. Joseph, Esq.

"Are you Catholic?" he asked.

"Yes."

"Oh, then you must have attended my Mass. I'm Father Car-
lyle Blake. Oh, I now recognize you. You're the son of Isabel,
one of our Sacred Heart Sisters."

Did Betty send an affirmation from the environment, an
omen of support for this book? Believe it or not, the only other
time I saw Ann after January 2008 was on Thanksgiving Day
2009. I'd been editing this chapter when I made a quick run to a
nearby grocery that happened to be located in one of her build-
ings, and clearly heard Ann's voice say, "I'm going to take a bag
of rice until later. I forgot my wallet."

"Ann!" I called out as I spun around. "Every time I write
about you and Betty, you appear. If you go now to my laptop,
you'll see your name on screen!"

"Oh my God," she uttered wide-eyed.

In the watchmaker's store going on two years before, the
good lady might not have noticed the mystery. This time she
couldn't ignore it.

Fortified by the fact Ann and Teacher Rita were her special
friends, in October of 1991 doubts shifted in favor of meeting
Betty Sperber. She granted an instant appointment. On entering
her office, her intensity was clear. She was having two conversations, both telephones to her ears. One balanced by a shoulder
prop, the other in her hand. The free palm went back to taking
notes after its firm grip. She was engaged in another of her
many efforts to restore a most pretty island's glory days. Times
when Sen. Edward "Ted" Kennedy in sandals, shorts, and T-shirt
leisurely pushed a supermarket cart next door to "JFK Housing
Project," named in honor of one of his assassinated brothers.
Ted was fond of socializing with natives in his getaway island,
second to none in pure beauty. Typical in size to others, St. Croix
yet appeared to loom large in the geopolitical sphere. During a
1990 criminal justice delegation visit to a youth facility in Kiev,
Ukrainian Republic, when told where my home was its director
responded with an air of friendly envy, "How lucky you are to
live in a resort."

Through our interpreter I tried to enlighten he used the word "resort" too loosely.

"Oh no," my host corrected, "I'm aware of your island. For me, all of it is a resort."

It occurred to me within his duties as colonel in the then-Soviet Union Army he'd reviewed satellite images of St. Croix, site of one of the world's largest oil refineries.

Perhaps, Victor Somme Sr. is in the best position to globally compare the island's charm. In forty years of air transportation employment he has amassed more than two million miles across Earth. Actually, he was the Alexander Hamilton Airport worker who answered the Australian radio host's telephone call on the day of Fountain Valley:

> I have to say when it comes to sunsets the four best I've ever seen were in Sydney, Auckland, a tiny town in the Mohave Desert near the Arizona-California border named Needles, and at Ham's Bluff in St. Croix. But if it comes down to serenity, nothing can compare to a Sunday afternoon drive along our South Shore Road.

Betty was at the forefront in restoring its reputation upheaved by Fountain Valley. Feelings among hotel, retail, and real estate groups were that the island's reputation was so badly mangled only time would heal it. For them, premature promotions could make matters worse. Lee Morris, my Continental teacher pal who'd slammed the Constitution, is also a longtime real estate agent. He had cautioned Betty, "Let sleeping dogs lie. Travelers will soon forget. If we move too soon, we might mess things up. But Sperber went right ahead contacting airlines and travel agencies. She was a one-man tourist department."

Earl Powell, past Hotel Association president, and who managed several hotels, added, "Betty Sperber and her 'Operation St. Croix' more than anyone or agency brought business back to the island. Betty invited travel agents to come down and held parties for them. She practically dragged Elizabeth Armstrong [of landmark Buccaneer Hotel] and myself to mainland trade shows and coached us how to answer hard questions about St. Croix as a premier destination."

On August 19, 2009 Rita de Chabert Shuster softly spoke, "Since you are still writing, I'll add Mrs. Sperber each month for quite some time used my home to hold parties for travel writers and agents she brought down to St. Croix. She wanted to show them that everything was okay in the island. Local hotels carried the expenses for their airfare, food, and the music. She made sure a cross section of the community was invited to mix with those agents."

Betty motioned to a chair next to her desk as I was about to sit on a small couch across from it. She paced back and forth within length of the telephone cords. Despite its small size, her office carried an aura of hugeness. Something was surreal about it, perhaps because for the first time I was seeking help from a high-profile Continental. One who lost her retirement investment by acts of a convict whose freedom she sought. I felt like a fish out of water. About ten minutes later, she directed her staff to filter further calls, and she shot straight to the point: "Rafie is my good friend. We've been writing and talking for years. Even if he did what they said he did—we never discussed the incident—he is a young man who came a long, long way and it does not make sense to keep him in that place when he could be out here guiding the kids that are getting themselves in trouble."

I wanted to jump in to say: *That's exactly what I came to tell you!* But her dream flow of words was so unforeseen I was flabbergasted. Mrs. Betty Sperber, of whom I'd been so judgmental, perfectly chanted the mantra Rafie and I coined over the years. How could a person whose nest egg had been broken by murderers be so forgiving? Perhaps she was the angel Rafie insisted she was. I saw Betty as often as our schedules allowed. She'd always reassured I could name-drop her to others. She clearly wished to see Rafie free no less than his family. Yet, she kept her sentiments at arm's length as was appropriate for someone without blood relations. In what turned out to be our last meeting the hospitality promoter was optimistic without being pushy: "I'm sure Rafie and you are covering all the bases. He asked me to look at the petition, but that's up to you. He wanted me to suggest some people who might offer support. Alex [Gov. Farrelly] and I talk often and I'm sure he'll consider what I've told him about your brother's maturity over the years."

As to the consideration of Rafie's petition by Gov. Farrelly and his inner circle during December 1994, I was later informed by an insider, "No name among your brother's supporters was mentioned as many times as was the late Mrs. Betty Sperber."

Betty, after all, was the centerpiece in reviving the industry instantly imploded by the crime. She rounded out the powerful support of Maj. Gen. Jean Romney of VI National Guard, federal and local wardens, Fountain Valley's attorney, a victim, Chief Deputy US Marshall Krim Ballentine, and other icons such as Delta Dorsch, whom Gov. Farrelly treasured as his adopted mother. Their help was simply blessed by a Jewish angel carried on Catholic wings.

Nine: Prison Saint Is Born

I believe that everything you do bad comes back to you.
So everything I do that's bad, I'm going to suffer for it.
But in my heart, I believe what I am doing is right. So I
feel like I'm going to heaven.

—Tupac Shakur

"Rafie was the best convict I ever met. Sorry, I meant to say 'person.' You know they call all of us who have been in prison 'convicts,' so I made the mistake and called him that."

A property crime repeat offender, who served time with him, uttered that praise. Other former, as well as current, inmates insist he changed their lives for the better. One warmly refers to him as "The Library."

I wondered how my brother could've been such a good person in prison, where kindness is taken for weakness of the most vulnerable kind. I ventured as far as to hint his small size made him so exposed as to hardly defend himself. His reply left me thinking of lessons young bears receive when foolish enough to try taking a badger's kill.

"Of course I was tested many times. The thing is, when that happens, you got to fight ferociously! Fierceness was the key. The edge I also had was that of a lifer with nothing to lose."

Just recently, a former inmate solemnly told me, "Twice I had to take out man [prisoner] who Rafie didn't even know was planning to kill him. He suspected I did it for him. Frifo tell me, 'I know you watching my back, but I had it under control. You got to stop thinning the population, brother.' I let him know I tell them to come at me instead, and each one made the mistake."

To repeat, surviving prison is an art in of itself. It's "gladiator school" full of zeal to take life so as to gain "rep." The higher the target in the pecking order, the further the killer moves up. Taking out an inmate like Rafie would have been more than worth it within those chilling rules.

Rafie saddened as he explained how vulnerable some prisoners became as they neared their "max out"—full sentence—date. They couldn't afford a "hit"—getting in trouble—which could cause them to do more time. In their last months, they'd request "PC"—protective custody—sneeringly referred to as "Punk City."

A most telling anecdote on how my brother ultimately dealt with the cruelty of prison life was conveyed by an ex-inmate:

> Rafie was like the head of Rastas and other fellows from the Islands. He was our teacher. When I first went in he said to me, 'In here, you have four weapons to choose from if you want to live and get out as soon as you can. You could use a pistol, that's a small shank [prison-made knife], or a rifle, which is a medium-sized one, or a machine gun, a long one. But the best weapon in here is the bazooka. That is your brains,' he told me while pushing his finger against my head, letting me see he was dead serious! He got me to come to his class, and to think before I say or do anything.

There are other jail-life stories Rafie detailed which are better not repeated here. Some can be found in Reuben D. Dowling's autobiographical *Mango Madness* and *Big Mango*, as well as in movies like *Tracks*. Suffice it to say Rafie couldn't believe I slept with my bedroom door open.

His fellow inmates were not the only persons impressed by him. In the mid-1980s, as federal public defender I needed immediate assistance. The Office of United States Courts sent to help me from Arizona Assistant FPD (now Judge) William Deaton. One of the first things we spoke about was *Fountain Valley*.

Michael A. Joseph, Esq.

"I recently attended a seminar on prison reform programs. Your brother's file was a case study. Never has the Bureau of Prisons seen an inmate confined for such violent crimes shown such rehabilitation as did your brother. His file is truly exceptional."

Not long after Deaton's remark, an FBI agent walking past me in the opposite direction on the sidewalk adjacent to my office, out of the blue offered, "This is off record. Do not give up on your effort to free your brother."

Warden R. H. Risen, US Bureau of Prison (BOP) Lompoc, California, said Rafie's behavior was "excellent" and that "he tutored two to three hundred prisoners working towards their high school degrees."

Rafie was more than teacher; he had the backs of the West Indians and Rastafarians in the prison. Another former inmate informed, "Your brother and Tupac Shakur's [step]father, Matulu Shakur, every morning would walk around the yard to talk about problems between the different groups. Rafie looked out for us and Matulu looked out for stateside black prisoners. Sometimes they had to go make peace with the white boys or Mexicans, or it was the other way around."

Meanwhile, Rafie was corresponding with a growing number of supporters, staying in touch with what was going on back home. After he was released, he amazed me with familiarity as to who were related to whom whenever he spoke with others. When I noted my puzzlement about his capacity to remember so many family relations, I learned he'd been by studying obituaries. It gave him a feeling St. Croix was, ironically, alive and well. He was anonymously provided over the years with subscriptions of *The St. Croix Avis*.

While I was federal public defender I could not officially represent Rafie, but luck was in play. J. B. Kiehlbauck, PhD, BOP's north central regional chief of psychology, in a January 5, 1979 memo informed:

Mr. Joseph is currently one of a select few men to have completed paraprofessional-level training. In all activities, he has distinguished himself for diligence, intelligence, personal insight, and growth, and ability to assist others with personal and interpersonal crisis. As a prelude to his ultimate release, in the interest of himself and family resources, and so that he might contribute to peers and the service system, it is the writer's recommendation that he be considered for return to Virgin Islands jurisdiction at the earliest time those authorities will consider accepting him.

Next to the governor's grace, that was the best document possible. I needed help to make greatest use of it. One afternoon years later, I was invited to sit for lunch with former local senator Leroy Arnold, and his Continental friend Attorney John Nichols on the balcony of Hamilton House Restaurant. Rafie's name came up, and I was only too glad to share the news of the BOP's memo.

"Regional Chief of Psychology Dr. Kiehlbauck recommended Rafie come home as a prelude to his eventual release. I need a lawyer to push it because I can't represent him."

To my astonishment John Nichols said he'd help. He was counsel to Rockefellers' Rock Resort Corporation, to banks, and to many of the businesses in the tourist industry. I simply could not believe my ears.

"I think I can help your brother, Michael. I did the corporate work for Fountain Valley. I will have to make a call first, but I don't think the fellows in the States will consider it a conflict. Come see me in about week."

I did. Rockefellers' mainland office had no issues with their local counsel's representation of Rafie. We instantly started a plan. John and then-governor Juan Luis had a warm friendship, but he needed a community elder who had Gov. Luis' confidence. John made sure the governor saw Dr. Kiehlbauck's memo. That elder cultural icon Leona Brady Watson nudged Gov. Luis to order the local prison to do as the BOP recommended. Soon after, Rafie was transferred to continue his sentence in St. Croix.

He wasted no time obtaining furloughs to further his education at nearby College of the Virgin Islands. This was done with assistance of parole board member Olric Carrington and CVI academic dean Arnold Highfield. They, like other bighearted benefactors, were in contact with Rafie for years prior to his transfer.

John Nichols was another matter. He'd come to Rafie's aid on sheer kindness, without particular feel for his new client. So, he thought it fitting Rafie obtain a furlough for Thanksgiving Day at his Queste Verde home. And it happened. It was a wonderful time for the best of our true selves. A stone throw away from where Maureen O'Hara once dined Hollywood legend John Wayne, Rafie relished his first home-cooked turkey in more than a dozen years. Our conversations were as splendid. The prisoner had read classic British authors and since John was a New Englander, the feast was garnished with chats about them. John's wife, Margo, and I relegated ourselves to being their bookends. It was a day of unabashed joy. Deep down, we were salvaging from misfortune the redemption of a human spirit.

The one thing not so generous on that Thanksgiving Day was time. John called the BOC to ask permission for an extension of two hours past Rafie's 6:00 p.m. curfew. Negative. On dropping him off to his cage at 5:59 reality sunk in; my brother was still incarcerated.

So he remained exposed to the hardships of prison life. His main peeve was the lack of predictability of local rules:

> I'm really glad to be back close to the family. But, the one thing I notice here is the rules change all the time. The 'Bulls' [federal prison guards] stateside can be dealt with because you know how they are coming even when you get transferred to another prison. Down here, certain days they'll tell it's OK to do this or that. Out of the blue, another guard will say something different. I've had some run-ins already. I feel I am being jerked.

And then Rafie had a confrontation with the wrong man: Director of Bureau of Corrections Edwin Potter. While catch-

ing an early morning seaplane flight to my St. Thomas office,
I thought I glimpsed my brother in a prison car. But it couldn't
be. After checking in, something told me to take a second look.

"What the hell, Rafie? Why are you handcuffed and sitting
here?"

"This morning they came and said they are taking me to
St. Thomas. I guess I'm leaving on the flight after yours," he
answered humbly.

His guard confirmed they were on their way to St. Thomas.
I moved on thinking BOC wanted him to set up a tutoring program at the detention facility there. Days later, almost in tears
his guard confessed he was on his way for a connecting flight
back to BOP Lompoc. Thank God it was not for misbehavior
involving violence. It was about sex. He was caught making love
to a BOC employee whom, Rafie told me, was a past girlfriend
of Potter. Instead of leaving well alone on being warned such
conduct in the future would result in return to Lompoc, Rafie
protested he couldn't be sent back for something "so personal."
My brother learned to too late the power of power.

I resumed private practice and more years of struggle to get
Gov. Alexander Farrelly's attention. Rafie and I decided to seek
a commutation of sentence to time served based on rehabilitation. Pardons are usually based on factual innocence, or unfair
convictions. We could have contended the latter, but Rafie's
reform was undeniable. Besides, while commutations are infre-
quent, pardons are extremely rare.

Luck, it's said, is being prepared when opportunity strikes.
Senate Judiciary Chairman Orrin Hatch, a Republican, offered
the chance. Because I'd been a legislative director on Capitol
Hill, I was asked to assist in the confirmation of Territorial
Court judge Raymond L. Finch to the federal bench. Gov. Far-
relly had forwarded his name to President Jimmy Carter for
nomination. Carter did nominate Judge Finch, but lost reelec-
tion and Finch was overlooked by successor President Ronald
Reagan. He was re-nominated by President George H. W. Bush.
Still, he was not moved into the Judiciary Committee because
President Bush lost reelection to President Bill Clinton. Presi-

dent Clinton accepted Judge Finch's nomination, yet again he was not moved into the committee.

On the first Saturday of November 1994 I happened upon Sen. Hatch in a health food store in Roanoke, Virginia, and simply told him of the glitch. I emphasized Judge Finch had been a Democratic nominee who was yet re-nominated by a Republican. I let Hatch know I was invited to meet President Bush as a gesture of appreciation for my father's starting the St. Croix Republican Club. Sen. Hatch was quite familiar with our first native federal judge, the Hon. Almeric L. Christian, so he knew the district of which I spoke. Without further ado, he promised he would look into the matter right away. "Send me a letter for my files," Hatch said as we parted. Two days later, on Monday, I did send the letter. On same day Gov. Farrelly got a call to have Judge Finch fly to Washington for a hearing on Wednesday before Hatch's committee. Finch appeared and was favorably reported out of Hatch's committee. On Friday he was endorsed by the Senate, and on same day Sen. Hatch sent me a letter stating, "There were no problems. Judge Finch was unanimously confirmed."

Before November ended, United States District Court judge Raymond L. Finch was sworn in. At the ceremony Gov. Farrelly, beaming with pride, finally accepted my request to meet with him to review Rafie's petition for commutation. Also at the ceremony was a Rafie supporter, retired warden Richard Schrader, a fertile author, poet in residence, and 1994 Humanist of the Year. He agreed to attend the meeting with me. Actually, I asked him to take the lead as a penal professional who'd interacted with my brother. When we met Gov. Farrelly, he was in a good mood and he and Schrader spoke on a first-name basis. In the presence of those elders I was nervous and at times referred to the governor as "Judge Farrelly." He didn't mind at all. He was the only person in the VI to be appointed a judge, elected as a legislator, and elected as a governor.

Perhaps because Gov. Farrelly "had been there and done that," not once did he telegraph his opinion on what he was being told. Excepting, he was impressed with Rafie's plan for continuing education in California if released. Gov. Farrelly referred to a particular letter he'd received. It was sent on June 3, 1991 from Chela Sandoval, an instructor at University of California, Santa Cruz, concerning Rafie:

> We met via Mr. Joseph's close association with one of the most respected members of the intellectual and academic community here in Santa Cruz, a former Crucian by the name of Rosa Maria Vilafane. I understand that Mr. Joseph is interested in studying at this university should he be released to do so, and we have a support system in place here to help him achieve his goals.

On December 19, 1994 Gov. Alexander A. Farrelly announced he commuted Rafie's eight consecutive life terms to the twenty-three years he'd served, "in the spirit of Christmas to give some of our brothers and sisters who have strayed a second opportunity."

The governor's religious tone was not at all pretentious. He grew up across from St. Patrick's Church, attended its school, and remained a devoted Catholic. Rafie had communicated with Bishop, now Cardinal, Sean O'Malley, and Cletina "Tina" Tuitt of the Sacred Heart Sisters. In spite she was a shotgun blast victim at Fountain Valley, Sister Tina appealed for Rafie's release. And prior to my meeting with O'Malley, Gov. Farrelly already consulted him concerning whether he should free Rafie.

On December 22 American Airlines landed with Rafie as a free man. Ti Lenhardt had boarded LaBeet on the aircraft he hijacked. Now, Ti greeted LaBeet's freed co-convict ten years almost to the day of that tragic flight.

Rafie's friend Clatus "Preevo" Prevost was driving past and saw us as were turning out of Alexander Hamilton Airport. He curved around and signaled us to follow his car. Preevo was special. He knew Rafie for years before Fountain Valley and befriended me because, he said, he really likes Rafie and glad I was helping him. In fact, Preevo liked to help everyone. His C&C Construction hired persons otherwise unemployable because of their prior contact with the law. His main contract was with Hess Oil refinery and with it he helped many get good-paying jobs.

Preevo was as serious as a rhino, yet his heart was a caring one. Rafie didn't have to tell me to follow him. It was automatic. At nearby Bethlehem Inn, my brother and his old friend toasted to freedom. Before chitchat, though, Preevo matter-of-factly uttered, "Rafie, I think you should get off this island as soon as you can. If you stay here you are going to die."

He relaxed when told by Rafie two professors at the University of California, Santa Cruz, awaited his arrival. UC–Santa Cruz was known for accepting Huey P. Newton, cofounder of the Black Panther Party, who in 1980 earned a doctorate there. Rafie, too, wished to be called "Dr. Joseph" in the field of social counseling.

But the dogs of war were let loose when the press for days in a row reported on the backlash to Gov. Farrelly's action. Many stores closed their doors for a while on Christmas Eve to allow their employees to join hundreds of protestors wearing black armbands. Mostly led by Continentals, they marched in the streets of Christiansted; Charlotte Amalie, St. Thomas; and Cruz Bay, St. John. Alexander A. Farrelly Criminal Justice Complex in St. Thomas was vandalized with spray-paint changing its name to "Alexander A. Farrelly Criminal Injustice Complex."

The local US Department of Justice office attempted to reverse Gov. Farrelly's release of Rafie. It was bizarre because the BOP, an agency of the DOJ, had certified him fit for freedom. But a Continental DOJ attorney didn't bother to consult BOP's file on Rafie and blindly told *The San Jose Mercury News*, "I consider anybody who could slaughter eight people and walk away extremely dangerous. People are angry and upset."

Rafie made it crystal clear he'd rather be killed than go back to *that place*. On the patio at the rear of my house surrounded by thick shrubbery, he scoped the area.

"I'm figuring a way out of here. If they come for me I'm going to run through those bushes and I'm not going to stop until they shoot me dead."

He left for California, but not for Santa Cruz. He was disheartened by law enforcers there. Sgt. Nancy Carroll of UC–Santa Cruz's security unit said to *The Mercury News*, "Of course we would have some concern if a murderer comes to campus. It's something we're watching."

And when informed of Rafie's intent to enroll at the university, the police chief of Santa Cruz City said to *The Santa Cruz Sentinel*, "This is the first I've heard of it. Boy, aren't we the lucky ones?"

On January 4, 1995 *The Sentinel* ran this headline: "MASS MURDERER COULD ATTEND UCSC."

On same day *The Mercury News'* front page blared: "ADVICE SOUGHT ON KILLER."

My brother believed he'd be better off at a girlfriend's in Santa Barbara. Due to wide coverage of the protests, that area was hardly different. On Fourth of July of 1995 he called me.

"I have a job, and everything was going well until today. My neighbor and I became friends. I helped him paint his house, and he helped paint ours. That's how good we are. He's having his barbeque and we are having ours. But he just came over to our fence looking at me funny and asked me, 'Are you that murderer the governor in the Islands illegally released?' One of the neighbors must have told him that. I couldn't even answer him. I walked off as if I didn't understand what he was talking about. I am so pissed how things got so twisted. I told my lady it wouldn't be fair to her to have the neighborhood spying on her house every time I go in or out. I'm coming back home."

He did and married his Seventh Day Adventist School sweetheart. In addition to having a home and a wife, other support was available. Edwin Callwood, a busy lawyers' investigator, often offered him work.

Rafie's closest friend was Angel Diaz, a former policeman and founder of popular La Reine Chicken Shack (domestic diva Martha Stewart's favorite island restaurant). Diaz, whose home was always open to Rafie, said he came by sometimes depressed: "Rafie felt he was getting nowhere."

Ernest Hemingway's *For Whom the Bell Tolls* posits that whoever takes life for any reason will not have peace until he pays penance. Whether as a pawn of war or otherwise, redemption was the price. That's the premise of Ubuntu. Rafie's in-prison contrition was officially facilitated, but when released he faced so many doubters it foiled his free-world restoration. According to a teacher, "Your brother came to Eulalie Rivera School to talk to the students about staying out of trouble. He told them about his time in jail and how most of the inmates were school dropouts. I was so very impressed. He really got their attention. Afterwards, I told him he should go to other schools and do the same thing. He said he wanted a counseling job but they turned him down."

Another difficulty he faced was that more than a few natives, most of them young, elevated him to somewhat of a hero "for keeping white people from taking over the island." This weighed heavy on him. For, he knew that while Fountain Valley's backlash was driven by the skin color drama, the massacre itself was by no means planned much less driven by race. But what he didn't find out was it had been precipitated by the great evils of war.

Penalties of Vietnam: the war that cursed our brother Edwin with such an irritability it led him to shoot his brother-in-law, kill his own wife, kill his mother-in-law, and then kill himself. It drove brilliant social activist Darwin King to scamper around a shopping center diving to the ground shouting, "Incoming! Incoming!" and caused his veterans hospital lonely death. It so warped Otto Jensen as to quietly sit in his truck and slit his own throat wide open. It pressed LaBeet to shoot at policemen arresting fellow Vietnam vet Esteban Davila for stealing to buy drugs to dull their war scars and which shooting led to Fountain Valley. It then drove Davila to serenely walk into a beach until he was far out enough to drown himself.

Five days before someone called to say, "Rafie is dead," I came across a picture of him, Robert Vaughn, DEd, and me. It was taken at one of several socials we attended with Dr. Vaughn, a Continental. An author, librarian, and photographer, he reached out to Rafie because he knew that he, too, had gotten a second chance—but for an unforeseen delay he would've been lunching at Fountain Valley same the time of the massacre.

Two days prior to seeing that picture, we were at a gathering of mostly businesspeople when Rafie asked to leave early for the reason that "People are smiling in my face, and then gossiping behind my back."

I explained to him it was harmless even if true. I was naive, he said: "I made it out of jail because I gained the ability to know what was going on around me."

After I took him home, and arrived at mine, he called to tell me, "Mikey, I have solved everything and I am going to go away."

I thought he meant he was returning to the States. But while staring at that photo, I suddenly realized what he was really saying about "going away." And it slammed me there was nothing I could do to save him. I cried out, "Rafie, I've lost you!"

I never saw him again alive or dead; I didn't view his body.

Instincts told me that something terribly wrong must have happened during the five days after I came across the photo of us. It took eleven years to find out what it was. On September 7, 2012 Jacqueline "Jackie" Sobotker, a library assistant, revealed it to me. On the afternoon of November 21, 1998, the day before he died, she and he were having a long chat while they sat on the upstairs steps of Grandfather's house. And then, a buff young man double-parked in front of them. What to others was no big thing, such as the stranger's bad parking, Rafie keenly avoided so as to not draw police attention. He didn't want any to think he was being cocky because he got out of eight life sentences. He calmly asked the young man to move the car further down the street. Jackie tells what then erupted:

> The guy let out a bunch of curse words at Rafie calling him an old this and that. Rafie didn't say a thing. When that rude boy started to walk around the cars to approach Rafie, I went down the steps in front of him. "Do you know who you are disrespecting like that?" I

told him who Rafie was and I hit him a slap! With that, Rafie got ready for him thinking he's going to hit me back, but the guy rushed into his car and sped off. When I got the call the next day that Rafie was dead, I said, "No! What nonsense are you telling me?" After I called around and found out it was true, I felt so empty.

After my brother parted from Jackie, he walked to the home where he'd been captured twenty-six years before. The predawn hours of November 22 found him on its living room floor resting at the feet of Mother, where he'd been reminiscing with her all night:

Rafie kept telling me how much he loved me, thanking me for raising him. And about how grateful he was we got him out of jail. He told me he can't stay in St. Croix, and he have to go away. We talked about when he was growing up and those kinds of things. I kept telling him to go inside and get some sleep. But he asked me to stay with him until the sun comes up. I just stayed there talking with him for hours. When the sun was coming up, he left.

Hours later Rafie injected himself with heroin "to go away." Uninvited violence that would've ruined twenty-three years of growth and blemish the reputations of good people who'd stood up for him had come much too close. As awful was his seeing an otherwise feisty young man running like a startled wild turkey upon being informed of his connection to Fountain Valley.

****

The Fountain Valley Five lead trial lawyer, also, was truly stunned by Rafie's release. William "Bill" Kunstler as a civil rights activist worked with the Freedom Riders who risked their lives in 1960s Deep South voting drives. He negotiated on behalf of prisoners at the deadly Attica Prison uprising in 1971. He won the 1972 Chicago Seven trial arising from riots at the 1968 Democratic Convention by unsettling the court into irreparable errors. His charisma even got him a part as the bigoted judge who sent Malcolm Little to jail in Spike Lee's biopic *Malcolm X*. Yet Bill could hardly speak when he called to learn how I was able to free Rafie. At first, he hinted I betrayed my brother's codefendants, but calmed down when I read portions of Rafie's petition. The support letter he found most persuasive was from his trial rival, their prosecutor, now-Superior Court senior judge Julio A. Brady.

Bill suddenly changed the subject to O. J. Simpson's murder trial. I asked his opinion of it.

"Ah, an LA jury will not convict O. J. once tampering with the evidence is proven."

"Why not, didn't that happen when the Five were tortured? Couldn't the court see it? As you know, Judge Young appointed me as a defense investigator and I brought others tortured to see you lawyers."

"But the evidence in the case was too overwhelming," he responded.

"That's what I mean. The evidence seems quite formidable against O. J. What is the difference for your confidence his jury will not convict?"

"Don't worry, O. J. is a celebrity. An LA jury will not convict a celebrity."

We ended our chat by agreeing that who goes to jail and who does not is at times unpredictable. Perhaps it's this elusive justice which keeps Ballantine, Smith, and Gereau in jail twenty years longer than was Rafie even though they have also changed for the better.

Then again, that justice or lack thereof often hinges on the decisions made by the attorneys and their clients. This was the situation when the Fountain Valley defendants framed their case as the "Fountain Valley Five" and proceeded as if they were a single defendant.

Alas, years ago the Hon. Julio A. Brady shared with me, "Had Gereau and Smith made motions for separate trials, I may well have dismissed those two because of insufficient evidence."

Ten: Rafie's Story

Note:
I received the following from my brother in 1991 dur-
ing his incarceration. Other than being formatted for
printing, it is verbatim. I offer no comment as to his
view on the state of St. Croix just prior to the murders.
Although we were like twins in many ways, we saw the
world at large through our own eyes.

A Prefatory Note

The case for which I have been imprisoned since 1972 happened in the US Virgin Islands, an otherwise quiet Caribbean group covering some 133 square miles, and located roughly one thousand miles southeast of Florida. The crime itself bore shocking effects and political overtones. It was vociferously denounced by a shocked public. And the case was highly sensationalized. The international press mentioned it, while the national and local media had a field day. But I have never before documented anything on the case or how I felt about it.

Why, then, do I now write what I call "My Story?" In the first place, it is indeed a story that needs to be told by someone who actually lived it. Although others have lived it along with me, I could not recount their experience. To do so would be presumptuous. Therefore, I write in the first person singular, relying on my experience, memory, and present-day outlook. And wherever I write in the plural form, it is a matter of public record or knowledge. At this time, too, for sound reasons, I confine myself to relating the case, distinct from the crime. In doing so, I shun florid narration. And for the sake of brevity, I avoid some details even where the reader might want more. But elaboration of those particulars would set well with perhaps a future larger text.

Nonetheless, it should become obvious that there has been something to say on the subject which, nineteen years ago, was inarticulately told in anger. But today, after the many years of personal growth and continued self-education, I can articulate the matter unburdened by negative emotions. And, despite any restrictions, the story hopes to soothe some curiosity. Its purpose has been to convey, however, that which I deem good for me and four officers in particular, even if in arriving at the good I have had to delve into some unpleasant remembrances.

But actual inspiration to write appeared while preparing a letter to Attorney Efia Nwangaza of South Carolina. The attorney got my name from a newspaper in 1990, and has since sent me a few pieces of mail. This good soul did not even know me, yet reached behind the prison walls to offer encouragement and help. I liked that. But, I never got around to writing her until I began a first letter in March 1991. In telling Nwangaza of me and my case, things long suppressed began to unfold. I was inspired to write, and this is the result.

Otherwise I keep my pen to myself, to letter writing and to checking the schoolwork of inmates whom I teach in the prison education program. I teach Adult Basic Education (ABE), General Educational Development (GED), and even some current events.

As much as to help others, I teach for personal satisfaction. Teaching gives me a sense of making amends for my past. I find it lifting to reach another person educationally, especially other prisoners. I see so much of the past undisciplined, misdirected me in them. And I know that education, the mental and moral development of a person, together with the pursuit of knowledge for the sake of knowledge, has benefitted me tremendously in these long nineteen years of incarceration. I, in turn, help who wants to better himself through education. I should feel well to reach especially a younger prisoner to develop within himself the desire for self-improvement. For his positive growth and newly acquired skills via education, and his elimination of

Michael A. Joseph, Esq.

errant values, old attitudes and behavior patterns will have a carryover effect on the community into which he is eventually released. This is my way of making amends—no matter how quietly or unnoticeably.

Recently, though, I got some acknowledgement for what I have been doing. An article in the November 24, 1990 *Santa Barbara News-Press* quoted the Lompoc, CA, US penitentiary education supervisor who said that I am "an excellent instructor. When Joseph is not tutoring other inmates, he's studying something else on his own." And I wonder whether Virgin Islands corrections would appreciate this.

And the Lompoc prison administration has been sufficiently satisfied with my "institutional adjustment" and scholastic achievements. It has written letters recommending my relocation to Virgin Islands prison. Lompoc's most recent letter to the Virgin Islands corrections director was in September 1990. But the director has not responded up to seven months later. I remain exiled to stateside prison.

Meanwhile, I hold to hope that people out there who care and understand will persuade the Virgin Islands government to return me to my native birthplace. There I could do for the prison education program what I am doing in federal penitentiary. My indigent family could visit me, as my kinsfolk cannot afford the cost of travel across the Atlantic Ocean and to this distant place in California. There also I may demonstrate my real worth as a person, distinct from an age-old violent image seemingly preserved for Virgin Islanders by my "out of sight, out of mind" treatment by the territory's correction bureau. And, finally, I would be in a position to exploit the sentencing judge's expedited/early parole recommendation and, if granted, someday live the responsible and productive life which, at thirty-nine, I have yet to live as an adult in free society.

I recognize, though, if I am to receive help from people out there, they should hear from me and know how I think today. So, I write my story.

Rafie O. Joseph
March 1991
Rafie's Story
Written in 1991 in Lompoc Prison*
This title is in his longhand.

Fountain Valley is the name of an estate in the countryside of St. Croix, Virgin Islands, a sunny Caribbean island whose native population is of predominantly African descent. The estate is a verdant piece of fertile land on which long ago rested slave plantations. Located in the northwest area close to the scenic rain forest it had now become the site of a plush golf resort for tourists. The tourist industry is heavily owned, managed, and patronized by whites, while the menial jobs are usually reserved for natives and Afro-Caribbean immigrants. Nineteen years ago, Fountain Valley Golf Resort was a thriving business owned by Rock (as in Rockefeller) Resorts, Inc. After what happened, it was sold and renamed Carambola (the name of a fruit that does not grow in the Caribbean).

In the late morning hours of September 6, 1972, five armed, masked men emerged from the nearby semi-surrounding hills and descended upon the resort. When they left, all the whites (seven) were dead and an immigrant worker lay beside them. Three to four other employees were shot mainly in the lower legs, while several others went unharmed. The establishment was also robbed. Such is the reported scenario of what had happened.

A massive manhunt was immediately under way. It scoured the eighty-two-square-mile island, concentrating mainly on the hills. Scores of US marshals, FBI agents, and other federal people were brought in to assist local police, while US Coast guard boats circled the tiny island clockwise and counterclockwise day and night. From dawn to dusk helicopters and small reconnaissance planes crisscrossed the skies, searching. The hunt was for five dissident natives.

The western town, Frederiksted, from where the suspects hailed, was continuously searched and kept under surveillance.

This town holds historic significance for major Virgin Islands freedom efforts. It is where the slaves rose up in 1848 to win their liberation from slavery throughout the then Danish West Indies. The revolt was led to a successful end by St. Kitts-born Moses "General Buddhoe" Gottlieb. Thirty years later, from Frederiksted, was also launched the famous "Fireburn" of 1878. Natives, in rebellion against their state of economic bondage, burned cane fields and attacked homes of sugar plantation owners in which several whites were killed. This fiery wave of insurrection affected some twelve miles of a fourteen-mile distance between Frederiksted and the eastern town of Christiansted. The rebellion was led by Mary "Queen Mary" Thomas and her comrades, Agnes and Mathilda, also called queens.

As I write, I reflect on an old song heard as a child. Its chorus asks, "Queen Mary, a-weh yo' a-goh?" (Where are you going?) and responds, "Meh a-goh buhn dong Bahsehn jailhouse!"

Queen Mary was on the way to her final object of rebellion: to burn down the Christiansted Bassin prison, which housed a large number of native men and women, many of whom had refused to work for a few-cents-a-day pittance that could not meet living costs at all. Queen Mary was captured near Estate Anna's Hope, a couple of miles short of her objective. Tied between two horses ridden by gendarmes or Danish police, she was dragged at a gallop to Christiansted. Then, tried by their oppressors, Queen Mary and her comrades were convicted and exiled to a prison far away in Denmark. They served time and were eventually repatriated to their native St. Croix. Today, Frederiksted is called "Freedom City" by its grassroots residents.

During the search of the town now, in 1972, a large number of Frederiksteders, especially friends and family, were forcibly picked up for questioning. Direct methods used by marshals and police intimidated the people. Martial law was in effect.

The search on foot and from the air and sea was on to find those five men by any and all means. Of the five, three had previously taken to the hills. At twenty years of age I had lived in the rain forest for a few months prior to September 6. Another two had also taken to the hills shortly before the incident. The local police were well aware of this.

Thirty-six hours after the attack two of the suspects, who had moved freely about the community until then, were arrested separately, one in Grove Place village, the other near Christiansted. Six days later, the remaining three fugitives including me, the youngest of the five, were captured in an old wooden building in Frederiksted where we had been holed up.

The fatigue-wearing, automatic-weapons-bearing search army had been baffled. How did the three elude this massive group of searchers that had everything cordoned off on the little island for almost a week? How could they possibly have made it into town without being seen or heard by anyone at all?

The three had been hemmed in at the end of the hills near the western shores. Their backs now to the sea and having no choice, they decided to push forward in the pitch of night. With moonlight blocked out by the forest's canopy of trees, they quietly slipped through the midst of their pursuers, using as a beacon the crackle of walkie-talkies and the nervous chatter of searchers camped in unfamiliar terrain. In spite of the low-flying aircraft continuously searching the hills the three spent the following day burrowed in treeless, low-brush terrain. Then, under cover of dark, they went unseen into Frederiksted. Dogs barked aggressively to alert the townspeople. But the three knew the backyards and crannies of their small town well. Thus, what would seem impossible was accomplished for at least a couple of days. And it held well until—it seems—someone noticed and reported an unusual movement at the previously checked, battened old house.

The capture was sensational. It was a clear day and just before high noon when the sun hung dead overhead. Helicopters hovered above and circled the aged structure, their loudspeakers blaring orders down to the people on the streets below. And, shouting impatiently, the searchers on the ground hurriedly ordered people from nearby homes. Soon the entire square block was empty save for the pursued and their pursuers. The latter all brandished varied weapons, and many wore grey bulletproof vests. They scampered about, ducking behind walls and anything that offered cover, as they surrounded the decrepit building in which the pursued were trapped. Clearly, the searchers seemed highly agitated, like teased dogs about to be unleashed. Some appeared more frantic than others and, if scared, understandably so. After all, nothing like this had ever before happened in the history of the United States Virgin Islands.

In 1917, during World War I the US had by threats and diplomatic negotiations finally arrogated the then-Danish West Indies from colonialist Denmark. The Danes were paid twenty-five million dollars for these three inhabited islands (St. Croix, St. Thomas, St. John) and the several surrounding islets. They were immediately renamed the US Virgin Islands. Their strategic location in the Caribbean Sea held much military significance for the United States. Naval bases were soon installed helping to, among other things, prevent further encroachment on the US Caribbean backyard by German submarines. Up into the 1930s, naval administration governed these militarily valued possessions. Economically they were, in the words of US President Herbert Hoover, a "poor yard."

However, by the late 1950s, with the tourist industry beginning to flourish in the hands of "Continentals" (white Americans) and land prices rising rapidly, all remainders of economic self-sufficiency, including sugarcane fields and subsistence farming, were being discouraged and/or removed. At the same time, an influx of large-scale corporations was underway to the harsh replacement of native-owned small businesses. The importation of foodstuff, especially from American-owned companies, increased dramatically to sustain what is today a totally dependent consumer population. The territory's license plates now proudly displayed the label "US Tropical Playground," later upgraded to "American Paradise."

By way of economic progress, local politicians passed "tax-holiday" laws to lure greater investments to the islands. Tourism benefitted from the exemptions. Also, a nascent industrialization was born with, for example, watch assembly factories, a bauxite processing plant, and an oil refinery. This was *prima facie* good economics for the American investors. Unfortunately, however, native business owners went unprotected and sadly many ended up government employees. Land also went unpreserved for locals so that many of them today can no longer afford a home of their own. Land prices and real estate taxes, together with building materials and other living costs, have become virtually oppressive to the average native now. Consequently, many Virgin Islanders have been emigrating to the United States in search of greener pastures which many never find.

The schools have been emphasizing the value of status-quo tourism, urging students to smile with the money-spending visitors. Yet, the education system has historically failed miserably to prepare or interest, especially secondary students, in management and ownership of the tourist industry from its onset. Otherwise perhaps today natives might be more involved in its advertisement, administration, and ownership. And Virgin Islands youths might have a deeper sense of dignity and a greater feeling towards inheritance of a community wherein tourism is the appointed economic backbone.

True, locals wave politely to welcome tourists and smile with a good heart, though at times duplicitously on the streets where seasonally they jostle with their guests for position on the sidewalk. Imagine how much more meaningful could be the smiles and welcome if natives were a substantive part of this private industry, how much more respectful of tourists youths would be could they speak of their families owning hotels and operating tourist-related businesses. Instead, they display their disenchantment in unacceptable ways. For example, not long ago some junior high schoolers were said to have sprayed tourists with mace and caused problems in and around gift shops on Main Street, a famous tourist thoroughfare. One may assume that this sort of behavior says more than meets the eye.

Tourism is said to be good for the islands and politicians exhort the public to support it, but do Virgin Islanders truly feel themselves psychologically and economically related to it? I recall how, as a youngster and wayward "street rebel," I felt in my heart that there was nothing in tourism for natives and that the community was "owned" by outsiders. For example, whenever I walked the streets with my shirt off or unbuttoned, the police insisted that I "dress properly." Of course, it is their duty to enforce such laws, but I always argued back that tourists often walked about shirtless or in brassiere-like tops and skimpy bottoms, yet no one told them to "dress properly."

In fact, my very first time in jail resulted from one such argument. It was on St. Thomas, where the majority of cruise ships come to port. An officer slapped my face in the middle of an argument about buttoning up my shirt on Main Street. I had just turned eighteen and had to sleep in jail that night. After that I started acting more and more like I had no reason to smile. Such attitudes are not the natural ways of Virgin Islanders. We are traditionally a friendly people, and God-loving community.

Anyhow, although the local government is making efforts to create low and moderate income housing, many natives remain landless and thus "homeless" in what is ironically called the "American Paradise." And, equally ironic, many of them seek refuge in the illusion that, as American citizens (since 1926), they are "better than" their fellow Afro-Caribbean West Indian people whom they contemptuously call "aliens." Thus, by some contrived consciousness and an illusory state of continued well-being, the natives have always been reported as being complacent, even happy.

It is understandable, then, why such surprise and great shock reverberated throughout the local and mainland communities when the Fountain Valley incident occurred. Indeed, this was a stunningly violent and awful tragedy that took innocent human lives and impacted painfully on many families and the community as a whole. It was a terrible crime and I shall always regret that it ever happened, that so many lives were lost.

But there were a certain few who quickly adjusted to the loss of lives, while assuming greater concern for the life of the tourist industry itself, the anointed icon of the islands' economy. Little attention, if any, was given to the cause of the incident. And fear generated by desecration of the icon amounted to public hysteria and was fed sensationally from government leaders and private concerns down to law enforcers, who were apparently made to feel responsible for what had happened. Now the police had set about to find those five men believed to have dared to desecrate the sacredness of it which act caused immediate collapse of tourism. Such daring men excited great anxiety and agitation, fear even, in their pursuers. And three of the five were still not apprehended.

Who knew what next the pursued would do, especially now that they were cornered. The agitated commands to "come out with hands up" blared from bullhorns above and on the ground. The door opened and the three men emerged with their "hands up" as ordered. No weapons could be found in the old wooden building.

Burning up from tropical midday heat within the closed tin-roof structure, I was shirtless in torn blue jeans and socks-less combat boots as I stepped into the sunlit dirt yard. The relieved, yet high-adrenaline police soldiers approached us cautiously and then suddenly rushed us. They shackled our wrists behind, chained our legs, and dragged us three into separate vehicles. They then took us to an unusual place.

It was not to the police station, or to the jail. It was to the site of the attack, to the Fountain Valley (now Carambola) Golf Clubhouse. As I would learn later, a temporary special interrogation center was set up here. As I limply negotiated my fettered steps through the patio and pro shop area of the resort, I saw smug faces that I recognized and others which I did not. Prosecutors, such as the then-Virgin Islands attorney general, Ronald Tonkin, high-ranking police officials and other government functionaries, both black and white, mingled in the area.

I was taken into an adjacent back room. With hands cuffed behind the back and feet chained, I was made to sit on a wooden chair. The interrogation began. Following the preliminary questions of name, next of kin, etc., I repeatedly told my interrogators that I would not answer their questions. I wanted to see a lawyer. I was adamant. This went on for about half an hour. The main interrogator was a Negro FBI. Getting no way, he left the room. I was now with four Virgin Islands policemen.

Michael A. Joseph, Esq.

These four repeated questions and accusations, and I likewise denied them. Soon they removed my boots and replaced
the chains on my legs with a pair of handcuffs that held my bare
ankles close together. Then one officer got behind the chair and
grabbed each side of my large bushy Afro, controlling my rising from the seat. To each negative response that I gave to their
questions, they banged me about the neck, arms, stomach, and
legs with fists and a police baton. Then the leader of the four
reached for an electric cattle prod. He applied this shocker to
every sensitive zone of my upper body, including the chest nip-
ples, the lips, and eyelids.

I screamed not only from pain but as though they should
have mercy. I was naive. For I had absolutely no idea that worse
would come. And what did come is something which I could
not at the time, not even by a figment of the imagination, have
thought humanly possible. Nor would I today, in maturity, and
especially since I have overcome its trauma, ever wish the experience on my worst enemy. And, just like I tried then, so would I
today prefer death to the experience. For what follows did in fact
happen—no matter how unbelievable or humanly unimaginable.

In a matter of time, my body had strangely become somewhat inured to the beatings, although not at all to the shocking.
But I remained defiant, responding to their questions with nasty
curses even about their poor mothers, who had nothing to do
with it. At one point the leader told me that I had "killed those
people like an animal." Where I got the calm and deliberateness
from, I do not know. But I defiantly looked him in the eye and
calmly, but as abrasively as possible said, "You is the animal
fo' wa yo' d'ween to me." He reacted with a punch to my right
cheek, drawing blood. I could tell that was not what he wanted
to do, lose his cool and draw blood. He backed away almost
instantly, as though in disgust with his reaction.

Then, a subordinate stepped closer to me. He drew a
revolver, cocked its hammer, and pointed the cold barrel onto
my right temple. He said if I did not talk, he would shoot and
then say I tried to escape. But by now I did not care. I began by
slowly pulling my head backward, feigning wide-eyed fear and

210

whimpering, "No, man, no . . . please, please!" until my head touched the chest of the one standing behind me. Then suddenly I jolted my head forward in collision with the cocked-hammer weapon. But the accident did not happen.

Noticing this move, the leader ordered the gun put away. He then reached for my crotch and tore wide open a small hole that was already in my pants. I wore no underwear and was exposed. He began to shock me down there. He would also squeeze my testicles in his large hand and, upon releasing them, apply the shocker. My screams and tears were genuine and involuntary, having nothing to do with begging mercy. Yet I continued to deny knowledge of what they asked about the events of the sixth of September.

Then I was taken down to the smooth concrete floor. The remains of my dungarees were pulled down to my ankles. The officer at my head kept my hair firmly in his grip and transferred me from chair to floor in this manner. After my trousers were pulled down, the one who had used the revolver tactic grabbed hold of my cuffed ankles. I was now being shocked down the legs and up between the buttocks, with the leader continuing to wield the electric prod. Meanwhile the fourth officer attempted to pry open my mouth on orders of the leader, who had tried to insert the shocker.

If any one of them was obviously reluctant to put me through this experience it was this fourth officer. He knew me. I had serviced his car before as an auto mechanic apprentice. Aside from this, it seemed that his heart was not into what they were doing. Not that he did not thump me earlier on. Now he was poking his index finger and thumb between my clenched jaw. When he almost succeeded in prying open my mouth, I bit down in desperation. My teeth cut my inner cheek, but squeezed his fingers good. He jerked them away, telling the leader that he could not get my mouth open, that I was biting. He was not really trying.

Throughout all this, the one with my hair in his grip and the other at my feet were struggling to keep me stretched out on my back. This position was quite uncomfortable, with the hands

Michael A. Joseph, Esq.

cuffed behind. And I just kept fighting back, jerking and biting, rather than to lie there passively.

Then the fourth laid a towel over my mouth and nostrils and helped the other two to hold me down. The leader began slowly pouring water from a silver basin through the towel and down my mouth and nose holes. They would let me up for air when I was near drowning. I would even fake drowning. But they seemed to know when it was for real. So the premature body jerks or sudden stillness did not work. They simply went about the task over and over, reminding me that they had all the water and time in the world. But, whenever they opened the door for one to fetch another basin of water or to let somebody in, I would scream to the top of my lungs even though they would not be doing anything to me at the moment. I just wanted the people in the pro shop, particularly the head honchos, to hear and come stop what I was going through. But nobody came to stop it.

I remember an officer coming into the room, apparently to see how things were coming along. There was a respite to retrieve more water. I knew the officer since childhood. His younger brother and I were close companions. I knew the officer's mother and family well. If someone should save me, it would be he. I lay naked on that wet floor at the feet of this man. Looking up at him and calling him by his nickname, I begged, pleaded, and literally cried for him to stop his partners from what they were doing to me. It was a personal appeal, reflecting our knowing each other's family. For one split moment it appeared to affect him and he looked sadly down at me. But he quickly composed himself and said he could do nothing unless I told them what I knew. He promptly left the room. I screamed again. The water had arrived.

Intermittently the prod was applied. It was more jolting now that my body and the floor were wet. But I kept denying knowledge of anything.

Then the treatment took another twist. I was forced to sit up. A plastic bag was placed over my head and the wet towel was wrapped around its end at my throat. Then—wham—the baton would be whacked across my abdomen knocking out the wind.

212

I sucked in air and the bag immediately stuck to my mouth and nostrils. In spite of the officers restraining me, at least once in desperation I managed to contort my body and somehow force my cuffed hands far enough up and around from my back for a middle finger to poke a hole in the bag, letting in precious air. This caused cuts on the wrists from strain on the handcuffs and a sore shoulder that did not hurt as much then as it would for many weeks later. Bags were changed and the treatment repeated over and over.

The water, plastic bag, and shocks were intermixed now. They used psychological means, too, such as showing me a bundle of weapons they claimed one of the codefendants had directed them to. They also told me a variety of things supposedly extracted from codefendants and persons who were previously picked up and released. Some of this information was lies which I could not bring myself to confirm and therefore tie myself into having actually shot anyone. But I did not know how long this thing would last. Throughout the ordeal I had really lost all sense of time. I had not seen food all day but was not hungry. I was just terrorized and too much in pain. Exhausted. The moment came when I could take no more. I agreed to give a statement in order to bring this thing to an end.

They pulled up my wet, mangled dungarees, removed the cuffs from my ankles, and took me out of the room and across the adjacent pro shop to a large restroom area. It was dark night outside. The head honchos seen in early afternoon milling about were no longer around. In the bathroom area sat the Afro-American FBI at a small table. I sat and was joined by one of the four local policemen.

The earlier questionings and various accusations had painted a picture of what happened during the attack of the golf resort. I told what I thought fit the picture but mixed with my truths. The FBI and the policemen wrote my statement. But the FBI man was not pleased with it and threatened to—in his words—"throw me back to the wolves." Not wanting this I quickly gave another version that fit exactly what I believed they wanted to hear. This time I tied myself into doing things I did not actually do. I refused to sign it. They threatened "to the wolves" again if did not sign. But they did not return me to room where I spent the afternoon.

They dressed me in clothes taken from the pro shop. An extra-large, expensive blue jersey swallowed my five-foot-seven, one-hundred-and-fifty pound frame, and lemon-lime Bermuda shorts reached baggily to my calves. I was barefoot. It must have been around midnight. (Although mine was a territorial crime, Virgin Islands capital crimes are heard in the US District Court according to a mixture of territorial and federal laws. Recently, though, the VI legislature decided with congressional approval that all territorial crimes will go to the territorial court effective October 1, 1991.)

I stood in chains before that judge and do not remember speaking. Perhaps a head shake or nod "yes" or "no," but I considered him part of the scheme, perhaps because he was white and whites had been killed. The two men arrested with me were also there. It was the first time I had seen them since we were taken to interrogation. I do not recall hearing them speak to the judge either. Judging from how they appeared, I knew they had suffered a similar fate as I.

Why was I so quiet? To think of it, I guess, one would have had to experience the depth of terror that I knew at that moment in order to appreciate my speech—lessness. But I remember of wanting to go straight to jail and into bed, instead of back to that dreaded place of interrogation. And only God could tell me that the judge did not know something was wrong. I knew that he observed my bruised and swollen cheek, how I was dressed, and my broken, flat spirit. He did not ask, though. And it is he who would later preside over my suppression of evidence hearing and the trial.

After the arraignment I was taken back to the Fountain Valley Golf Club interrogation center and into the same room. Now, they wanted to know about some "Two-Fifty Savage" gun. I knew of no such weapon. I was falling asleep during questioning. They beat me and used the electric prod. I still denied knowledge of the gun, and just could not stay awake.

214

They took me out of the room and into the pro shop. The two codefendants were shackled to green cots at separate corners of the large shop; they were resting or sleeping. Away from them, I was placed flat on my back on an army cot. And spread-eagled, all four extremities were handcuffed to it. The police said I could sleep. I dozed off instantly. But I was awakened just as quickly with a rifle butt slamming into my groin. A sharp pain sped throughout that area. I screamed and bawled as I strained against the shackles to reach at my groin. I knew nothing about a "Two-Fifty Savage." Each time I dozed off, the rifle butt blow was repeated. Then one of the codefendants shouted across the shop for them to leave me alone. Apparently trying to save me from further punishment, he hollered, "De di'n doh noht'n! I kill ahll de people. I kill ahll de moddaf . . . people!" But they did not pay him any mind. The policeman slamming my groin was the one who had held onto my hair throughout the earlier sessions. A couple of other officers stood about. Eventually I said that I knew where the gun was, although I knew no such thing. I just wanted to sleep and be left alone. I was painfully worn out. I told them the gun was stashed in the hills. As it was almost dawn they decided to let me sleep for a moment, and when enough light was up, they would take me for this mysterious "Two-Fifty Savage" gun.

I took them several miles to a foothill where I pointed out a concealed "Four-Ten" shotgun. They jumped at it, cradled it, certain they had the murder weapon. This was okay with me because I knew the shotgun could not be connected to any crime. Besides, I figured, I would be spared any more of that I had gone through.

They drove back smugly to the place of interrogation. I do not recall being hungry. But I know that they never offered me any food to find out if I wanted to eat. Still in leg chains and handcuffs from the drive, they put me to sit on the cot. They asked me to sign the statement given the previous night. I refused. They threatened and cajoled, left and returned. I still refused. Then they were actually going to take me back into that dreaded room. At that point I decided to sign it. The thought of going back into that room did something to my mind and soul. At this point I would sign anything they put before me. I signed the statement but with R-a-p-h-a-e-l rather than with "Rafael," the only way I spelled and wrote my name as phonetically taught to me by my father since I was five years old. To this day, the police, the courts, and prison system spell my name with the "ph." After I had signed the statement, codefendants and I were kept chained spread-eagled to the army cots.

In the early afternoon, I saw a government doctor. A couple of the officers escorted me into the restroom area to this gynecologist. He appeared to be a Spaniard. I humbly showed him my cut wrists and bruised cheek. I told him that I ached all over and wanted to go to a hospital. He felt about my body, perhaps for broken bones, documented nothing, gave me some aspirins, and left. (Almost one year later this good doctor told the court I was constipated.)

Later on in the day, the three of us codefendants were flown by seaplane to the archaic fort in St. Thomas, forty miles from St. Croix. The two other codefendants, who had been arrested earlier, were already at the fort. Dressed in green jumpsuits, we were kept in separate but adjoining cells. The three of us who were captured together were kept handcuffed (hands in front) in the cells. We were isolated from other prisoners. We hollered to one another and learned that all five had suffered the same or similar fate in interrogation.

I was extremely depressed for the first couple of days, saying very little and barely eating the slop fed through the bars by the police officers. They actually required me to eat and use the slop pail with my hands cuffed. For the first few days I was not allowed out of the cell. There was no flush toilet, shower, or running water in the cell. The slop pail was stinking. No family member or friend was permitted to visit during those first few days.

I was visited by a Continental, court-appointed attorney shortly after I had arrived at the fort. He had flown in from St. Croix. Subsequently I saw an intern and a nurse whom had never seen before or would ever see again. The nurse was a St.

Thomian and the novice doctor was an African American. I told of my bodily aches and showed them the now partially scabbed, lacerated wrists, which were aggravated by periodic rubbing of the handcuffs. They, too, ignored my complaints, wrote down nothing, gave me a couple of tablets, and left. I was messed up about this. I felt that I was being treated like the worst thing on earth, and as though there was a conspiracy going on. I bristled at every police and government worker with unbelievable anger and hatred.

Then came time for the Five to go for a preliminary hearing downtown. Legs chained and hands cuffed, we went into the courtroom in the smelly jumpsuits. The judge was a Crucian (St. Croix born) who has since retired. He ordered the chains and handcuffs removed in the courtroom. This done, what happened next was an expression of rage by five very bitter young men who felt the entire world was against them and who didn't care about the consequences of their action.

One of the Five launched into a tirade of what he was going through in raw West Indian dialect laced heavily with abusive language. Each of the codefendants joined in cursing out his feelings. There was confusion. The judge ordered quiet, but pandemonium broke loose. We turned over benches, physi-cally struggling with the marshals and police, nastily cursing them, the judge, and the establishment. Outnumbered, we were subdued, chained up, and removed from the courtroom. I had absolutely no respect for the court or government people at the moment.

But this judge was different. He seemed to know that some-thing was wrong and wanted to find out. We were brought back into the courtroom after the benches and everything had been set back into place. Judge Almeric Christian, the only native federal judge the Virgin Islands would know to this day, sug-gested that the shackles could be removed if we agreed not to explode again. The judge told us to take our time and explain what was wrong. We agreed.

Atrociously inarticulate at the time, I talked angrily and rapidly in my Crucian dialect in a single but not necessarily ordered flow: "Dey bete me up . . . Po' wahta dong meh throat . . . Shahk meh . . . cohva meh head wid plastic . . . Cyan see meh modda an' dahta . . . Deh gahmeh lakkup widda han'cuff. . . Ah huhtin in de nite an' cyan bade oh noht'n an' eatin' bahd," etc., etc. The other four told their part, too. Judge Christian was concerned mainly with the treatment at the fort. In no uncertain terms, he ordered better treatment which we promptly got. No more all-day confinement or handcuffs in the cells. We also got visits right away and fresh fruits.

But tension and bitterness remained high between the police guards and us. Fights were regular. One night we refused to lock in. A terrible fight ensued in which we commandeered the only entry to our isolated section of the fort. The police, tired of being repelled, simply hurled canisters of tear gas into the cellblock and made us spend the rest of the night in the fumes. We were removed the next morning, and electric fans were used to blow away the remnants of the gas. Sometimes we were provoked. But often we were the ones creating problems, perhaps as a general "payback" which some officers innocently could not understand. How five men could be so tenaciously rebellious against the larger group, the odds, was unbelievable. It was as though we were fueled by purely negative emotions which, paradoxically, gave us a feeling of being "right." Beaten down, we would rise again to fight, to curse, to defy. And we felt right to carry on like this. We seemed to strengthen one another in this mind-set.

In December they split us up by transferring one codefendant and me to the Christiansted penitentiary—the very one that Queen Mary had set out after. We mixed with sentenced prisoners who stood by us. I got along relatively well, except when a young Hispanic guard fired several rounds from his tower at a codefendant and me in the open yard. Shots literally whizzed by us, pinging off a background wire fence, as other prisoners scampered for cover or dove to the ground. The guard claimed that we were picking up a small brown envelope thrown over the prison perimeter fence to us by a passerby. No such envelope was ever found, although the officer could have been correct.

But to fire shots so loosely in the prison yard! It is a miracle no one got hit. The then-acting warden, I think, Police Captain Andino, immediately removed the guard from the prison reservation. He was fired. Then, by April 1973, all five codefendants were removed to a brand new isolated structure at Estate Anna's Hope, St. Croix. It was a small concentration-like camp with no other prisoners. That same, belligerent mind-set was revived, especially after the suppression of evidence hearing.

The suppression hearing began shortly after the move. We each took the stand and told the court of the torture in detail. My attorney, Frank Padilla, surprised me when he pulled a plastic bag from his back pocket and told me to put it over my head to show the court how the police had done it. I refused hysterically. I could not believe he was crazy enough to expect me to put that bag over my head.

Anyhow, one police officer named Tony Powell surprisingly admitted on the stand that he was present in the restroom where a codefendant was being tortured. He admitted to punching the codefendant, but denied participating in the other atrocious treatment which he said he witnessed. (Powell did not stay in the police long after his testimony.)

A recently returned Vietnam veteran, Dennis McIntosh, at the time employed at the VI Department of Public Works, took the stand. He told of helping a friend, a police officer, build a house. While working on the new house, the officer had told McIntosh of having witnessed the torture. Of course, when called to the stand, the officer denied it. (After his testimony, McIntosh did not last as a government employee.)

I think it was during this time that nationally renowned defense attorney William Kunstler put one of the four prosecutors on the stand. Somehow Kunstler had managed to obtain information concerning a conversation at the district attorney's office between a prosecutor named Sax and one of the police officers who had tortured me. Kunstler asked Sax whether it was true that the officer had admitted that codefendants were tortured; that the treatment was necessary because the natives were his people and he knew how to deal with his own kind

219

Michael A. Joseph, Esq.

(Sax was Anglo-American); and whether the officer said he thought I would have been the first to break, but that I was the last. Prosecutor Sax did not deny that there was a private conversation between him and the officer, or that the officer possibly said these things. Sax, however, said all this with a big "but . . ." Mr. Sax explained that he could not clearly understand what the officer was saying because during the conversation, there was construction work going on outside the office window and a jackhammer was making noise.

The FBI agent who had interrogated me admitted on the stand that I had asked to speak to an attorney. He said, however, that I later voluntarily gave him the statement and helped find the shotgun. His one admission of my asking for a lawyer gave credence to the rest. No other officer admitted anything. They all said that everything went according to law and that the five codefendants were cooperative. The judge believed them.

Judge Warren H. Young ruled that he did not believe we were tortured, or coerced in any way. He agreed, however, that my right to an attorney was violated. Accordingly, the judge threw out or suppressed any evidence the police claimed they got from me, including the statement and the shotgun. But the judge held in evidence any statement and other materials extracted from the other defendants. This included four so-called confessions and weapons which would be later used in a trial. Judge Young was the same one before whom I had dispiritedly stood in terror for arraignment on the darkest night of my life.

After the unfavorable ruling, the codefendants became ever more unruly and intolerant. All through our stay at Anna's Hope we had problems with the prison guards who transferred from the Christiansted penitentiary to watch and feed us. The food was cooked and sent down from the penitentiary. At this point we did not tolerate the slight provocations which we had managed to ignore during the suppression hearing. For example, some guards had made a custom of holding back our food and serving it greasy cold and sometimes contaminated. It appeared that a few "old-school" officers found it okay to agitate and oppress us. After all, the media had sensationally popularized the hateful, terribly violent image of the hateful killer monsters who deserved absolutely nothing good and our own behavior had furthered that ugly image. So, a few ignorant and unprofessional guards thought that any mistreatment was justified.

I must not give the impression that the majority of local prison guards thought or behaved this way. But our behavior, or the orders of a willful officer, drew them into problems with us. Nor did their leader, then-assistant warden Richard A. Schrader, condone mistreatment. From my personal observation, Mr. Schrader is a kind man. In fact, he amazed me by not being vindictive even after I had, for instance, outright disrespected him, or had a fight with one of his officers.

And fight we did. We were downright rebellious, bitter, and angry. We defied any officer, rule, or regulation. We dared the guards to make us do anything in the camp we did not want to do. This caused problems, as the officers attempted to enforce rules and regulations. Just one of us would defy an instruction and the rest of us invariably endorsed his defiance. This attitude often caused conflicts within myself, as though the heart was telling me to do one thing and the mind another. Evading these inner discords, I would act defiant even if reluctantly. So, right or wrong—remember we were always "right"—we defied our keepers in unison. Win or lose, we fought with such heart that we often held ground against the odds until more officers arrived. Things got so out of hand that all of us, officers and prisoners, ended up in closed court before Judge Young. The judge ordered the Department of Public Safety, which in those days governed the prison system in addition to the police, to altogether remove itself from our keep.

A set of US marshals was now put in charge of Anna's Hope camp. And the court made certain concessions, such as more and better visiting privileges and allowed our food to come from a native restaurant. The federal officers were all large African Americans. The ones who were not solid and six feet were sturdy and robust. Things changed. But we were in such a state of rebellion, we put on some heavy fights even with those marshals.

Michael A. Joseph, Esq.

I had gotten to like one of them, though. Of course I could not admit this. I was supposed to hate all police. In fact, whenever I was seen chatting with him you could hear the curses of my codefendants. I was checked. I tried to psych myself into anger with the marshal and say nothing to him for a couple of days. But I liked him. It is natural for a person to be attracted to human love and compassion, which was what that marshal displayed to me. He would talk with rather than at me. I never got the feeling that he was judging or condemning me. I was awed by his discernment of the inner conflicts I struggled with, although I never confirmed that his analysis of me was correct. In fact, I denied that he knew what he was saying. But, in looking back, that marshal was like the counselor or clergyman that never visited the camp. And he never gave up, as seen in the letter he wrote to me a few years after I was convicted and exiled to a US prison. Oddly, although brief, our best chats took place not necessarily at the camp, but when he was escorting me from the transport van or the holding cage into the courtroom and back.

The trial commenced mid-1973. It was the same judge again. The Honorable Warren H. Young, born and reared in suburban America, could not relate to or understand the defendants well, especially our Caribbean dialect, and cultural grassroots ways. We were aliens to his upper-class values and customs, to his political outlook and racial upbringing. Besides, the Five were convinced that the judge had conspired to keep a lid on the torture, and that he had in effect arrived at a conviction with the ruling that it did not occur. Nothing could make us five unlearned, misdirected, angry young men believe otherwise.

It was a jury trial that lasted over a month. The trial was a tumultuous one. It was characterized by frequent outbursts fraught with curse words and scuffles with marshals in the courtroom. Then, chained and cuffed, we were brought back into the courtroom individually, and sentenced to eight consecutive life terms each. I was the last to go back in. I had noticed that each time a codefendant was removed from the holding cage, he was not brought back in. So, I expected to meet them in the courtroom, but they were not there when I arrived.

222

Judge Young was sitting at his bench, waiting for me. A small number of spectators—some crying, and some smirking—were in the courtroom, too. The judge asked if I had anything to say before sentencing. Wrapped in leg and waist chains I stared at him and angrily said that there was nothing I could say which he did not already know. This I recall saying. *The San Juan Star* quoted me as saying that "the war has just begun," or something to that effect. Perhaps I did say something like that. But I was certainly not quoted accurately, since I did not speak like that and the words "has begun" sound much too proper for me at the time. Anyway, arrogant and in anger, I turned my back to the bench as the sentence was imposed. Brash and ignorant immaturity, neither the sentence nor anything else happening in my life would sink in until I began to grow away from the mentality that dominated that phase of my life.

After sentencing, I was taken through an unusual exit of the courtroom and ended up in a red, white, and blue US mail van. It was snugly backed up to an unused side exit downstairs to receive me. The other codefendants were already sitting chained up in back of the windowless van. We could not see outside. Our supporters awaited our exit in front of the courthouse where, as usual, the Ford van that regularly transported the Five to and from the courthouse was parked. The supporters could see the mail wagon driving away from the hither side, but had no idea we were tucked into it. It appeared to be picking up or delivering mail. The mail van slowly drove away as it secretly took us to a seaplane that flew us to Puerto Rico, to the Rio Piedras Penitentiary, in transit to five separate US prisons. Thus, within an hour of being convicted, we were sentenced to life in prison and exiled off island.

While I was in solitary confinement at the Rio Piedras Penitentiary, my trial lawyer, Ronald Mitchell, visited me. I learned that at least four jurors had recanted their verdicts. Within hours of the court's release of the predominantly native jury, a juror named Rodgers went to a Frederiksted activist to dictate a renunciation of his "guilty" verdict. Rodgers swore to and signed the statement. By nighttime that same day, the jury foreman, Allick, went literally crying to his brother-in-law, a former legislator, to tell of his experience during the deliberation. Mr. Allick was against conviction until he received information that, if he did not change his vote to "guilty," he himself would be tried and jailed for perjury. Allick had failed to admit during voir dire examination that one of our defense attorneys was his godfather. Allick, too, now prepared and signed an affidavit renouncing his verdict.

Two female jurors also renounced their verdicts under oath. A young lady named Isaac had been the last one to change her vote to "guilty" when she, too, was told she would be charged and tried for perjury. Isaac had failed to admit during jury selection that her uncle had fathered a child with my elder sister. And juror Boulware stated that she eventually changed her "not guilty" position when she was informed, during the deliberation, that a charge against her daughter, that had been dismissed without prejudice, would be brought back up. The daughter, a college student, had been accused—unfairly, and on the basis of hearsay—of having given some after-the-fact help to persons who, as a political act, committed the first-ever bank robbery in the US Virgin Islands. This robbery took place on St. Thomas in 1970. All the people charged with it were in some way affiliated with the Frederiksted-based United Caribbean Association (UCA), a political organization for Virgin Islands self-determination, led by Mario Moorhead.

I understood why those jurors had changed their votes to "guilty." They felt they had to protect themselves and families from felonious records and possible prison terms. And I truly admired their courage for coming forward at once to renounce the verdict and the deliberation process.

It was revealed that one juror, who was the ex-wife of a police officer connected to the Fountain Valley case, would become ill during deliberations. In illness, she would be taken by the marshals from the deliberating room or from the hotel where the jurors were sequestered. Each time the sick juror returned she would pass on some tidbit of information concerning who would be charged and jailed for perjury or retried on old charges if their verdicts were not changed to "guilty." An evidentiary hearing brought these allegations to the fore. If this juror did behave as alleged, I could understand that too. After all, her ex-husband supported her children. Had we won the case, a slew of lawsuits would have followed and some police officers would likely have lost money and jobs that put bread on the table. Judge Young ruled against the jurors' renunciations.

The Fountain Valley case, resulting from a territorial or state crime tried in US District Court, was appealed to the Third Circuit US Court of Appeals in Pennsylvania. The conviction was affirmed. A writ of certiorari was filed in the US Supreme Court, pleading that the case, which was so full of discrepancies, be heard. The Supreme Court denied certiorari without an opinion. It is interesting that the United States Supreme Court would not hear a case as nationally known and sensationalized as the Fountain Valley case. One riddled with errors and discrepancies. Equally curious is why the Supreme Court would deny certiorari without an explanation.

In 1977 attorney Frank Padilla returned to my aid and filed a motion for sentence reduction or modification. Then, in a February 1978 memorandum, the sentencing judge, Judge Warren H. Young, refused to reduce the eight consecutive life terms. But, to my welcome surprise, he also suggested expedited/early parole for me alone. This recommendation implied that Judge Young had seen something in me or in my relation to the case to merit my eventual freedom. I have used the recommendation as incentive. And, frankly, I wish Judge Young was alive today to realize practical justification for his suggestion of leniency in my case.

Anyhow, by 1978, five years after arriving in the USA, I had begun to get over the dark anger, bitterness, and hatred which had consumed me. I was in a federal penitentiary with no other Virgin Islander, and to this day I travel my own path. I was growing on my own. I spent most of the first two years in some form of disciplinary lockup. During the initial phase they shipped me around a lot, so I was riding buses from state to state and prison "hole" (solitary) to prison hole. At times I would end up in a prison that I had passed through a couple of trips previously. All this was hard in a strange land, since mail sent to me at one prison would get to me while I was on my way to another. My family did not know where I was at any one time. The bus rides were mostly through East Coast and Midwest states. But I used the "bus therapy," as federal prisoners call it, to some educational benefit. I got to see some of America's most beautiful and resourceful landscape and, for the first time, I recognized some of the poverty in its countryside as I sat at bus windows gaping out. Seeing barefoot, snot-nosed white children who reminded me of the children back home, I realized for the first time that not all white people were rich.

I then spent the next sixteen months in solitary confinement at the notorious Leavenworth, Kansas, US penitentiary. I met all manner of men and freaks and witnessed seamy sides of man hitherto unimaginable to me. Today nothing fazes me.

I set out to study. I wanted to learn to read, write, and express myself better.

When I got out of the hole and into Leavenworth's general prison population, I was the youngest among the hardest of men there. And although I had a lot to learn in the sagacious ways of survival among such men, I was much sharper in the book sense than when I had first arrived in America. By the late 1970s I was reading Immanuel Kant and Bacon with a dictionary, and going to bed trying to figure out what they were saying. I enrolled in the education program and acquired a high school equivalency diploma (GED) and eventually a college degree in business administration. But independent study had perhaps the greater impact. For instance, Kant had put me on the path to governing my own life by principles founded on reason. And Francis Bacon checked me on my energies expended in dwelling on revenge.

I really used to spend a lot of time dwelling on how I would have liked to "pay back" those four Virgin Islands police officers who took me through the torturous experience. I spent many nights angrily plotting all sorts of ingeniously evil schemes for them. But, as I grew personally, intellectually, and spiritually, I found myself thinking less of wanting to hurt them, and more of wanting to understand why these publicly trusted four human beings behaved like they did.

As I recall Bacon to say, to dwell on revenge is to waste energies which otherwise could be put to positive use, and to execute revenge is to step down to the level of behavior of the one upon whom revenge is exacted. For me to desire revenge would be to step backward two decades into a life and mentality that I have worked so diligently to grow away from in maturity.

No, it was not revenge that I wanted anymore, but understanding of their behavior. In this way I could come to forgive those four men—just like I want to be forgiven for any harm or wrong which I indirectly or directly have done to any individual, family, or community in my misdirected adolescence.

I am aware that in order to truly appreciate forgiveness one must know how to forgive. And as I deeply desire forgiveness, so am I convinced those four officers want to forgive themselves and to be forgiven as human beings. They, like I, cannot forget what happened because it is not something you can simply will yourself to forget. I am sure they have contrived ways to suppress reflection on wrongdoing in order to escape its depressing recall. But it is only to face oneself, and to pray and/or talk it out, even indirectly, that we could all remove the depressing effects, if not the memory of our unacceptable conduct. And it must be done with fervent commitment to never again pass the path that caused our yearning for forgiveness.

It was not out of raw wickedness that those four men put me through such a God-forbidden experience. We must understand the times back then: the fear and hysteria in the atmosphere; the public outcry and loud demands for justice against the perpetrators of the Fountain Valley crime; the burden of responsibility placed squarely on the shoulders of the local police force to produce, as the adrenaline flowed within its ranks; the eagerness of the interrogators to break the case wide open and thus please the public and their superiors, etc., etc.

The officers were anxious to allay certain fears, both real and imagined. I vividly recall how zealously they tried to get me to

227

tell of two mysterious Cuban revolutionaries. I caught hell for not knowing who in the world were Pablo and Raul. I could not convince the officers that I knew no such names or Cubans. The interrogators kept insisting that I knew two Cuban revolutionaries who were involved in the attack on the golf resort. When finally they got through with me, I did not ever again want to hear the names Pablo and Raul, whoever they were supposed to be.

It seems that someone had given them information about possible Cuban involvement. The officers were so eager to burst open the case and please everyone that they went about this in a manner that was illegal and morally unacceptable. They apparently held that the end result of their conduct was to the common good. But to indulge in immorality does not contribute to society's improvement. Nor was their behavior, I am sure, conducive to their long-term inner peace. Neither did it ultimately enhance their careers.

None of them amounted to much on the police force. In fact, they are no longer with the department. Two of them retired with no more than a low grade or rank above their rank in 1972. The other two, for whatever reasons, left the force prematurely. It appears, then, they were not ultimately rewarded for their conduct, even though the judge's disbelief initially protected them. But not proving in a court of law that a thing happened does not necessarily mean that it did not happen, and vice versa. Perhaps the powers that be had some indirect confirmation that the police conduct did occur.

I know for sure that the matter weighed heavily on one of the four officers up to thirteen years later.

In November 1984 I was moved from federal prison to the Virgin Islands. I did so well coordinating the education program in the prison that I was allowed to go and speak to auditoriums full of sixth graders at a couple of St. Croix public schools. (I had acquired a certificate in paraprofessional counseling after three years training under a federal prison psychologist.) Eventually, in 1985, the warden granted me a short furlough. I spent the day at my mother's house and on the way back to the prison, my brother wanted to stop at my younger sister's home for a little while. My sister's husband is a veteran on the St. Croix police force. They had a visitor. Another officer was sitting at a table on the front porch. I had to pass by him to enter the house. Not recognizing the stranger, I said hello to him on my way in. Pointing to the officer, my brother-in-law asked me if I remembered him. I could not recognize the face, so he said the visitor's name. I was in good spirits, happy all over for the first time in thirteen years to be spending a brief outing with my family. I spontaneously reached out and shook the visitor's hand, inquiring about his well-being. He was one of the four officers.

I held his hand, which hung limply in mine, and noticed his heavy countenance. He was not all relaxed and we both knew what produced that obviously concerned expression on his face. But I was not about to let anything spoil my day, not even by leaving him with his uneasy feelings. Instead, I looked him in the eye with friendliness and said something like, "The past is past. I've grown away from the past and don't want to be held to it, forget the past. I'm looking to the future. I want to get out of prison and will need people like you to help me." Instantly a bright smile came upon that brother's face. His hand now gripped mine as he assured me that I could count on him. Noticeably relaxed, he began to tell me that he had heard of the good things I was doing with the prison education program and encouraged me to keep up the work towards eventual release. At first he had been so silent. Now he was talking with such ease.

He was a happy man. Had he been wicked, he would not have been so instantly relieved and felicitous. I, too, was glad for the chance to meet and talk with him. We did not talk outright about what happened many years ago. But we did deal with it through feelings exchanged and understood only by the two of us at that particular moment. He knows that I hold no ill will toward him. And I felt good about that.

I do know that my greeting had been completely spontaneous. Had I held malice or ill will towards that officer, the vibes would have manifested in some way right then. But I could find no hostile feelings and bad thoughts in my heart and mind towards the four officers, or anyone else for that matter.

For this reason I deliberately decline to mention any of the four officers' names, or the names of anyone else whose mention here could cause the slightest negative effect. I want them all to live their lives in the now and not to be judged by the past.

I ask no admission of them but that they face themselves. I assure them that I have been doing so for many years now. May they know that I, too, seek forgiveness. And that I understand. This understanding shines a welcome light on the darkness that once consumed me. May a similar light shine within them and others toward me too.

Epilogue

I did not intend to write an epilogue. But Discovery Channel aired "Moby Dick" about the facts behind Herman Melville's 1851 classic *Moby Dick*. And I saw an imperative parallel.

The program revealed that a stupendous bull whale twice attacked the *Essex*, a whaler out of Nantucket Island, battering away more than twelve feet off its bow. The *Essex* quickly sunk some one thousand miles west of South America. The cabin boy later wrote a book about it.

He penned how the crew harangued the youthful captain into reversing his order to navigate their lifeboat with the currents and winds toward the island of Tahiti. They claimed it was infested with cannibals. That prejudice led them to try to reach South America against the elements and they all starving to near death. To survive, they, themselves, became cannibals. The cabin boy recounted his revulsion at the picking of straws to kill and eat fellow crew. In time, he picked the short one and had to kill his only boyhood friend. When rescued, the few survivors were sucking on dry bones for last bits of human marrow.

On return to Nantucket, the captain became a detached lantern-bearing night watchman insanely hoarding food. The cabin boy could not fathom the contradiction of expressing one's good heart with the sheer horror it could bring. He articulated that tragedy in a single poetic line: "Oh, how many good hearts have ceased to be in consequence of it."

So piercing was that insight, I drafted an epilogue based on Rafie ceasing to be in consequence of his good heart. I told friends my book finishes in "a whale of a story." Strangely though, microcassettes of long nights of dictation sat in my car's glove box. A draining feeling enveloped me, and then I had an epiphany. I was portraying Rafie only as player on the stage of

231

Michael A. Joseph, Esq.

Fountain Valley. And I remembered the words of our physical education teacher: "What bothers me, though, is the loss of Rafie. Rafie had so much to offer. What a shame!"

Sometimes, rather than waiting out doubts of his fellows, one chooses to cease being on seeing in himself life's innate worth.

Our teacher's sadness inspired a description of my brother within a different syntax:

So Long Song In Another Key

In Rich Fertile Heat Of Life's Core
Traveler is Conceived To surface Unafraid
Complete
Cuddling Crater's Edge He dipped the Glow
And Kindled his Tip To Blow at the Wind
Browsing Horizon
Ideal paths he Trekked Save Teasing Vices
In Bold Smoke Rings
Pleasing face Smiled Soothing Singe
Of Wishful Thinking In quest of Core Harmony
Paradoxical Stumble Marooning Pocketful
Of Sparkle
Freefalling into Rich Heat
Beckoned To Bypass Besieged
Crater's Edge
Floating into Core's
Vastness
Finally
Harmony

Notes

Overture
1. Nobel Laureate John Steinbeck (*American Literature,* McDougal, Littell & Co., 1989 pg. 426).
2. *The Laws of the United States Territories and Affiliated Jurisdictions* (Stanley K. Laughlin, Lawyers Cooperative Pub., 1995 pg. vii, hereafter *"Laws of Affiliated Jurisdictions* at . . .").
3. *Alexander Hamilton* (Ron Chernow, Penguin Press, 2004 pgs. 8; 697, hereafter "Chernow at . . .").
4. Chernow at 26.
5. *Id.* at 29.

   Alex Hamilton's tribute to St. Croix was initially published in 1840 in a biography of him by eldest son James. While Alex is assumed to have been born in the British colony of Nevis, Chernow says he found no documentary verification other than the fact he did migrate at eight years old from that island to St. Croix. There is oral history Alex was the son of George Washington. It is verified Washington visited Barbados with his father when he was about fourteen. Several students of Caribbean history believe Alex as a result may have been born in Barbados or Aruba. An elder informed me Alex's actual age was altered by two years to hide that truth. Chernow noted this alteration, but offered an alternative basis for the enigma of the real birth date (1755 or 1757?). He says Alex lowered his age because he was embarrassed to appear "older" than his college mates.
6. *Id.* at 8.
7. *The Virgin Islands Daily News* (March 5, 2006). As for hedonism in St. Croix, consider this: "In Herrhut, Germany, in a museum hangs a large oil painting with blue background and a stately black man clasping a Creole hymnbook . . . The portrait is titled *The Black Evangelist,* the title given to Cornelius, a master mason who laid the cornerstones for six early Moravian churches."
8. Chernow at 8.

PART ONE
Chapter One
1. *New York Daily News*: "Slaughter in Paradise" (July 17, 2005).

2. *Government of the Virgin Islands v. Gereau,* 11 VI 265, 272 (3rd Cir. 1974).
3. *St. Croix Avis* (February 29, 2004).
4. *America's Virgin Islands: A History of Rights and Wrongs* (William W. Boyer, Carolina Academic Press, Durham, NC, 1983 pg. 313, hereafter "Boyer at . . .").
5. *U S Constitution, Article 1: Section 2 Clause 3; Section 9 Clause 1.*

    Madison's quotation is from *The Summer of 1787* (David O. Stewart, Simon and Shuster 2007, pgs. 69; 305–06). General information about, and quotations from, the framers are supplied by and thus credited to *The Summer of 1787*, and *The Federalist Papers* (James Madison, Alexander Hamilton, and John Jay, edited by Isaac Kramnick, Penguin Books 1987).
6. *Webster's Dictionary of the American Language* (2nd ed. 1972); *Black Skin White Masks* (Frantz Fanon, Grove Press, NY, 1967 pg. 194, hereafter "*Black Skin* at . . ."). Fanon says this reveals a "[m]oral consciousness . . . fracture[d] . . . into a bright part and an opposing black part. In order to achieve morality, it is essential that the black, the dark, the Negro vanish from consciousness. Hence a Negro is forever in combat with his own image." That's more reason to stop identifying US citizens as "black."
7. *See, Dorr v. United States,* 195 US138 (1904) (no right to jury trial).
8. The "unincorporated territory" doctrine, by which such basic rights are denied, first appeared in *Downes v. Bidwell,* 182 US 244 (1901) (Justice White's reliance on the Northwest Ordinance of 1787 is found at pg. 320); *St. Croix Avis* (October 1, 2006); *Virgin Islands Daily News* (January 30, 2007).

    On behalf of the VI Humanities Council, in January 1993 Prof. Paul M. Leary of UVI prepared a lecture on the political status of US islands. It should be consulted for a more detailed view on this American anomaly. However, Leary is in error the Supreme Court achieved unanimity on the "unincorporated" doctrine. When the court last visited the issue, Justice Oliver Wendell Holmes concurred in the unanimous judgment *only*, declining to join in the opinion upon which it was based. Prior to that, Justice John Marshall Harlan had consistently rejected it.
9. *The Caribs: A Proper Perspective,* No.1 (Jalil Sued-Badillo, Foundacion Historia de Puerto Rico, Inc., 1986 pg. 4); *King Leopold's Soliloquy* (Mark Twain, 1905; 2nd ed., Int'l Pub., 1970). Twain condemned the genocidal colonization of Africa, a damage no less than was the Jewish Holocaust. And Sartre's prose begs this question: Is current African barbarism proof European racism actually created monsters? *King Leopold's Ghost* (Adam Hochschild, Mariner Books, 1999 pg.146), sounds the pathos of Africa through Joseph Conrad's Mr. Kurtz's death-

bed utterance: "The horror! The horror!" Oliver Stone's Vietnam movie *Apocalypse Now* invoked same words, whispered by Kurtz (Marlon Brando) as his last, to convey the great evils of war.

10. *Intelligence Report* (Editor's Page, Southern Poverty Law Center, Fall 2006).
11. "Forgotten Genius" (February 8, 2007 pbs.org).
12. Chernow at 185. George Washington's refusal was beyond modesty. A kingdom would've been contrary to his Freemason beliefs, which questioned the absolute power of monarchs as far back as the days of African Pharaohs.
13. *500 Nations Productions* (an eight-video film series by Jack Leustig, hosted by Kevin Costner, Vol. 2, 1994, hereafter "*500 Nations* at . . .").
14. US Const. Art. II, cl. 2.
15. *The Federalist Papers* (Penguin Classics, 1987 pgs. 31–36).
16. *Patriots* (A. J. Langguth, Simon & Shuster, 1988 pgs. 296–97; 368, hereafter "*Patriots* at . . .").
17. 500 Nations, at Vol. 2.
18. *The Fire Next Time* (James Baldwin 1963).
19. *500 Nations,* at Vol. 3.
20. Chernow at 211.
21. *Time* (July 4, 2005).
22. *4 American Jurisprudence—Proof of Facts, Schizophrenia* (Bancroft-Whitney, 1960).
23. *VI Daily News* (March 8, 2007).
24. *World's Great Men of Color* (J. A. Rodgers, Collier Pub., Vol. 2, pg. 169).
25. Chernow at 376 (emphasis added).
26. *VI Daily News* (March 8, 2007).
27. *Laws of Affiliated Jurisdictions,* at vii. How telling are word subtleties. Justice King, in decrying the fact US tropical areas are taken for granted, bit the bait by repeating the adjective "insular." The standard meanings of insular include "narrow-minded," "limited," and "inward-looking." Ergo, I inserted "tropical" next to "insular" as I'm sure that better fitted Justice King's context.
28. *St. Croix Avis* (May 21, 2006).
29. Epigraph from *The Hopi* (Frank Waters, 1963).
30. *VI Daily News* (July 13, 2006).
31. *500 Nations,* at Vol. 2.
32. *Id.*
33. *The Caribs: A Proper Perspective* (Jalil Sued-Badillo, Foundacion Historia de Puerto Rico, Inc., 1986 pg. 4). Other historians describe Caribbean aboriginals in several ways. Personal observations of Las Casas to the contrary, the Caribs are said to have been combative and raider of the Arawaks, tagged also as Tainos or Lucayans.

Advances reflective of Las Casas' civility were made. Instead of Catholic conversions resulting in slavery, Spanish Florida started in 1693 to grant sanctuary to slaves fleeing south in the first Underground Railroad, and freed those who converted to Catholicism. It was the same way in Puerto Rico when Denmark colonized St. Croix in 1735. Runaway Crucian slaves sailed to Puerto Rico, and by becoming Catholic converts they were given freedom. As such, they started there the community of Louisa Aldea.

34. *Salt River in St. Croix: Columbus Landing Site?* (Wilfredo A. Geigel, Esq., El Libro Inc., Puerto Rico 2005 pg. 31, hereafter "*Salt River* at . . ."). Geigel is the past president of the Historical Society of Puerto Rico. Research on that rape incident and on the word *cuñeo* may be worth a thesis. People of St. Croix with Puerto Rican and Taino ancestry vent *cuñeo!* as an expression of disgust. This may be rooted in the oral history of the rape in 1493 by navigator Michele de Cuñeo.

35. Chernow at 581; 678.

36. *Scott v. Sandford*, 60 US 393, 403–04; 407 (1857) (overruled by the Thirteenth Amendment).

37. *Africa Counts: Number and Pattern in African Culture* (Claudia Zaslavsky, Lawrence Hill Books, 1973 pgs. 109–110). African children's games depend on the arithmetic arrangement of objects.

38. Chernow at 26.

39. *Wonders of the African World* (Luis B. Gates, Alfred A. Knopf, NY, pg. 9); *The African Origins of Civilization* (Cheikh Anta Diop, Lawrence Hill Books 1974 pgs. 27–28). Did the African three-in-one gods Iris, Horus, and Osiris offer a template for the American tripartite scheme of checks and balances? Freemason founders surely were exposed to that trinity and the equilibrium it embodied.

40. *St. Croix Avis* (June 25, 2006). A discussion of Danish slave laws which permitted their freedom in St. Croix is found in *The Umbilical Cord* (Hon. Harold W. L. Willocks, VI, 1995 pg. 95).

41. *Saint Croix 1770–1776: The First Salute to the Stars and Stripes* (Robert A. Johnson, Author's Publishing, VI, 2007). Others say France was first foreign port to salute the "Stars and Stripes" flown by the ship *Ranger* on February 14, 1778. Johnson explained to me the latter salute came after the Revolution was well underway.

42. *Patriots,* at 124.

43. *Id.*

44. Chernow at 641.

45. *Id.* at 677–78; 689. Aaron Burr grew a murderous rage against Hamilton because he blocked his paths to the presidency by supporting Jefferson in 1801, as well as to the New York governorship. The West Indian was

a curse, a hypocrite, author of all his misery. That's how Burr saw things in the spring of 1804 according Chernow.

46. *Id*. at 680–85.
47. *Id*. at 675; 692. In tow with his aristocratic pretence, Burr was not above uttering the words "nigger whore." A story in the *American Citizen* alleged Burr threw a *nigger ball* supervised by his slave Alexis, to woo free African voters to his Richmond Hill estate. It was highlighted by Burr's dancing with, and seducing, a *voluptuous black woman*.
48. *Id*. at 689.
49. *Id*. at 690.
50. *Id*. at 717.
51. *Id*. at 711.
52. *Id*. at 730.
53. *Id*. at 130.
54. William Faulkner: *Nobel Prize Acceptance Speech 1950* (*American Literature*, McDougal, Littell & Co., 1989 pg. 618).
55. Chernow at 131.
56. *Id*. at 337–38.
57. *Vision* (Government of VI, Winter 2006).
58. *Salt River,* at pgs 2–3.
59. *Pioneers of Negro Origins in California* (Sue Bailey Thurman, Acme Publishing 1952).
60. Chernow at 733.
61. *In the Tiger's Jaw: America's First Black Marine Aviator* (Presidio Press, Novato, CA 1998 pg. 257).
62. *Time* (July 29, 2002).

PART TWO

Chapter Three

1. *Fading Back: A Personal Look Back Into the History of the Virgin Islands Police Department, St. Croix District* (Police Commissioner Elton Lewis, VI, 2003 pg. 62).
2. *Mango Madness* (Reuben D. Dowling, VI, 2004 pgs. 90–91).
3. *Black Skin,* at 7; 217–19.
4. *Massacre in Paradise: The Untold Story of the Fountain Valley Massacre* (Hon. Harold W. L. Willocks and Myron Allick, Jury Foreman, Fountain Valley Trial, VI, 1997 pg. 35, hereafter "*Massacre,* at . . .").
5. *Laws of Affiliated Jurisdictions*, at 68.
6. Boyer at 279–280.
7. *Id*. at 312.
8. *Id*.
9. *Massacre*, at 33.

Michael A. Joseph, Esq.

10. *Fading Back*, at 61.
11. *Bowling for Columbine* (Oscar-winning movie by Michael Moore, 2002).
12. *VI Daily News* (July 7, 2006); *St. Croix Avis* (October 25, 1972).
13. *A Short History of the Deer of St. Croix* (George A. Seaman, VI, 1984).
14. *Government of the Virgin Islands v. Gereau*, 10 VI 53, 84 (DC VI 1973).
15. *Id.* at 84 n. 4.
16. *Massacre*, at 18.
17. *Id.* at 95.

Gratitude

I contemplated long: How do I identify by name the count-less those who helped Rafie regain freedom; the uncountable those who made this book possible; the many who in the last twelve years left this life and for whom I tried and tried to get it done before they departed? The numerous who asked time and time again, "When is the book going to finish?" my answer to which was, "We are in the same boat!" for by that question *you* became the oars with which I rowed to the shore of its comple-tion. I entreat your good natures to forgive my incapacity to identify by name *all of you* to whom I'm forever grateful.

Review Requested:
If you loved this book, would you please provide a review at Amazon.com?

CPSIA information can be obtained at www.ICGtesting.com
Printed in the USA
LVOW06s1818300315

432568LV00035B/77/P